BEST DAY HIKES IN CONNECTICUT

WELCOME TO THE AMC

Welcome to the Appalachian Mountain Club! Founded in 1876, we are America's oldest conservation and recreation organization. We promote the protection, enjoyment, and wise use of the mountains, rivers, and trails of the Appalachian region. The AMC has twelve chapters from Maine to Washington, D.C., comprised of tens of thousands of outdoor enthusiasts like you.

By purchasing this book you have contributed to our efforts to protect the Appalachian region. Proceeds from the sales of AMC Books and Maps support our regional land conservation efforts; trail building and maintenance; air- and water-quality research; search and rescue; and environmental education programs for school-age children, at-risk youth, and outdoor enthusiasts.

The AMC encourages everyone to enjoy and appreciate the natural world because we believe that successful conservation depends on such experiences. So join us in the outdoors! We offer hiking, paddling, biking, skiing, and mountaineering activities throughout the Appalachian region for outdoor adventurers of every age and ability. Our lodging destinations, such as our state-of-the-art Highland Center, are Model Environmental Education Facilities, demonstrating our stewardship ethic and providing a place for you to relax off-trail and learn more about local ecosystems and habitats, regional environmental issues, and mountain history and culture.

For more information about AMC membership, destinations, and conservation and education programs, turn to the back of this book or visit the AMC website at www.outdoors.org.

AMC'S BEST **DAY HIKES** IN
CONNECTICUT

Four-Season Guide to 50 of the Best Day Hikes
from the Highlands to the Coast

Including Mount Misery • Bear Mountain • Bluff Point

RENÉ LAUBACH
CHARLES W. G. SMITH

Appalachian Mountain Club Books
Boston, MA

The AMC is a non-profit organization and
sales of AMC books fund our mission of
protecting the Northeast outdoors. If you appreciate our efforts
and would like make a donation to the AMC,
contact us at
Appalachian Mountain Club,
5 Joy Street, Boston, MA 02108.

http://www.outdoors.org/publications/books/

Front-Cover Photographs: Couple Walking Through Woods © Randy Faris/Corbis;
    Woman Skiing © EcoPhotography/Jerry & Marcy Monkman
Title Page Photograph: Hemlock Forest in East Haddam, CT © EcoPhotography/
    Jerry & Marcy Monkman
All interior images and back-cover photos copyright of the authors unless otherwise noted.

Distributed by the Globe Pequot Press, Guilford, Connecticut.

Library of Congress Cataloging-in-Publication Data
Laubach, René.
  AMC's best day hikes in Connecticut : four-season guide to 50 of the best trails from the highlands
to the coast / by René Laubach and Charles Smith.
    p. cm.
  Includes bibliographical references and index.
  ISBN 978-1-934028-10-0 (alk. paper)
  1. Hiking--Connecticut--Guidebooks. 2. Trails--Connecticut--Guidebooks. 3. Connecticut--
Guidebooks. I. Smith, Charles W. G. II. Appalachian Mountain Club. III. Title. IV. Title: Best day
hikes Connecticut.

GV199.42.C8L38 2007
796.5109746--dc22
                        2007026878

The paper used in this publication meets the minimum requirements of the
American National Standard for Information Sciences—Permanence of
Paper for Printed Library Materials, ANSI Z39.48-1984. ∞

**Due to changes in conditions, use of the information
in this book is at the sole risk of the user.**

Printed in the United States of America.

Printed on recycled paper.

10 9 8 7 6 5 4 3 2 1

RENE'S DEDICATION

For my late Mother
Irmgard Buttler Laubach
who encouraged and nurtured
my love of wild things with her love and caring

CHARLES'S DEDICATION

René Laubach has been a good friend of mine for over ten years. We have worked on many books together and have shared stories of the marvelous aspects of creation we have discovered along the way. His knowledge is vast and his trustworthiness is more so (Proverbs 18:24). I dedicate my portion of this work to my friend René with a heartfelt thank you (John 11:41).

TRIP LOCATOR MAP

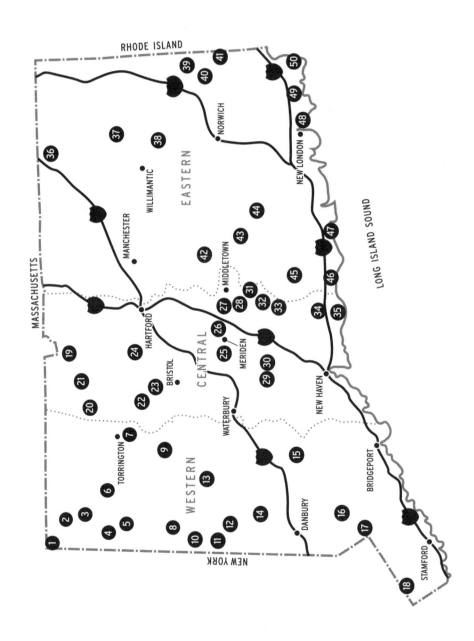

CONTENTS

NATURE ESSAYS

AT-A-GLANCE TRIP PLANNER

#	Trip	Page	Difficulty	Distance
1	Mount Frissell	2	Difficult	4.2 mi
2	Bear Mountain	7	Difficult	6.0 mi
3	Lion's Head	12	Moderate	1.9 mi
4	Sharon Audubon Center	17	Easy	2.5 mi
5	Pine Knob Loop Trail	24	Moderate	2.6 mi
6	Cathedral Pines and Mohawk Mountain	28	Moderate	3.7 mi
7	Wolcott Trail and Burr Pond	34	Easy	2.75 mi
8	River Road	41	Easy	3.0 mi
9	Mallard Marsh and Little Pond	46	Moderate	4.7 mi
10	Macedonia Ridge Trail	52	Difficult	6.4 mi.
11	Mount Algo and Indian Rock	60	Difficult	7.6 mi
12	Candlewood Mountain	65	Moderate	3.0 mi
13	Mount Tom State Park	73	Easy-Moderate	1.1 mi
14	Sunny Valley Preserve	78	Moderate	3.4 mi
15	Kettletown State Park	86	Moderate	3.5 mi

Elevation Gain	Estimated Time	Winter Hike	With Children ?	Trip Highlights
617 ft	3.5–4.0 hrs	snow-shoeing		a walk on the wild side, state high point
1,560 ft	3.5–4.5 hrs			mountain vistas from state's highest peak
536 ft	1.5–2.0 hrs			incomparable vistas, spring wildflowers
210 ft	2.0 hrs	snow-shoeing	yes	scenic pond, wetlands teeming with wildlife
700 ft	1.5–2.5 hrs	snow-shoeing		beautiful views of Housatonic Valley
740 ft	2.5–3.5 hrs			tornado ravaged old growth pines
80 ft	1.5 hrs	snow-shoeing/ X-country ski	yes	massive glacial boulders, luxurient azalea and laurel blooms
20 ft	1.0–1.5 hrs	snow-shoeing/ X-country ski	yes	longest river walk along the AT
40 ft	2.5 hrs			abundant aquatic wildlife, 1.2 mi boardwalk
761 ft.	4.0–5.0 hrs			rocky outcrops with steep scrambles, excellent vistas
900 ft.	5.0 hours	snow-shoeing		a rocky ridgeline to bucolic views of the Housatonic River Valley
640 ft	3.0 hrs			granite promontories, Kelly slide
395 ft	1.0 hr	snow-shoeing	yes	panoramic views from stone tower
350 ft	2.0 hrs	snow-shoeing		forest with a primeval feel, Lake Lillinonah, ledge vista
400 ft	2.0 hrs	snow-shoeing		wonderfull hilltop view of Lake Zoar

Elevation Gain	Estimated Time	Winter Hike	With Children ?	Trip Highlights
230 ft	2.0 hrs	snow-shoeing		rocky ridges and a scenic overlook
50 ft	1.0 hr	snow-shoeing/ X-country ski	yes	lovely woodlands and old pastures, laurel thickets
180 ft	2.0 hrs	snow-shoeing	yes	massive hardwoods, fine birding
400 ft	2.0 hrs	snow-shoeing		miles of trails, fine view from Barn Door Hills
650 ft	3.5-4.5 hrs			incredible mountain views, Manitou stones
450 ft	2.0-3.0 hrs			ridge-top views and an historic boulder cave
200 ft	2.0 hrs	snow-shoeing/ X-country ski	yes	fine wildlife viewing, great vista, and waterfall
300 ft	3.0 hrs			picturesque ledges, tight squeezes, and historic Tory Den
500 ft	2.0-2.5 hrs			Heublein Tower features fantastic views, King Philip's cave
700 ft	3.0-3.5 hrs			traprock ravines, beautiful Meri-mere Reservoir, views from the Hanging Hills
377 ft	2.0-3.0 hrs			challenging climb to a memorable view, a lovely, quiet lake
610 ft	2.0-3.5 hrs			some of the most exciting cliff walking in CT
100 ft	1.5-2.5 hrs	snow-shoeing		waterfalls and giant laurel
620 ft	3.0-4.0 hrs			rugged rocky scrambles, views galore, Indian Rock
500 ft	2.0-3.0 hrs			views from an overlook and a stroll through a chestnut grove
120 ft	0.5-1.0 hr		yes	rock carved in a bear's likeness
100 ft	1.0 hr		yes	rocky shelter used by Native Americans, blueberries
430 ft	1.0-2.0 hrs	snow-shoeing		basaltic cliff walk with great views, wildflowers
120 ft	2.0-3.0 hrs	snow-shoeing		granite outcrops amid oak/hemlock forest

Elevation Gain	Estimated Time	Winter Hike	With Children ?	Trip Highlights
40 ft	0.5–1.0 hr	snow-shoeing	yes	large, brackish water pond, mysterious rock carvings, great birding
100 ft	4.0–4.5 hrs	snow-shoeing		carnivorous plants and eye-popping laurel bloom
120 ft	1.5 hrs	snow-shoeing/ X-country ski	yes	author Edwin Way Teale's "Old Farm"
240 ft	2.0 hrs	snow-shoeing		striking fall foliage along scenic Little River Valley
10 ft	0.5 hr	snow-shoeing/ X-country ski	yes	lovely native rhododendrons
170 ft	1.0 hr	snow-shoeing		panoramic views, plentiful wildflowers and songbirds
130 ft	2.0–3.0 hrs	snow-shoeing/ X-country ski		mountain laurel in abundance
170 ft	1.5 hrs	snow-shoeing		signs of glacial action, colonial era settlement
170 ft	1.5 hrs	snow-shoeing	yes	hemlock ravine and brook, huge glacial erratic
300 ft	2.0 hrs	snow-shoeing		huge hemlocks along the Eight Mile River, Chapman Falls, and "devil's" potholes
175 ft	3.0 hrs			ledge outcrops, rock overhangs, crevices, cliffs, and caves
20 ft	2.0 hrs		yes	rocky shore, wonderful wildlife viewing
100 ft	1.0 hr		yes	tidal marsh, woodland giants
100 ft	2.0 hrs			scenic rock-strewn coast, barrier beach, and salt marsh
70 ft	1.5 hrs		yes	varied natural communities, great birding
65 ft	3.5 hrs			tidal wetlands, important bird area

PREFACE

PARAPHRASING A WISE MAN: WALK AND YE SHALL FIND. Indeed. Walking is what humans do best. We were born to walk. Just lacing up your hiking boots should get your blood pumping with the thrill of anticipation. And so we have written this book in order to pass on our own thrill of discovery.

It is true that Connecticut has no true wilderness, but within the borders of this small, populous state is a surprising number of wild oases teeming with life. Though it seems counterintuitive, the state is in many ways wilder today than it was 100 years ago. The nearly wholesale abandonment of agriculture during the nineteenth century has resulted in the regrowth and maturation of the state's woodlands. It was once said that a New England farmer's chief crop was rock. Not such a far-fetched notion perhaps. That sea change in vegetative cover has permitted bobcats, ravens, wild turkeys, coyotes, fisher, and a host of other creatures to recolonize a landscape from which they had been extirpated.

Reminders of the state's farming heritage are everywhere, from old milldams to countless miles of monumental stone walls still coursing through woodlands now coming of age. We've come to think that as the decades follow each other in timeless fashion, the natural world is shrinking back into fewer and smaller natural refugia where wild things cling to a tenuous existence.

Without question, two of today's major threats to biological diversity are habitat loss due to sprawl and the insidious march of invasive, exotic species that gobble up the landscape like some sci-fi monster.

But while development has degraded many landscapes profoundly and forever, much of Connecticut is wilder today than when our grandparents' grandparents were young.

Concomitant with this re-wilding of Connecticut has come increased public awareness and improved public access to these natural wonders by means of a growing web of public and private trails—many maintained by dedicated volunteers. From short, easy strolls to long, arduous hikes with serious elevation gain, Connecticut's hiking trails have a great deal to offer. Thus, a life of exploration awaits you.

So go forth in search of wild things. Whether that quest carries you to the top of one of the nutmeg state's traprock ridges, among its towering forest giants, along a shrubby field humming with insect activity in mid-summer, or to the remaining natural tidal estuaries, enjoy and appreciate the bounty that is ours.

Know that Connecticut's wild places are not here by accident. It has taken the dedication, perseverance and hard work of many caring individuals over many decades to conserve and care for what we enjoy and benefit from today. As beneficiaries of that legacy, it's up to all of us to preserve our natural heritage for this and succeeding generations.

HOW TO USE THIS BOOK

EACH WALK BEGINS WITH A LISTING OF IMPORTANT FACTS, which includes a rating of the terrain covered, the distance of the walk in miles, the elevation gain along the hike, an estimated time range needed to complete the walk, and the United States Geological Survey (USGS) topographical map and other maps that you may also wish to consult.

Of these criteria the time and terrain ratings are subjective. The approximate times for completing each walk are based on a relaxed pace that allows for plenty of observation and hanging out. Most people can finish the hikes in less time than we have allowed, but we hope they won't want to.

The ratings for the type of terrain covered include easy, moderate, and difficult. In general the terrain rating is a reflection of the total length of the walk, the elevation gain, and any unique features—such as scrambles or very steep sections—of that hike. Remember that a faster pace makes any walk more difficult and that it is possible to encounter poor footing on all trails, regardless of rating. The listing of important facts is followed by a Directions section, which provides driving directions to the trailhead.

The Trail Description is a guided tour of the entire hike. Landmarks are used as reference points, so you can know where you are along the walk at almost any given time. Plants, rock formations, animal burrows, and the like are described in the text in relation to where they appear along the trail, which makes it easier to find these things as you walk along. A section of More Information follows the Trail Description and provides contact information for the appropriate managing agency, entrance fees, visitor center hours, dog regulations, and restroom availability.

TRIP PLANNING
AND SAFETY

WALKING OR HIKING IN CONNECTICUT OFTEN TAKES YOU AWAY from the conveniences many have grown dependent on. We are, to be blunt, a wimpy bunch of folks when compared with the animals of the woods that thrive all by themselves through storms and snows. It takes many years to become as self-reliant as nature originally intended us to be, so in the meantime it is prudent to bring our technological crutches with us where we walk.

Always leave word with someone about where you are going and when you plan to return. Since getting lost is almost always a possibility, be sure to leave sufficient time to complete the hike before darkness sets in. Every time you go for a hike you should have a day pack with you to carry the ten essentials. The ten essentials are the ten commandments of hikers and will go a long way to making you more self-reliant in the woods. They are:

1) Extra clothing. What you bring depends on the season of the year and where you are going. Some of the staples include rain gear, hats and gloves, fleece or wool sweaters, and socks. Bring clothes made of fibers that retain their insulating value when wet, such as fleece and wool, instead of those that lose it, such as cotton.

2) Food and water. High-energy food such as cereal bars or gorp (a blend of chocolate, raisins, and nuts), along with at least one quart of water

or sports drink per person (on long hikes you can need easily twice this much). These items help replace what hiking depletes from your body. Bring more than you think you will need.

3) Sunglasses and a whistle. Sunglasses are needed in the winter when the combination of snow and sun can bring on snow blindness. The whistle is used in case you get lost and need to communicate with rescuers. The sound carries farther than a yell. Whistles are used only in emergencies.

4) Multitool. This wonderful invention combines folding pliers with a knife blade, screwdrivers, awl, and other goodies. The Swiss Army knife was its inspiration but multitools are even more versatile.

5) Fire starter. Campfires are not a part of the wilderness experience anymore, but they do have a place in some emergencies. The simplest fire starter to bring with you is a small candle.

6) Matches. It doesn't do much good to have a candle if you can't light it.

7) First-aid kit. Pick up a hiker's first-aid kit (specifically designed for treating the troubles encountered in the woods) from a good outdoor recreation store.

8) Flashlight. Sometimes it gets dark a lot faster than you think it is going to. A flashlight will go a long way to helping you find your way back in the dark.

9) Map. Know where you are and where you are going. Never go anywhere without one.

10) Compass. Learn how to use one and don't go anywhere without one of these either.

FOOTWEAR

You can wear hiking boots to play tennis or wear sneakers to hike the Appalachian Trail (AT), but why would you? Woodland trails are best negotiated in a pair of hiking boots. They give good footing and protect your ankles from twisting. Today you can get hiking boots that are hybrids between cross-trainers and sturdy leather boots. They are light and versatile and usually meet the challenges of the Connecticut trails quite well. Under the boots should be a good pair of hiking socks made of a fabric other than cotton.

LYME DISEASE

Named after Lyme, the Connecticut coastal town where it was originally identified in 1975, Lyme disease is by far the best known of several diseases borne by ticks. It is one of the fastest spreading infectious diseases in this country, with cases reported in all states except Alaska. Lyme disease is caused by a bacterium and borne by the black-legged tick. The hosts of this tiny tick, formerly known as the deer tick, are white-tailed deer and white-footed mice. This tick is very much smaller than the American dog tick and the wood tick. Black-legged ticks may be active any time the temperature is above 32 degrees Fahrenheit.

Black-legged ticks have a 3-stage, 2-year life cycle. At each stage the ticks require a blood meal. Larvae are most active from late July to early September, peaking in mid-August. Some years you encounter a secondary peak from mid-June to early July. Larvae molt into nymphs over the winter. Nymphs are most active from May through August. In late summer nymphs molt into adults that are about 2 millimeters in length.

The classic symptoms of Lyme disease include a red, circular rash at the site of the bite. Early symptoms may resemble those caused by the flu. Later symptoms may include arthritis and heart and neurological problems.

Lyme disease can be successfully treated with antibiotics. A new vaccine to combat the disease is under development.

The following precautions can help you avoid Lyme disease:

- Wear light-colored clothing.

- Tuck shirts into pants and pants into socks. Wear closed shoes.

- Spray pants with a commercial tick/insect spray that contains no more than 33 percent DEET, being careful not to get the repellent directly on your skin.

- Stay on trails and away from branches, brush, and tall grass.

- Check your clothing for ticks periodically. The black-legged tick larva may be no larger than the period at the end of this sentence.

- Conduct a thorough tick check after you return home. Be sure to examine your scalp, back of the neck, armpits, groin, and behind the knees. Also check beneath elastic bands.

If you find an attached tick, remove it carefully by grasping it with very fine tweezers by the head and gently pulling it straight out. Be careful not to break off its mouthparts. Wash the site with an antiseptic. Watch for signs of a rash. You may want to save the tick for later identification by your physician if symptoms appear.

Note that dogs can also contract Lyme disease.

With all that said, do not let the fear of contracting Lyme disease keep you out of the woods. Instead, be sure to take the sensible precautions listed above and be alert for signs of potential symptoms of the disease.

1

WESTERN CONNECTICUT

THE NORTHWEST HILLS ARE HOME TO THE CONNECTICUT SECTION of the Appalachian Trail (AT), which weaves through about 50 miles of beautiful woodlands and mountains from the New York border to the Massachusetts state line in the southern Berkshires. Along the way many walks show you some of the best sections of the Connecticut AT, from the easy stroll along the Housatonic River outside Kent (Trip 8) to the views from Lion's Head (Trip 3) and the stone pyramid atop Bear Mountain (Trip 2). If this touch of wilderness isn't quite wild enough, you can even ascend a rugged trail through three states to a lonely perch of rock that marks the highest elevation in the state (Trip 1). The walks in western Connecticut also include the oasis-like sanctuaries of Greenwich Audubon (Trip 18) and Weir Nature Preserve (Trip 17) in and around the southwest panhandle and the unforgettable forests and wildlife surrounding the White Memorial Conservation Center (Trip 9) and Sharon Audubon Center (Trip 4). To top it off, you can visit a grove of ancient pines pillaged by a tornado (Trip 6). Whichever walk you choose, in whatever season, the western region of this beautiful state is a fascinating place to explore.

TRIP 1
MOUNT FRISSELL

Location: Salisbury
Rating: Difficult
Distance: 4.2 miles
Elevation Gain: 617 feet
Estimated Time: 3.5–4.0 hours
Maps: USGS Bash Bish Falls—MA, CT, NY; Mount Washington State Forest map available online

No other place in Connecticut is as lofty or as wild as the forests of Mount Frissell. Here the highest elevation in the state hides among dense thickets of mountain laurel, and black bears and bobcats still stalk the woods. If you want to walk on the wild side, this walk is for you. This out-and-back hike to Mount Frissell passes through three states, over three mountains, and offers unforgettable views.

DIRECTIONS

From the junction of Routes 41/44 in Salisbury, proceed south on Route 44 for about 100 yards to the Salisbury Town Hall, where it meets Factory Street. Turn right (west) onto Factory Street (which becomes Mount Riga Road). At 1.3 miles, the road becomes gravel, and at 1.6 miles it enters the Mount Riga Forest Preserve at a gate (seasonal road). The road turns sharply right at the South Pond dam and then continues north, becoming Mount Washington Road. The trailhead is on the left at 7.1 miles.

TRAIL DESCRIPTION

The Brace Mountain Trail is unblazed but easy to follow. The South Taconic Trail is marked with small white blazes, and the Mount Frissell Trail is blazed in red.

From the parking area on East Street (called Mount Washington Road in Connecticut), near the Connecticut–Massachusetts state line, the Mount Frissell Trail heads northwest on an old woods road, then turns left (south) into dense shrubby woods. The path crosses into Connecticut, setting a course toward the steep slopes of Round Mountain.

Round Mountain is one of the highest peaks in the state; it's just a dozen or so feet lower than famed Bear Mountain a short distance to the east. The trail's

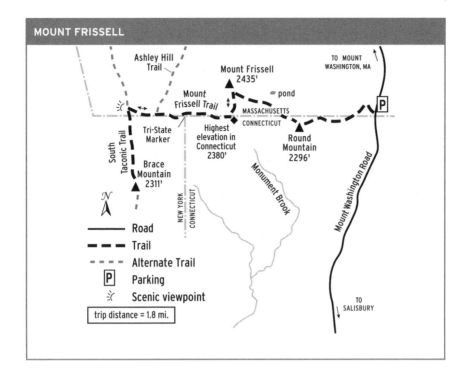

MOUNT FRISSELL

Ashley Hill Trail

Mount Frissell
▲ 2435'

TO MOUNT
WASHINGTON, MA

Mount
Frissell Trail

pond

MASSACHUSETTS
CONNECTICUT

P

Tri-State
Marker

Highest
elevation in
Connecticut
2380'

Round
Mountain
2296'

South Taconic Trail

Brace
Mountain
▲ 2311'

𝒩

NEW YORK
CONNECTICUT

Monument Brook

Mount Washington Road

—— Road

■ ■ ■ Trail

- - - - Alternate Trail

P Parking

☼ Scenic viewpoint

trip distance = 1.8 mi.

TO
SALISBURY

easy grade changes quickly at the foot of Round Mountain. The path climbs moderately up the east slope for a while before becoming steep and strenuous as it traces a course more northwestward toward the summit. As the trail nears the crest of the mountain, the grade eases and the path enters the grassy open area of the summit (2,296 feet) about 0.7 mile from the trailhead.

The trail leaves the summit to the northwest, descending gradually at first and crossing back into Massachusetts, where the path begins a steeper descent. The path drops to the saddle between Round Mountain and Mount Frissell. A side trail right leads to a vernal pond less than 0.1 mile to the northeast. The Mount Frissell Trail now climbs from the saddle up the eastern face of Mount Frissell. The trail gains 300 feet in less than 0.2 mile, making the ascent short but steep. Just before reaching the summit (1.2 miles), the grade relaxes. The view from the open eastern ledges and nearly constant breeze make this spot a place to linger and have lunch. Mount Frissell (2,453 feet) is one of the more remote mountains in the Berkshires; it is a place to savor the vast privacy that only wilderness can offer.

The summit of Mount Frissell is in Massachusetts. The highest point in Connecticut is farther down the mountain. From the summit, the trail descends through scrub and mountain laurel thickets to an overlook on the eastern side

The end of the trail runs along a beautifully isolated grassy ridge.

of the mountain. Here the trail turns right (west) and continues a few yards to a stone pile (1.3 miles) on the side of the trail. A metal United States Geological Survey (USGS) marker fixed to the bedrock identifies this location as the point of highest elevation in Connecticut at 2,380 feet, some 64 feet higher than the top of Bear Mountain (the highest summit in Connecticut).

From the USGS marker, follow the trail west as it snakes through thick stands of laurel and wild azalea and descends bedrock outcrops. Wild blueberry grows from fissures in the bedrock, and oak and maple grow in the more sheltered spots. The next landmark (1.7 miles) is a cut-stone pillar astride the trail that marks the point where New York, Massachusetts, and Connecticut meet. This area was once a source of great friction among the three states, even leading to violence and bloodshed. By the time the marker was placed in the late 1800s, however, New York and Massachusetts had settled their differences, and both state names were chiseled into the rock. Connecticut was the lone holdout in the dispute, and its name is notably absent from the stone, though someone has scratched "Conn" on the marker.

Continuing west, the path passes on the right (north) the intersection with the Ashley Hill Trail, which leads in 3.4 miles to the Mount Washington State Forest Headquarters on East Street in the town of Mount Washington, Massachusetts. To the left (south), an unmarked trail enters private land. The trail passes through groves of oaks growing amid a forest of boulders and outcrops,

CLIMBING THE TACONIC KLIPPE

As you hike up a steep, rocky summit trail, you may not care whether you're walking over igneous basalt or metamorphic schists. To paraphrase Freud, sometimes a rock is just a rock. However, rocks have more to tell you about the natural world than anything else you commonly bump into. Many are tens of millions of years old, and some are closer to a billion. You just can't be that old and not have a good story to tell. Such is the case with the Taconic Klippe.

The Taconics are a narrow range of mountains that straddle the borders of Vermont, New York, Massachusetts, and Connecticut. Near the tristate boundary of Connecticut, Massachusetts, and New York, the principal peaks are Mount Brace (2,311 feet), South Brace Mountain (2,304 feet), Round Mountain (2,296 feet), and Mount Frissell (2,453 feet). The Taconics are incredibly old. The trails that lead to the highest point in Connecticut traverse rocks that took their present form during the Taconian mountain-building event, which began 445 million years ago. At this time, Europe and North America began to drift toward each other. The pressures that resulted caused volcanic islands to form off the coast and the Taconic Mountains to begin to rise. Around 435 million years ago, the volcanic islands were pushed against the mainland, and the Taconic Mountains reached their ultimate height, probably near 20,000 feet.

The continuing drift of the European continent against North America formed huge thrust faults and dislodged a gigantic section of the earth's crust, called a klippe. This enormous section of land, which now reaches from the Hudson Highlands to Ticonderoga along Lake Champlain, then slid westward in huge earthquake-induced landslides. Hundreds of millions of years of erosion have worn down these impressive peaks to one-tenth their original height. The rock is primarily gneiss (pronounced *nice*), which formed miles beneath the earth's surface after being subjected to intense heat and pressure. Knowing all this does not take away the burning in the legs as you climb the mountainside, but it does give you something to think about.

producing a unique and lovely landscape. At 2.1 miles, the Mount Frissell Trail breaks out of the dense woods and ends at the South Taconic Trail. This is another beautiful spot, perched at the steep edge of the escarpment. The views out over New York's Harlem Valley are gorgeous, and the open grassy ridge is comfortable and relaxing. A nest of signs conveys a number of options to continue the hike both north and south.

Following the South Taconic Trail south (left) for 0.5 mile leads to the rocky cairn and grassy bald atop the summit of Brace Mountain, one of the nicest spots in the Taconic Mountains. Turning north (right) and hiking 2.9 miles leads to the summit of Alander Mountain, with long runs of open ridge and perhaps the best views in the Berkshires.

From the end of the Mount Frissell Trail, turn around retrace your steps east to Mount Washington Road (East Street).

MORE INFORMATION

Restrooms are available at forest headquarters. Leashed pets permitted on trails. Mount Washington State Forest, East Street, Mount Washington, MA 01258; 413-528-0330; http://www.mass.gov/dcr/parks/western/mwas.htm.

—C. S.

TRIP 2
BEAR MOUNTAIN

Location: Salisbury
Rating: Difficult
Distance: 6.0 miles
Elevation Gain: 1,560 feet
Estimated Time: 3.5–4.5 hours
Maps: USGS Bash Bish Falls—MA, CT, NY

This is one of the most popular hiking destinations in the state. A grand stone pyramid crowns its summit, offering unrestricted views of broad valleys, shimmering lakes, and rugged mountains across three states. In addition to the vistas, this hike takes you on a long loop through ancient forests where animals such as fisher, deer, and coyote roam to an unbeatable view from the state's highest summit.

DIRECTIONS
From Salisbury and the junction of Routes 41/44, take Route 41 north for 3.5 miles to a parking area on the left. A blue sign for the Undermountain Trail is near the large parking area. During periods of heavy use, vehicles are often parked along the road, making conditions along Route 41 more dangerous.

TRAIL DESCRIPTION
The hike over Bear Mountain is on the Undermountain and Paradise Lane Trails, both blazed with pale blue markers, and the Appalachian Trail (AT), blazed in white rectangles. Turns are noted by two stacked blazes, the upper blaze offset in the direction of the turn. All trail junctions are signed.

From the parking area on Route 41 in Salisbury, the Undermountain Trail immediately passes a kiosk on the right where trail maps and other information are available. Opposite the kiosk is a short path that leads to a privy. The trail heads west and begins a gentle climb into a forest of red and white oaks, ash, and hickory, all shading clumps of witch hazel, mountain laurel, wild azalea, and striped maple. Evergreen Christmas fern shares the forest floor with mats of partridgeberry, sprigs of wintergreen, and isolated specimens of rose twisted-stalk and wild sarsaparilla. Rose twisted-stalk is a plant that favors the cool climates of mountain slopes from southern Canada south along the spine

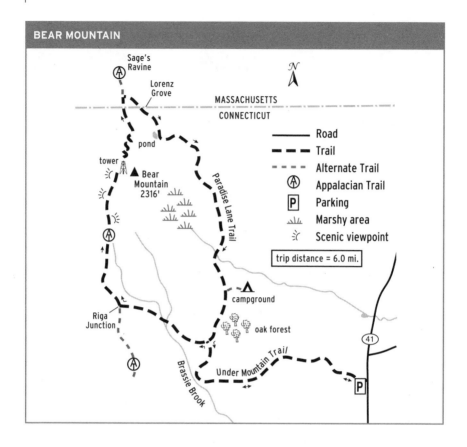

BEAR MOUNTAIN

Sage's Ravine

Lorenz Grove

MASSACHUSETTS

CONNECTICUT

pond

tower

Bear Mountain 2316'

Paradise Lane Trail

Riga Junction

campground

oak forest

Brassie Brook

Under Mountain Trail

	Road
	Trail
	Alternate Trail
Ⓐ	Appalacian Trail
P	Parking
	Marshy area
	Scenic viewpoint

trip distance = 6.0 mi.

41

of the Appalachians. The foot-tall herbaceous stems grow in a pronounced zigzag pattern, with each zig and zag accented by a solitary deep green leaf. In late spring through early summer, small deep-pink, pendant, bell-shaped flowers appear along the stems.

The moderate but relentless climb becomes steeper as the path slabs the eastern slope of Riga Ridge. Along the trail are a number of interesting plants including selfheal, a member of the mint family with short, square stems; lilac flowers (in summer); aster; and spotted wintergreen, with lance-shaped green leaves decorated with a central white stripe. Look for red efts through here as well. These little salamanders and are colored bright orange.

After passing the sign welcoming you to Appalachian Trail Lands, the trail swings past Brassie Brook, climbs a series of stone steps, and intersects with the Paradise Lane Trail at 1.1 miles. Continue on the Undermountain Trail through woods of birch, hemlock, beech, and maple. The path is level here and soon crosses Brassie Brook near a cluster of mossy boulders and small, quiet pools. On the low, easternmost boulder is a small bronze plaque that reads:

In memory of
Dave Gilman
a teacher and friend
as long as the mountain laurel
shall bloom your spirit and wisdom will abide in us all

From Brassie Brook the path proceeds through areas dotted with hobble-bush, laurel, wild azalea, wintergreen, and trailing arbutus. Hobblebush, like rose twisted-stalk, prefers cooler climates. In spring, this gangly shrub bears wide, flat clusters of white, hydrangea-like blossoms. The tall, open woods yield to swampy thickets of summersweet, laurel, and striped maple. This wet area is crossed on two log bridges lined with tall ferns and clusters of blue-bead lily.

A short distance farther, the path climbs to Riga Junction and the junction with the AT (1.9 miles). Turn right (north) onto the AT and proceed through low, wind-stunted woods of maple, birch, and oak with an understory of laurel, honeysuckle, sassafras, and chestnut. For a short way, the terrain is level. Soon after passing an unmarked woods road to the left, the grade becomes steep as the path ascends the southern slope of Bear Mountain. The thin mountain soil, studded with boulders, can no longer support the trees that thrive on the

Hikers perch atop the stone pyramid on the summit of Bear Mountain.

lower-elevation slopes. In their place, red maple, bear oak, chokeberry, blueberry, and pitch pine—plants adapted to more severe conditions—dominate.

The trail winds up the mountain, passing a large boulder on the left whose top offers a fine view to the south, west, and east. You don't need to climb it, however, because a short way farther up the path are bedrock outcrops, each with a view nice enough to stop and celebrate. Ravens make frequent flybys, and in fall the stunning foliage serves as a backdrop to a steady stream of migrating raptors. The path now becomes rocky, with a beautiful southern view a nearly constant companion. Reindeer moss, named for its antler-shaped stems, grows in the sheltered crevices of rocks, as does three-leafed cinquefoil, a subalpine wildflower with small white summer blossoms and crimson autumn leaves. As the path becomes more level, it weaves through oak and pitch pine thickets before reaching the stone pyramid atop the mountain's wooded summit at 2.7 miles.

The top of the stone monument offers a spectacular view. To the north are the rounded profiles of Mount Race (2,365 feet) and Mount Everett (2,602 feet). The pure blue bodies of water to the east are the Washinee and Washining Lakes, together called Twin Lakes, some 1,500 feet below. To the west-northwest are the summits of Round Mountain (2,296 feet) and Mount Frissell (2,453 feet). The closest mountain to the southwest is Gridley Mountain (2,211 feet), while due west is Brace Mountain (2,311 feet). On clear days, the Catskills are visible far beyond the profile of Brace Mountain.

At the base of the stone monument is a stone plaque that proudly proclaims the summit of Bear Mountain as the highest point in Connecticut. This plaque has been a source of misunderstanding for more than a century. In 1885, when the plaque was carved and placed, the summit of Bear Mountain was indeed the highest surveyed point in the state. Unfortunately, not all of the state had been surveyed in 1885. Years later it was determined that the highest ground in the state actually lay on the south slope of Mount Frissell (see Trip 1), a short distance to the west.

From the summit, continue north along the AT, which quickly begins a steep 600-foot descent of Bear Mountain's northern slope. It is helpful for hikers to remember that in New England the north faces of mountains are commonly steeper and more rugged than the south sides. This is because of the erosive action of glaciers that moved repeatedly over the landscape from north to south during the last ice age. The path winds around many rock outcrops and windfalls on its way to the level col far below. The descent is especially slippery when ice, rain, or fallen leaves cover the rocks. When the trail finally levels out, it passes the unmarked Northwest Road on the left (this leads to

Mount Washington Road, also known as East Street, in about 0.7 mile) and heads gently downhill near the boundary of Massachusetts and Connecticut. A few yards farther north, at 3.2 miles, is a sign welcoming you to the fragile environment of Sage's Ravine. The Sage's Ravine campsite with tent platforms is 0.7 mile north along the AT. Paradise Lane Trail leaves right (southwest) toward Route 41.

Turn right onto the Paradise Lane Trail and into a stand of hemlock and white pine called the Lorenz Grove; its name is explained by a nearby bronze plaque honoring Edward Lorenz for his work in protecting this land and his dedication to the Connecticut Chapter of the AMC. Many of the trees in this grove have the sinuous scars of lightning strikes on their trunks. On sunny days, this is a pleasant place to linger. If dark clouds are on the horizon, however, this is not a place to seek shelter. From the grove, the trail enters a clearing of scrubby bear oak and blueberry with a nice view of Bear Mountain to the southwest. The clearing yields to woods of red maple and serviceberry, also called shadblow, a small gray-barked tree covered with lacy white blossoms in early spring.

A small, attractive woodland pond is passed on the right, followed by a wet, boggy stretch where gray birch, pitch pine, and bear oak mingle with the long fronds of pasture brake. The path then proceeds through a series of long, fairly flat stretches where moist fields of ferns alternate with forested, rocky uplands. Near a large tree, a side trail on the left leads to the Paradise Lane campsite at 4.1 miles, where overnight camping is permitted. The path now comes to a broad, open forest of low, thick-trunked oak trees. These trees look no different from the hundreds of others along the trail, but they are far older, many more than 120 years old. The grassy woods are home to turkeys, coyotes, deer, bobcats, red squirrels, porcupines, raccoons, deer mice, pileated woodpeckers, and fishers.

From the oak forest the path descends gently, crossing some stone walls before meeting the Undermountain Trail at 4.9 miles. To return to the parking area, turn left onto the Undermountain Trail and continue downhill for 1.1 miles, reaching Route 41 at 6.0 miles.

MORE INFORMATION

The Undermountain Trail begins in Mount Riga State Park, c/o Macedonia Brook State Park, 159 Macedonia Brook Road, Kent, CT 06757; 860-927-3238. A privy is available at the trailhead. This section of the AT is maintained by the Connecticut Chapter of the AMC; 860-742-8243; www.ct-amc.org.

—C. S.

TRIP 3
LION'S HEAD

Location: Salisbury
Rating: Moderate
Distance: 1.9 miles
Elevation Gain: 536 feet
Estimated Time: 1.5–2.0 hours
Maps: USGS Bash Bish Falls—MA, CT, NY; Sharon—CT, NY

Lion's Head, named for its feline profile, is one of the more popular spots along the Connecticut section of the Appalachian Trail (AT). It is a place of incomparable vistas and friendly hikers. This out-and-back walk takes you on scenic trails populated by many species of songbirds and wonderful spring wildflowers.

DIRECTIONS
From the junction of Routes 41/44 in Salisbury, proceed south on Route 44 for about 100 yards to the Salisbury Town Hall, where Factory Street meets Route 44. Turn onto Factory Street and follow signs toward Mount Riga. Bear right onto Bunker Hill Road. Follow Bunker Hill Road to its end, about 0.95 mile. Park in the designated hiker parking lot; *please respect the landowner's private property* and park only where the signs indicate.

TRAIL DESCRIPTION
The Lion's Head Trail is marked with pale blue blazes, while the AT is blazed with white marks. Turns on all trails are noted with stacked double blazes.

From the northeast corner of the parking area, follow the gravel path north through a field of sensitive fern, goldenrod, and isolated islands of willow, alder, apple, and red cedar. Just beyond a shed, the trail turns left (west) and follows a wide cart path lined with barberry and honeysuckle bushes beneath the spreading boughs of wild apple, cherry, and ash trees. The apple trees are covered with blush-white, lightly fragrant flowers just after Mother's Day each year. The blossoms attract bumble- and honeybees as well as hummingbirds.

The cart path heads down a gentle grade and crosses a small brook where sweet violets bloom in spring and veeries and wood thrushes sing on warm summer mornings. From the stream, the trail ascends gradually near a stone wall, climbing through a young, mixed hardwood forest of red oak, cherry, red

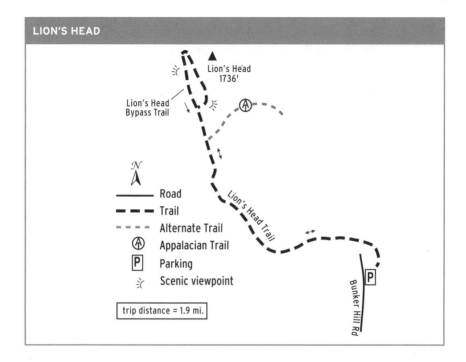

LION'S HEAD

Lion's Head
1736'

Lion's Head
Bypass Trail

Lion's Head Trail

Bunker Hill Rd

Road
Trail
Alternate Trail
Appalacian Trail
Parking
Scenic viewpoint

trip distance = 1.9 mi.

maple, apple, and black birch, with a scattered understory of striped maple. As the woods open into a fairyland of ferns, trilliums, and Canada mayflowers, the grade becomes moderate. Paper and gray birches begin to appear, and yellow-throated vireos can be seen clinging to pliant branches of understory shrubs as the birds hunt for food.

Just after crossing a stone wall, the grade becomes a bit easier and the path wanders between a fence line on the right and a field of ragged boulders to the left. Soon the blue-blazed Lion's Head Trail intersects the white-blazed AT and the path becomes a bouquet of blue-above-white blazes. Continue uphill through thickets of mountain laurel, wild azalea, blueberry, and wintergreen. As you continue to gain elevation, the character of the forest begins to change. Hemlock, oak, and white pine appear, shading boulders of metamorphic schist. The pale pink blossoms of wild azalea, which grow near the boulders, flower in late spring.

At a level spot on the hillside, the Lion's Head Bypass Trail continues straight ahead (north). In bad weather, the route over Lion's Head can be dangerous; the Bypass Trail was created to give hikers a safer path over the mountain. It also is a handy alternate route for those who think the steep scramble up to the overlook is a bit more than they can tackle.

The combined Lion's Head/AT turns right at the Bypass Trail, and you immediately scramble over steep, rocky terrain to the lookout. The top of Lion's

Painted trillium is one of the many spring wildflowers that bloom along the Appalachian Trail near Lion's Head.

Head (elevation 1,738 feet) is formed of rounded bedrock with small depressions and fissures filled with scree. The environment up here is unusually harsh. The nearly constant wind desiccates most plants, and the thin, nutrient-poor, rocky soil dries out quickly. The plant community that thrives in such rigorous conditions has developed the means to cope with the extreme climate. Pitch pine is the dominant conifer; its twisted branches and trunk look like a natural bonsai. Laurel is also common here; its leaves are coated with a waxy cuticle, inhibiting moisture loss. Smaller plants grow on the ridge, including three-leafed cinquefoil. This low-growing subalpine plant has white flowers perched on a slender, 4-inch-tall stalk in summer. The rich, glossy green leaves turn an intense scarlet in late summer and fall.

The views from the overlook are as interesting as the plants. To the east are the famous Twin Lakes of Salisbury. The closer and smaller of the two is called Washinee Lake, while the larger one is Washining Lake. To the northeast is a small body of water called Fisher Pond, which lies on the eastern flank of Mount Riga. All the hills and ponds that highlight the eastern view are set on the wide valley of the Housatonic River; its wide, fertile floodplain stretches for miles to the east.

HUMMINGBIRDS

Few creatures are as magical as hummingbirds. With plumage dyed in iridescent colors, they are like rainbows on the wing. About fourteen species of hummingbirds breed in North America, yet only one, the ruby-throated hummingbird, breeds in the eastern United States.

Ruby-throated hummingbirds are not the most colorful of hummingbirds, but they are the flashiest dressers of any bird east of the Mississippi River. The males are decked out with sparkling green feathers on their back and sides that shimmer like rhinestones, a snow-white breast, and a bold ruby-red patch beneath the chin. The females, which don't need to wear neon to get a male's attention, are more modestly attired with yellow-green feathers on their back and a white breast and throat.

Hummingbirds are tiny things, reaching only 3.5 inches when full grown. They are spectacular fliers and zip around forests and gardens with amazing speed. Hummingbirds can also hover and are the only birds that can fly backward. All this hyperactivity burns a lot of calories, and hummingbirds seem in a constant search for food. For entrées they like to nibble on small flying insects, which they grab and consume in the air. For dessert, the birds visit flowers to sip the sweet nectar.

Hummingbirds are migrants, spending their summers up north and wintering in the tropics. In late summer or early fall, ruby-throated hummingbirds travel south to their wintering grounds in Mexico, Belize, and Guatemala. There, these adaptable birds visit many habitats and are one of the few species that seem to thrive in previously deforested areas in the first stages of regrowth.

In addition to viewing hummingbirds in the wild, you can attract these magnificent birds to your yard by planting some of their favorite flowers in the garden. These include bee balm, cardinal flower, blazing star, fuchsia, hollyhock, foxglove, scarlet sage, spider flower, and petunia.

To the west you can hear the steady roar of Wachocastinook Brook as it pours from South Pond about a mile west of the overlook. Farther to the west are the tall, rounded hills of the Taconics. To the southeast, Wetauwanchu Mountain looms against the horizon, and to the south, Red Mountain forms the skyline.

From Lion's Head, the trail follows the rocky ridge through brushy stands of bear oak, pine, serviceberry, and blueberry. Before long, the Lion's Head

The summit of Lion's Head is crowned by a sign nestled among the branches of a pitch pine.

Bypass Trail enters left. Continue along the AT for a short distance to a rounded rock shelf and another beautiful view, this one to the north. Bear Mountain lies straight ahead, with Mount Race just to the right. Just beyond Mount Race is Mount Everett, the highest mountain in the southern Berkshires. On clear days, just to the right of Mount Race, the saddle-shaped form of Mount Greylock, the tallest peak in Massachusetts, is visible some 70 miles away.

Some attractive, ephemeral wildflowers grow in the nearby hardwood forest; gaywings are one of the most unusual and enchanting species. These diminutive plants produce small, bright pink blossoms shaped like tiny airplanes. Return to the parking area the way you came.

MORE INFORMATION

Because this trail crosses portions of private property it is important that hikers use the trail only during daylight hours and that they stay on the established trail and carry out all litter. Camping, fires, motorized vehicles, mountain bikes, and horses are not permitted. Hunting and tree cutting are prohibited. This section of the AT is maintained by the Connecticut Chapter of the AMC; 860-742-8243; www.ct-amc.org.

—C. S.

TRIP 4
SHARON AUDUBON CENTER

Location: Sharon
Rating: Easy
Distance: 2.5 miles
Elevation Gain: 210 feet
Estimated Time: 2.0 hours
Map: USGS Ellsworth, Sharon Audubon Center Trails map (available online)

This is a loop hike on a diverse rural property of 1,147 mostly wooded acres that features scenic Bog Meadow Pond, abundant wildlife, and teeming wetlands.

DIRECTIONS
In Sharon, from the gray granite clock tower at the intersection of Routes 4/41/343, turn onto Route 4 and travel east for 2.35 miles. Turn right off Route 4 into the Sharon Audubon Center property and bear right for less than 0.1 mile to the parking area.

TRAIL DESCRIPTION
From the map kiosk near the parking lot, follow the sign for Ford/Hal Borland Trail, crossing the wooden bridge over Herrick Brook. Ahead is the Explorer Hut. Examine the brook banks for signs of nocturnal foragers such as raccoons. Reach the Deer Trail junction at the hut and turn left to follow its rectangular red blazes among hemlock, sugar maple, red oak, and yellow birch—all but oak are northern hardwood forest indicators. Chunks of gneiss (pronounced *nice*) rock jut from the forest floor, while skunk cabbage, cinnamon fern, and sensitive fern grow in the gurgling brook's drainage beneath hemlocks. Red trillium (wake-robin) and jack-in-the-pulpit line the chipped path.

Emerge from the forest at the Ice House. The stone spillway of Ford Pond is just ahead to the left. Turn right, pass the Ice House, and follow the Bog Meadow/Fern Trails, which fork left away from the old road track. In late spring, wild raisin shrubs are studded with clusters of lacy white flowers. Later, its blue-black fruits provide food for wildlife. The dam's rock wall is on the left, and Ford Pond is visible as you reach the top. You find a nice view of the pond from the bridge over the spillway. The hills just beyond form an attractive

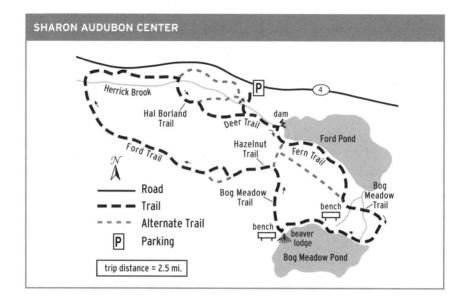

SHARON AUDUBON CENTER

Herrick Brook

Hal Borland
Trail

Deer Trail

dam

Ford Pond

Hazelnut
Trail

Fern Trail

Ford Trail

N

———— Road

- - - Trail

- - - Alternate Trail

P   Parking

trip distance = 2.5 mi.

Bog Meadow
Trail

Bog
Meadow
Trail

bench

bench

beaver
lodge

Bog Meadow Pond

backdrop. The pond surface is covered with yellow-green filamentous algae, fertilized by Canada geese. Water-loving birds such as red-winged blackbird, warbling vireo, and tree swallow sing breeding songs in spring and early summer here.

Walk right and back to the Bog Meadow trailhead. As you enter the woods, turn left onto the green-blazed Fern Trail to follow the pond's edge closely (the Bog Meadow Trail continues straight). Pretty royal fern joins sensitive fern in damp soil, while Christmas and evergreen wood fern form clumps amid the rocks. Hay-scented and interrupted fern thrive nearby on higher ground. Cinnamon fern also is abundant; tapping its tawny, fertile fronds in spring liberates a cloud of rusty spores. Beavers girdled some red maples along the water's edge long ago. Their old bank lodge is visible on the far shore. One uncommonly large American chestnut tree is protected from the rodents' sharp incisors by a wire cage. The wonderfully fragrant, carnation-like aroma you smell in late spring emanates from the delicate pink blossoms of mountain azaleas. Reach the Fern Trail/Bog Meadow Trail intersection and continue straight on the Fern Trail. The path divides briefly to bypass a long-fallen casualty.

A mid-June visit featured glimpses of a male yellow-bellied sapsucker drinking from rows of oblong sap wells he had drilled in a young black birch. After the sapsucker left, a ruby-throated hummingbird took its turn lapping up the sweet liquid, rich in oil of wintergreen, as it hovered on whirring wings. Sap provides a vital early-season nutrition source for hummingbirds after they first return from the south. Continue by swinging away from the pond, through red oak, red maple, and witch hazel growth. After 0.5 mile, reach a four-way intersection with the white-blazed Hendrickson Bog Meadow Trail and turn left. Witch hazel, from which the astringent is distilled, is abundant, along with beaked hazelnut.

Very soon you reach a soggy area bordering a stream. Cross a wooden bridge where skunk cabbage, wetland ferns, and golden ragwort, sporting egg-yolk-yellow blossoms, thrive in the dampness. At the end of the board-walk/bridge, a boulder has sprouted delicate maidenhair fern. Wild geranium blooms in late spring along the trail. Cross another small stream on stepping-stones. In spring and early summer, gaudy Baltimore orioles and well-camouflaged red-eyed vireos sing from a small fern-filled clearing. The trail swings left and soon reaches a fork with Woodchuck Trail on the left; continue on the Bog Meadow Trail.

Pass a big rock outcrop on the right. A rocky slope rises up to the left, and then the trail bears right past highbush blueberry shrubs to Bog Meadow Pond, a far more natural scene than Ford Pond. Green frogs croak their comical banjo-like gulps, and swamp sparrows sing their cheery musical trills from the lush bordering vegetation. Tussock sedge clumps dot this marshy end. A forested ridge looms 400 feet above the pond—a wild and idyllic scene. To the right of the path grows one of the most luxuriant stands of skunk cabbage and cinnamon fern I have ever seen. It is reminiscent of the Carboniferous Age! The path actually follows the top of an earthen dam, and soon you'll reach a concrete outflow piled high with old beaver cuttings.

Cross the outflow on a short boardwalk. A thick, hairy poison ivy vine climbs a tree to the right; some also grows along the ground, where red maple is the dominant tree. Watch for turkey vultures rocking on the rising air currents over the ridge and listen for the wild cries of ravens. The trail then passes through a small but dense stand of giant reed. Leafy twigs recently cut by beavers float on the water as you reach a boardwalk where a bench makes a perfect place to enjoy a snack. While I was eating lunch, red and black ants tended their aphid "cows" on an arrowwood bush immediately behind me. The ants protect the aphids from predators for the aphids' honey dew-like secretions, an arrangement that seems to suit both well. On the opposite "shore," a red maple swamp covers an area larger than the pond itself.

Continue down the boardwalk to a T-intersection with the Oak Trail on the right. (The 100-foot-long left branch ends at the water's edge in a wide deck with benches.) After leaving the boardwalk, turn left to continue on the Bog Meadow Trail along the shore. Witch hazel is still very common, and red oak is now the most dominant large tree. One has a wood duck nest box attached. These are definitely drier woods, with hickories and bracken ferns

A wild and idyllic scene awaits hikers along the Bog Meadow Pond.

appearing. Pass through a gap in an old stone wall where chipmunks seem to be the prevalent life-form. In late spring, black cherry, black raspberry, and diminutive bluet all bloom along it. Paralleling the wall, the sun-bathed path is alive in early summer with butterflies basking and seeking nectar.

A bit farther along is an old beaver-cut area now lush with sedges and shrubs. Reenter shaded woods, where pink-blooming wild geraniums are plentiful in June. An imposing rock wall, 10- to 12-feet thick and waist high, is now close at hand. What effort must have gone into constructing it! The evocative aroma of pine pitch fills the air as you reach an intersection amid white pines nearly 1.0 mile from the parking area. Turn right onto the Bog Meadow Trail, but before following it, walk left 150 feet to the shore and bench to examine the active bank beaver lodge. It is anchored by a large, multi-trunked red maple.

Be alert for the pungent smell of beaver castoreum. Beavers secrete the substance to mark their territories against intrusion from neighboring clans. Return to the main Bog Meadow Trail. Walk up a slight hill to emerge at the edge of a field studded with pairs of bluebird nest boxes. In summer, nesting tree swallows poke their bi-colored heads out of the boxes. This small, sandy meadow has scattered red cedar (a sign of former pasturing) and gneiss rocks. Pass through another gap in a rock wall and soon reach the four-way intersection with the Oak Trail. Continue straight on the white-blazed Bog Meadow Trail downhill under oaks and maples with a few hickories and white pines. Below the trees witch hazel, beaked hazel, and chestnut saplings grow. Sessile-leafed bellwort, or wild oats, is one of the most common forbs in these oak woods. It reveals its modest, pale yellow pendant flowers in spring.

At a junction just before a large rock outcrop, 1.1 miles from the start, turn left onto the Hazelnut Trail. Almost immediately cross old Bog Meadow

Road in a slight depression and continue straight uphill. To the left stands a collier's hut replica and demonstration charcoal mound. In late spring, white-blooming starflower brightens the forest floor under the oak, maple, birch, and hickory. New York fern and wild sarsaparilla are abundant. The Hazelnut Trail splits and rejoins a short distance farther along. The right fork is fairly wide and shaded. Gradually climb through oak woods and soon reach the intersection of the Hazelnut and Ford Trails. Turn right onto the Ford Trail. Listen for scarlet tanagers singing continuously from the oaks in early summer.

The trail is narrow and bordered by lowbush blueberry and soon starts downhill steeply. After undulating, it enters shady hemlock woods virtually devoid of ground cover and then descends more steeply again. The increasing volume of vehicular traffic foretells the nearing highway. "No Hunting" signs mark the sanctuary boundary to the left.

Continue fairly steeply downhill into maple, ash, and birch forest. Bear left at a boulder and pass an old hemlock snag riddled by cavernous pileated woodpecker excavations. At the bottom of the hemlock-shaded slope, Herrick Brook carries water from Ford Pond. Amble downstream along the bubbling brook to a wooden bridge over it, scanning the mud for tracks of deer and other woodland denizens. Walk through skunk cabbage—its bruised leaves emit a fetid odor. Enter a small clearing much warmer than the dank forest. The trail bears right, close to the highway. Continue through two tiny clearings and reenter woods. Oriental bittersweet, draping the woodland edge, is characteristic of disturbed areas like this.

Here an exquisitely camouflaged American woodcock burst from its daytime ground roost one June day. The bird sat tight until I was within 5 feet of it. These plump, long-billed "shorebirds" extract earthworms from moist soil with their marvelous, flexible-tipped bills. Pass an old wooden gate near the road, where Japanese barberry, another invasive exotic, proliferates. The trail drops below the road, and in its soft, dark mud you can spot the cloven-hoofed tracks of white-tailed deer easily. Fallen hemlocks are numerous. At 2.0 miles, come to a T-intersection with the red-blazed Borland Trail—named for the late Connecticut naturalist and nature writer Hal Borland. Turn right to move farther away from the busy roadway. You'll pass a big uprooted hemlock and walk through a moist area where blue violets bloom in late spring.

Cross Herrick Brook on a wooden bridge and pass beneath an overhanging grapevine. Climb the hill shaded by hemlocks. Among the evergreens stand a few big old pioneering yellow and black birches. Climb moderately and level off on the slope's flank. The explosive, sneezy "song" of an Acadian flycatcher may find your ear here. Hemlock ravines are favorite haunts of

HOW SWEET IT IS!

Sapsuckers are unique among woodpeckers in that they are adapted to exploit an abundant resource unavailable to other members of their tribe. They drill rows of small holes through the outer bark of maple, birch, and other tree species with sweet, high-calorie sap, and then repeatedly visit the sap wells to lap up the liquid as well as the insects that have been attracted to its flow.

I was fascinated to witness the comings and goings of a pair of yellow-bellied sapsuckers on a 4.5-inch diameter black birch during a mid-June visit. The sap wells covered a grid 18 inches high and encircled the trunk about 9 feet above the ground. Each hole was horizontal, and some were quite large for sap wells (0.75 inch by 0.25 inch). They were drilled all the way to the inner bark, or cambium (growth), layer. The upper, 8-inch-high portion of the grid was obviously fresh and appeared wet from the flow of sap. The lower portion was old and dark, no longer producing. Both birds fed only from the fresh, top portion of the well field.

The male sapsucker, distinguished from his mate by a red throat, made squeaky, mewing sounds as I watched, while a ruby-throated hummingbird buzzed in the immediate vicinity awaiting its opportunity to feed. On at least one occasion I saw the tiny hummingbird sampling the sweet fluid on hovering wings.

After the male sapsucker left, his mate appeared and took her turn, wicking up the sweet, oily sap with her bristle-tipped tongue. Then the male returned. With my wristwatch I timed the length of their visits to the well field and the intervals between visits. The intervals between visits ranged from 3.5 to almost 10 minutes, with 5 to 6.5 minutes being most common. The male did not remain long when he returned after only 3.5 minutes had elapsed since his previous visit. Perhaps that wasn't sufficient time for the wells to have filled again.

Both male and female generally spent about 3 minutes engaged in lapping up sap at each visit. On two occasions I witnessed the male arriving with a bill already loaded with insects. He had probably collected these from one or more additional well fields in the vicinity. He proceeded to dab his already insect laden bill into the sap wells, seemingly in an effort to soak up as much of the sweet fluid as possible. Both sapsuckers flew off each time in the same direction, and I concluded that they were returning to their nest cavity to feed their ravenous young.

this little neotropical migrant. Follow the red-blazed trail uphill amid large, moss-covered boulders. Black-throated green and black-and-white warblers sing in summer where the boulder-strewn slope rises to the right. Enter birch, maple, and oak woods as the trail levels off. Continue straight onto the Deer Trail; ahead is the brown Explorer Hut. Listen for the soothing sound of water flowing over the Old Mill Race spillway. Stay right of the hut, turn sharply left around it, and then go right to recross the small wooden bridge that leads up the steps and back to the parking area. The Center's natural history museum has live raptors. An outdoor aviary is also available.

MORE INFORMATION

Trails and Raptor Center are open dawn to dusk. Non-member fees are adults $3, children and seniors $1.50. Visitor Center and Nature Store open Tuesday through Saturday 9 A.M. to 5 P.M., Sunday 1 P.M. to 5 P.M. Closed Mondays and major holidays. Restrooms are located in the Visitor Center. Leashed dogs are allowed on certain trails, as marked. Sharon Audubon Center, 325 Cornwall Bridge Road (Route 4), Sharon, CT; 860-364-0520; http://www.sharon.audubon.org/about/about_trail.html.

—R. L.

TRIP 5
PINE KNOB LOOP TRAIL

Location: Sharon
Rating: Moderate, with challenging sections
Distance: 2.6 miles
Elevation Gain: 700 feet
Estimated Time: 1.5–2.5 hours
Maps: USGS Ellsworth

Within the Housatonic Meadows State Park, this is a lovely loop walk over rugged hills, along a brook, and through pine and hemlock groves with beautiful views of the Housatonic Valley.

DIRECTIONS
From the junction of Routes 4/7 in Cornwall Bridge, proceed 1.0 mile north on Route 7 to the parking area on the left.

TRAIL DESCRIPTION
From the parking area in a mixed grove of sugar maples, the trail enters a shady woodland with false Solomon's seal, jewelweed, and jack-in-the-pulpit beneath the leafy canopy. Jewelweed is a succulent herb that grows in shady, moist places. The flowers are rusty orange or pale yellow and delicately hang from the plant on filament-like stems. When the leaves of the flowers are held underwater, the undersides of the leaves shine with silvery color—the reason for the common name jewelweed. In late summer, the small, ripe seed capsules will pop open in your hand, a trait that gave the plant its other common name: touch-me-not. Jewelweed is also a traditional remedy for poison ivy.

The path crosses Hatch Brook on stepping-stones and briefly parallels a stone wall before crossing the brook. Here the Pine Knob Trail splits. You will be returning on the trail straight to the north. Turn on the trail to the left (northwest), which now climbs along the crest of Hatch Brook Ravine. Along the way, the path passes through groves of hemlock sprinkled with isolated specimens of oak, ash, and maple. The brook is a noisy, cheerful companion as it trips over stones and ledges in a seemingly endless series of small cascades. As you walk above the stream, look for the slender, ghostly white stems of Indian peace pipe popping through the leaf litter of the forest floor in late summer. Look also for patches of minty wintergreen as well as tangles

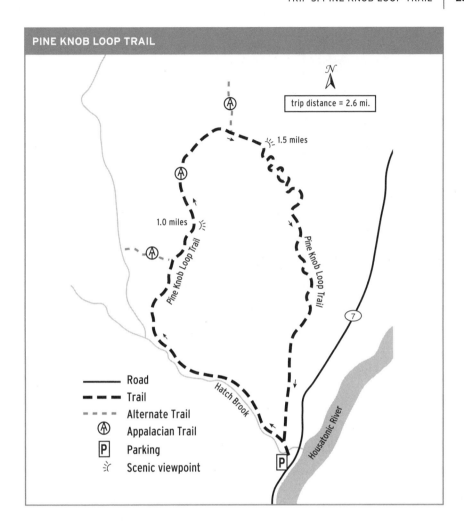

PINE KNOB LOOP TRAIL

trip distance = 2.6 mi.

1.5 miles

1.0 miles

Pine Knob Loop Trail

Pine Knob Loop Trail

7

——— Road

▬ ▬ ▬ Trail

- - - - Alternate Trail

Ⓐ Appalacian Trail

P Parking

Scenic viewpoint

Hatch Brook

Housatonic River

P

of maple-leaf viburnum, mountain laurel, and witch hazel. The white flowers of mountain laurel bloom in late spring, while the spidery yellow blossoms of witch hazel appear in early fall.

The trail then levels out and comes to a beautiful section of brook. The streambed is a bedrock shelf pocked with small potholes. Skunk cabbage, Christmas fern, princess pine, and trillium decorate the ground, while the sweet songs of veeries and warblers float through the trees. This is definitely a small patch of paradise. You will pass some large, interesting boulders. The path then begins a moderate climb through woods of maple, oak, and hemlock, with Canada mayflower, ground cedar, and Indian cucumber-root beneath.

At a small, level spot, the Pine Knob Loop Trail intersects the white-blazed Appalachian Trail (AT). Turn right (northwest) onto the AT, which leads up

The crest of Pine Knob is a rocky, forested ledge overlooking the Housatonic Valley.

the rugged slopes of Pine Knob. As it gains elevation, the path weaves through boulders where wild geranium, with loose clusters of nickel-sized lavender flowers in spring, grows around the rocks. Wood thrush can also be found here hunting for insects beneath the umbrella-shaped leaves of wild sarsaparilla. The path then begins a steep, rocky climb that leads to the first overlook, passing beneath hickory, oak, and maple, with blueberry, wild rose, and stump sprouts of American chestnut lining the treadway. The rocky ledge offers a nice place to rest and enjoy the broad southwest view of Mine Mountain with Dean Hill beyond. Turkey vultures frequently glide by, reminders that some creatures have found easier ways to reach the mountaintops.

From the overlook, the trail continues to climb for a while before leveling out at the ridge top. This is a lovely stretch of forest with hemlock, chestnut oak, and black birch sheltering lady's slipper, mountain laurel, wild azalea, and lots of chipmunks. These cute little striped rodents aren't as vocal as red squirrels, which also live here. Instead of the scolding chatter of red squirrels, chipmunks—actually a type of ground squirrel—let out a sharp chirp to warn other chipmunks of trespassers and then scurry for shelter.

The trail now comes to one of my favorite places in the northwest hills, the summit of Pine Knob. This small wild plateau, sprinkled with tussocks of grass and rugged, rocky outcrops, has a rough-hewn beauty all its own. In winter, you find nice views through the leafless trees out over the wooded Housatonic

Valley. From Pine Knob, the path descends steeply to a forested, level area where the AT leaves left (north) and the Pine Knob Trail turns right (south-southwest). This is a lovely walk through tangled thickets of mountain laurel and delicate plants of trailing arbutus that grow along the side of the trail.

The path then makes a brief scramble to a gorgeous, rocky overlook carpeted with blueberry, huckleberry, dogbane, and sweet fern. Pitch pine, chestnut oak, and white pine cling to the steep slope. Below, the Housatonic River Valley flows south, framed by the forested flanks of Mine Mountain, Dean Hill, and Coltsfoot Mountain. Phoebes, cardinals, wood thrushes, and chickadees call from the trees, while hairy woodpeckers leave small, frayed excavations in nearby tree trunks. This spot is a lovely place to linger and relax before beginning the descent to the parking area.

From the overlook, the trail turns left and falls steeply down the rough hillside. Near a large rock formation, the grade moderates, descending through deep woods of oak and mountain laurel. The path then approaches the edge of a cliff, which it follows past a century-old red cedar to a slender stream and a small, mossy waterfall. From here, the terrain becomes gentler, and the trail crosses a series of streams and stone walls as it meanders through the cool shade of tall, white pines. A west loop portion of the Pine Knob Trail leaves right. Continue straight along the Pine Knob Trail (southwest) past the trail loop junction. After you cross Hatch Brook, the parking lot is just a few yards farther.

MORE INFORMATION

Housatonic Meadows State Park offers opportunities for fly fishing and canoeing and features a campground near the Housatonic River with bathrooms and showers. Leashed dogs are permitted on the trails, but not in the campground. The park is open from 8:00 A.M. to sunset. No charge. Housatonic Meadows State Park, c/o Macedonia Brook State Park, 159 Macedonia Brook Road, Kent, CT 06757; 860-927-3238; http://www.ct.gov/dep.

—C. S.

Location: Cornwall
Rating: Moderate, with challenging sections
Distance: 3.7 miles
Elevation Gain: 740 feet
Estimated Time: 2.5–3.5 hours
Maps: USGS Cornwall

Change eventually comes to everything. Such is the case with Cathedral Pines and Mohawk Mountain (elevation 1,683 feet). These beautiful places lay in the path of a train of tornadoes that swept through the hills in the summer of 1989. In the forests, and in the human communities around them, things have not been the same since. Still, mountain views and ancient trees filled with songbirds await you.

DIRECTIONS

From the junction of Routes 4/125 in Cornwall, turn onto Pine Street (opposite the spot where Route 125 meets Route 4). Proceed past the Cornwall Town Library to a stop sign at the intersection with Valley Road. Turn left onto Valley Road and proceed 0.2 mile. Veer left onto Essex Hill Road and drive 0.2 mile to a small parking area on the left near a large boulder.

TRAIL DESCRIPTION

This out-and-back walk is entirely on the Mohawk Trail, which is blazed with pale blue marks. Turns are noted by two stacked blazes, the top blaze offset in the direction of the turn.

From the parking area, follow the pale blue blazes south past a large pine windfall. This area was once the heart of Cathedral Pines; today the tree trunks of this formerly great forest are heaped one atop the other in disarray. Beneath them grow the first wave of trees and other plants that constitute a first-succession woodland. Pin cherry, which bears candy-scented blossoms in May, is joined by saplings of hemlock and red maple, as well as thickets of honeysuckle, raspberry, and elder. In the few remaining spaces, goldenrod, dandelion, wild strawberry, and trillium grow.

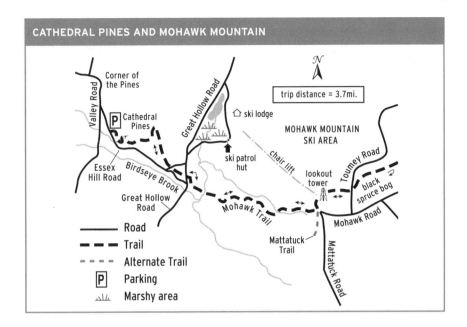

Succession woodlands are wonderful places to look for birds, and a typical spring day here will find red-winged blackbirds, goldfinches, catbirds, chickadees, warblers, blue jays, and sometimes the honk of Canada geese or the shrill call of a red-tailed hawk.

The path heads uphill past a small, bubbling brook and ascends a staircase of wooden steps set into the hillside. Soon the open landscape yields to a deep forest of towering white pine and hemlock. Spared the wrath of the tornadoes, these trees are all that remains of the Cathedral Pines (see essay in this chapter). The evergreen canopy is high overhead, and the massive, majestic trunks inspire humility in many of the hikers who pass through.

Continue uphill into a hemlock grove where deer are frequent visitors and pileated woodpeckers carve large, rectangular holes in the trees. The path crests the top of a rise and then descends into a shallow swale before again heading up the rocky hillside past an enormous white pine on the right. Starflower, partridgeberry, and Canada mayflower grow along the ground, while chipmunks scurry for shelter in the crevices of nearby boulders. The path then enters another section of forest damaged by the tornadoes, with blowdowns of hemlock sheltering crowds of pin cherry that grow up through the fallen trunks and branches. Turning south, the path merges with an old woods road and gently descends through the hemlocks, keeping a stone wall in sight to the left. Eventually the hemlocks yield to a

JULY 1989

Cathedral Pines is a blend of tall, straight-trunked white pine and hemlock ranging in age from about 100 to 300 years old. Some of the oldest trees began growing here about 1676, at the end of King Philip's War. In 1883, the forest was purchased by the Calhoun family, who protected it from logging until they donated the 42-acre grove to The Nature Conservancy in 1967. In 1980, a small tornado damaged some of the trees, but the majesty of the pines remained largely untouched. At the time, people breathed a sigh of relief that the storm had mostly missed this priceless legacy. Others believed that the trees were so massive and strong that storms were not a threat to them. What no one could possibly know, however, was that Cathedral Pines would nearly disappear in less than a decade.

The morning of July 10, 1989, was a typical summer day, with warm temperatures and fair skies. It was not typical in other ways. The humidity was high, and the water vapor collected energy from the sun and warm atmosphere like a battery storing electricity. In the early afternoon, a disturbance in the atmosphere began to tap that stored energy. Mountainous dark clouds began building over the upper Hudson Valley of New York, and a line of thunderstorms began to build into the sky. As the squall line matured, the thunderstorms became well defined and distinct. The entire assemblage rolled southeast toward the Taconics and Berkshires.

As the storm front passed over the southern Berkshires, it filled the sky with heavy, swirling clouds and gusty winds, turning the late afternoon into twilight. When it entered Connecticut, the weather radar at Albany detected the hook-shaped radar echoes from the storm cells that are the signature of a tornado. The swirling cloud bank had become a rotating cloud wall, then a funnel cloud that barreled through the sky toward Cornwall.

At 4:30 in the afternoon, two fully formed tornadoes touched down on Cemetery Hill in Cornwall, destroying acres of forest. One storm headed southeast toward the village center, while another rolled south toward Corner of the Pines and the great old forest. The storms lasted just a few horrific minutes. But in some ways they have never gone away.

The tornadoes of that July afternoon in 1989 destroyed something older than the town of Cornwall, older than the state of Connecticut, older even than the country. Cathedral Pines had been nearly completely destroyed. Only a few of the oldest trees survived.

Today the massive fallen trunks are being covered slowly by vigorous young hardwoods. When pine forests are damaged severely, they often do not regenerate, but simply disappear. In their place grow stands of hardwoods instead of pine. And that fact of succession—that this spot may never again host such a grove of trees—is the deepest wound, for it steals away hope. Then comes the realization that the storms not only stole the present and the past, but robbed the future. Not even centuries will bring back Cathedral Pines, a fact that makes the small surviving grove that much more precious.

mixed hardwood forest of ash and red maple with thorny barberry bushes beneath. Deer trails cross the path here and there, and wild turkeys come through in groups of ten or more.

At the junction with Essex Hill Road, turn left (west) onto the road and follow it a short distance to a stop sign. Turn right (south) onto Great Hollow Road and proceed to the base of the hill. Here the trail turns left (east-southeast) and follows a private driveway past a residence on the right. Continue across a wooden bridge into an open field marked with ruts of an old logging road.

Follow the wide, grassy path uphill past horsetail, dandelion, apple, willow, and weeping bushes of multiflora rose. Catbirds and phoebes sing in the trees, while hawks often soar in ever-widening circles overhead. As the path continues uphill, it enters an area of near-complete devastation that marks the primary debris field of the tornadoes. It has been many years now since the storms, and the woods are a chaotic riot of trees and shrubs crowding each other for space and light. Direct signs of the tornadoes still exist, but are often overgrown by the young forest. Broken trunks and a few tall dead trees remain as reminders. **Caution!** This area has an abundance of ticks, and it is common to encounter them on the trail. Use bug repellent and check yourself frequently.

The path climbs the slope of Mohawk Mountain through a seemingly endless area of blowdowns, saplings, and songbirds. Indian paintbrush blossoms here in summer, and the tart clusters of wild grape that hang from sapling white birch ripen in early fall. The path then leaves the sapling woods and enters a grassy field with pleasing northwest views. Quarry Hill is the small hill to the north, and White Rock is the ridge to the northwest, with Coltsfoot

Tornadoes wreak destruction but also create new habitats for countless species.

Mountain beyond. The field is home to woodland jumping mice, little brown furry things with 6-inch-long tails, and eastern coyotes, which hunt the mice and other rodents. Deer, rabbits, and grouse visit now and again, and if you believe some of the local folks (and there is no reason not to), the nearby hills are home to a few mountain lions.

From the field, the trail continues uphill, briefly passing through scrubby woods before entering a more mature hardwood forest. The path crosses a small brook where colonies of trillium and wild oats bloom in spring beneath the branches of alder, black birch, cherry, and red maple. After crossing a second stream and skirting a ski trail descending from the Mohawk Ski Area, the path enters a beautiful woodland savanna framed by stone walls, with large ash and maple trees above soft woodland grasses. Warblers and thrushes are here in spring and summer, which adds to the beauty of this charming spot.

The path then turns left and climbs repeatedly over stone walls as it meanders past oak, white pine, ash, and black birch to the junction of the Mohawk and Mattatuck Trails.

Turn left (north) onto the Mohawk Trail and proceed about 20 yards to the top of the chair lift and some beautiful views. To the left is a low stone tower that kids like to play on; it offers limited views. The best view is from the head of the grassy ski trail just beneath the lift. To the north are the Taconic Mountains, including Mount Race and Mount Everett in the Berkshires. To the northwest are the Catskills of New York. In fall, when the foliage is at its peak, this is an especially nice place to be. From the ski lift, it is a short walk along the trail to Black Spruce Bog. This fragile ecosystem is home to many plants common to more northerly climates. A boardwalk guides you over the moss-covered boulders and roots where black spruce and leatherleaf grow. After returning to the ski lift, you can retrace your steps to the parking area.

MORE INFORMATION

Leashed dogs are permitted on trails. Free admission. Mohawk State Forest, 20 Mohawk Mountain Road, Goshen, CT 06746; 860-491-3620; http://www. ct.gov/dep.

—C. S.

TRIP 7
WOLCOTT TRAIL AND BURR POND

Location: Torrington
Rating: Easy
Distance: 2.75 miles
Elevation Gain: 80 feet
Estimated Time: 1.5 hours
Map: USGS Torrington, Burr Pond State Park map available online

This is a loop hike along the scenic Burr Pond shoreline, part of an 1,800-acre recreational complex, that features massive glacial boulders and luxuriant laurel and azalea blooms.

DIRECTIONS

From the center of Torrington, drive north on Route 8 to Exit 45 (Kennedy Road). At the end of the ramp, turn left under the highway, then right at Winsted Road; follow it for almost 3.1 miles to Burr Mountain Road on the left. Follow Burr Mountain Road for 0.5 mile to the park entrance on the left. Drive 0.2 mile to the gravel parking lot on the left.

From the north, take Exit 46 off Route 8 in Torrington. At the end of the ramp, turn right onto Pinewoods Road. Drive 0.25 mile to the first stop sign and turn left onto Winsted Road. Follow Winsted Road for 1.0 mile to Burr Mountain Road at the blinking yellow signal. Turn right and follow Burr Mountain Road for 0.5 mile to the state park entrance on the left.

TRAIL DESCRIPTION

Cross the paved road toward Burr Pond to pick up the blue-blazed Wolcott Trail, named for the Civilian Conservation Corps' (CCC) Camp Wolcott. The trail enters hemlock-birch (both gray and black) woodland with a mountain laurel shrub layer and then almost immediately splits. Turn right (north) and walk along the east shore of the pond, built in 1851 by Milo Burr to provide power for a tannery, three sawmills, and America's first condensed-milk plant, owned by Gail Borden (1857). Chalky gray birches with straight boles contrast aesthetically with the dark trunks of eastern hemlocks. Gneiss (pronounced *nice*) boulders with alternating gray and white banding protrude from the forest floor. In June, mountain laurel shrubs, especially those receiving ample sunlight, are heavy with nickel-sized pink-and-white blossoms. Bird song fills

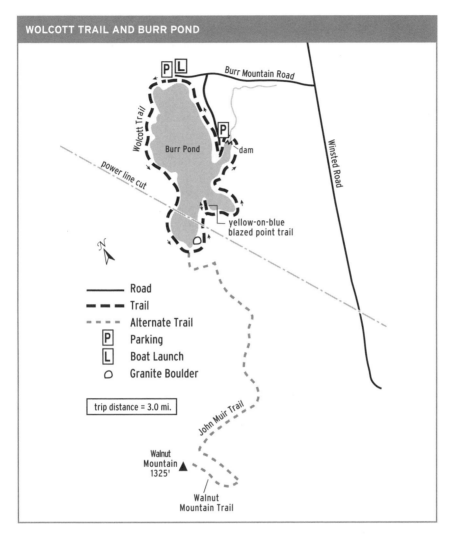

WOLCOTT TRAIL AND BURR POND

the air, virtually the only sound that disrupts the stillness. Listen for the voices of tufted titmouse, American goldfinch, white-breasted nuthatch, tree swallow, great crested flycatcher, and song sparrow in early summer. On a calm day, the flat surface of 0.75-mile-long Burr Pond serves as a mirror for the tranquility of the shore.

The level trail enters shadier hemlock woods that also contain red oaks. Some hemlocks are imposing at 2.5 feet in diameter. Pass a rock outcrop located to the right as American beech, yellow birch, and white ash trees appear. Witch hazel and young gray birch are part of the understory. One big, smooth gray beech is disfigured with carved graffiti as high as an adult can reach. It will remain visible for the remainder of the tree's life. The trail swings left as you parallel Burr Mountain Road. In early July, the sweet fragrance of azaleas hangs heavily in the still air. The pond is visible through the numerous yellow birches. Ducks often loaf on the nearby boulder islet that protrudes from its surface.

Cross a small boardwalk bridge over a tiny stream and enter a damp, overgrown area where gray catbirds fuss at intruders. Elderberry, yellow loosestrife, and meadow rue bloom in early summer, while tall sedges and sensitive fern are non-flowering indicators of damp soil. Arrive at the boat-launch parking area, which the trail crosses. Enter black birch and white ash woods and pick up the trail on the far side. The showy rose-purple blossoms of purple flowering raspberry add color to the scene in early summer. Cross a small bridge over a rocky stream. Some very large red and black oaks appear as a house up and off to the right comes into view. A resort facility follows.

Walk under hemlock, beech, oak, and red maple as the path swings slightly left. American beech—which, like hemlock, is very tolerant of shade—joins its evergreen partner at this northern end of Burr Pond. Six-and-a-half-inch redeyed vireos sing their monotonous phrases loudly, but invisibly, from the forest canopy. Now cross several small bridges over a boulder-strewn feeder stream and then almost immediately a second shallow flow. The leathery fronds of evergreen wood fern poke up from the scant soils atop the rocks. Red trillium (also known as wake-robin and stinking Benjamin) and Christmas fern, another evergreen, thrive in the moist, organic soil below.

Pass a large dead hemlock snag amid sizable live specimens of the same species and reach a wet area of cinnamon fern, elderberry shrubs, hemlock, and smooth winterberry. The acidic soil here is a rich, almost black, muck. Goldthread, a 6-inch-tall wetland indicator, sports three shiny, evergreen, scalloped leaves. The yellow-orange runners by which it spreads give it its name, and its white, star-shaped flowers appear in spring. Two vines, one poisonous, also grow here. Virginia creeper has five leaflets and smooth stems, whereas the infamous poison ivy has three leaflets and hairy stems.

Now reenter higher, drier hemlock woods and pass a house-sized glacial boulder adorned with rock tripe (a leafy lichen) and mosses. The boulder's flat face holds a memorial brass plaque 12 feet up honoring Phil Buttrick (1886–1945), a forester and later secretary of the Connecticut Forest and Parks Association who supervised the work of building Camp Wolcott. Pass over more short bridges over feeder streams. Water striders skate over the dark waters, supported by the water's elastic surface tension. Note the old beaver cuttings within a pond inlet close at hand on the left. The yellow flowers of bullhead lilies protrude above the pond's surface in summer. Indian

Look back over your shoulder at the power line cut for a stunning view of Burr Pond through hemlocks.

cucumber-root, which grows from an edible tuber the size of your little finger, sports rather small greenish-yellow blossoms and thrives in moist rich soil. The public beach is visible across the pond. Pass through an area of hemlocks whose lower branches are all dead and then by a very big red oak with a gneiss boulder behind it.

American beech predominates again as the hillside rises gradually. White pines become numerous and are then displaced by hemlock. Here I watched a red squirrel as it gathered dry beech leaves from the ground and took them in its mouth up a nearby tree, presumably for lining its nest. The forest floor is dotted with rounded gneiss boulders. Catch a glimpse of Burr Pond to the left through an opening, while up ahead a power-line cut comes into view. The ground below your feet is cushioned with a bouncy layer of decaying hemlock needles. Enter the sunny north-south power-line cut, which stimulates plant growth and insect diversity. Black-throated green warbler, veery, ovenbird, song sparrow, and cedar waxwing are all in full voice here in late spring and early summer. Cross a small rocky streambed, nearly dry in summer, and re-enter mostly hemlock-beech woods.

The trail rises gradually, passing through a small boulder field of now familiar gneiss rock. A red oak with five trunks stands on the left; its central

THE ICE SHEET COMETH

The area around Burr Pond and indeed the north-south-trending depression it now occupies are peppered with stones that were swept along by, and in fact became the scouring grit for, the advancing Pleistocene ice sheets that left their permanent marks and products on the New England landscape between 400,000 and 13,000 years ago.

Huge cabin-sized gneiss and granite boulders enhancing the rough terrain of the area were transported to this locality by a massive sheet of glacial ice more than a mile thick that eventually overspread the region three times during what is popularly known as the ice ages. The last of these ice ages, when mean annual temperatures were only 5 degrees lower on average than today's temperatures, began to reverse a mere 16,000 or so years ago.

The ice sheet formed over millennia, as summers became gradually but steadily cooler. The length of time between the end of one winter and the beginning of another is usually about 7 months today; during the ice ages this hiatus of warm weather separating seasons of snowfall became ever briefer, until they had dwindled away altogether. Snow fell nearly year-round. It had barely begun to melt when a new winter season descended. In time, snow accumulated ever deeper, compacting to form ice under its own crushing weight. As the ice sheet inexorably ground its way southward, it flowed over the land's surface with an incredible abrading force, wiping clean whole areas of their soils, vegetation, and animal life and leaving gouges, scratches, and rock debris (glacial till) behind.

Ahead of the ice sheet tundra-like conditions prevailed. Bitter winds and frigid temperatures made southern New England a very different place from what it is today. But eventually the climate began to ameliorate. Summer returned and lengthened over the centuries until ice no longer covered the land surface year-round. As the ice sheet retreated, it left vast deposits of rock, gravel, sand, and silt behind—material brought here by the ice from farther north.

The biggest and heaviest objects were first to be dropped by the shrinking ice sheet. Some boulders the size of houses were left oddly perched on native bedrock of a different composition altogether from the relocated fragments. These glacial erratics still dot the countryside of New England today.

Smaller stones were dumped later. The actions of water and ice rounded the rocks as they ground against each other and the bedrock and as they were tumbled in cataracts of foaming meltwater. Yankee farmers used the more manageable stones to construct the walls, or more properly fences, that are so much a part of the New England landscape today.

Outwash streams carried most of the finer materials away from the glacier's decaying mass. These deposits, some literally thousands of feet thick, are still mined today in Connecticut for their water-sorted deposits of sand and gravel.

terminal bud was destroyed long ago. Cross a smaller boulder field and over a little dry brook bed, after which the trail rises and bears left. You can still spy the pond through the trees, although you are farther from the water now on this sloping hillside. Pass over a boardwalk and come to a trail junction on the left. Going straight would lead you to the Muir Trail, past a swamp, and to the wooded summit of Walnut Mountain (1,325 feet), where a limited vista is possible—an optional round-trip extension of 5.0 miles. For this walk, however, turn left to continue around Burr Pond. Descend gently along the rocky slope through oak, birch, and hemlock. The Wolcott Trail continues to be blue blazed as you enter a hemlock grove; from this vantage point, a massive granite boulder rears up to the left like a mammoth, pyramidal black arrowhead, apex skyward, at the first short side trail. Standing on end, it is fully 15 feet high. Return to the trail and continue downhill. A stunning view of Burr Pond lies ahead and below as the deep forest gives way to the light-filled power-line cut.

Cross the open swath and reenter the forest, passing a large boulder on the right. The pond is visible downslope through the trees on the left. Princess pine, a 6-inch-tall club moss that resembles a miniature evergreen tree, flourishes below the maple and birch, oak, and hemlock. Reach a yellow-on-blue-blazed trail on the left that ends at the tip of a rocky peninsula jutting northward into the southern end of the pond. Turn left to follow the short side trail as it winds down under hemlocks, past large boulders, through laurel thickets, and up and over a bedrock outcrop to a very picturesque view of the pond.

Highbush blueberry, mountain laurel—blooming abundantly from mid-June to the beginning of July—and small hemlock have found a foothold on this rocky promontory. The look and feel is reminiscent of northern New England.

Return to the main trail, turn left, cross a small drainage seep, and bear left as the trail continues to hug the shoreline. Lovely black-throated blue warblers prefer to nest in these mixed woodlands, which offer nesting sites in laurels and hobblebushes. Follow the path through a mass of boulders that came to rest along what is now the shoreline of Burr Pond; pass a particularly sizable one to the right. The runners and dime-sized, paired leaves of partridgeberry grace the edges of the path through these mixed hemlock-deciduous woods, in which rocks abound. Arrive at the cemented rockwork dam built by the CCC in the 1930s; the stream feeding the reservoir, Burr Mountain Brook, flows over the dam's spillway. Cross the brook on a small newly constructed wooden bridge built on top of a previous concrete-and-iron bridge foundation. The new bridge is capable of supporting heavy vehicles. Turn left after crossing the bridge toward the parking area. Do not continue straight on the wide Pond Road. Reach an iron gate at the park picnic area, make a sharp right turn, and continue for a short distance uphill, following the blue blazes through hemlocks back to your vehicle.

MORE INFORMATION

Burr Pond State Park is open 8:00 A.M. to sunset. It offers bathrooms, a picnic shelter and tables, swimming beach, boat launch, and food concession. Mountain bikes are permitted on the trails. Leashed pets are allowed in the picnic area and on the trails, but not on the beach. Vehicle fees are charged from Memorial Day through Labor Day: Weekends/holidays $7 resident, $10 nonresident; weekdays $6 resident, $7 nonresident. Burr Pond State Park, 385 Burr Mountain Road, Torrington, CT 06790; 860-482-1817; http://www.ct.gov/dep.

—R. L.

TRIP 8
RIVER ROAD

Location: Kent
Rating: Easy
Distance: 3.0 miles
Elevation Gain: 20 feet
Estimated Time: 1.0–1.5 hours
Maps: USGS Kent, Dover Plains—NY, CT

Decades ago, a road hugged the western bank of the Housatonic River as it flowed south from Cornwall Bridge through Kent. Much of that road was abandoned long ago, and the old roadbed is today an especially lovely part of the Appalachian Trail (AT). The path is well worn and easy to walk, emulating the wide, shallow river that flows alongside in a relaxed, unhurried gait. Approximately 8.0 miles of trail run along the river, making it the longest river walk on the AT. The section described on this walk is only a portion of trail following the river and has been selected for its attractive scenery and manageable length.

DIRECTIONS

From the junction of Routes 7/341 in Kent, take Route 341 west across the Housatonic River. Take the first right after the bridge (Skiff Mountain Road). Proceed for 1.1 miles to a junction with River Road. Turn onto River Road and proceed for 2.7 miles to the gate and parking area. **Caution!** River Road is quite narrow; please be careful and courteous when driving on it. Note—River Road is generally not maintained in winter, so it may be impassable in snowy or icy conditions.

TRAIL DESCRIPTION

The entire AT is marked with white blazes and is easy to follow. Access trails are marked with blue blazes.

The parking area on River Road is not just a place to leave the car, but an area with attractive wildflowers. Queen Anne's lace mingles with the yellow blossoms of false sunflower and the lavender flowers of wild bergamot. Wild bergamot, also called bee balm, is similar to the species cultivated in perennial gardens. The leaves have a minty fragrance. Bee balm is also called Oswego

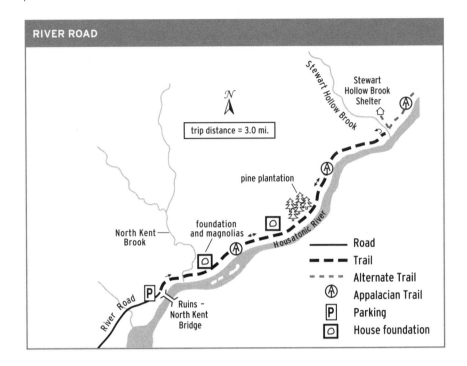

tea in honor of the Oswego Indian Nation of New York. In colonial times, the Native Americans used bee balm to make a soothing, tasty tea. The Native Americans shared their tea with the colonists, who used it as a substitute for East Indian tea. Bee balm's whorls of lilac-colored blossoms bloom in summer to fall and are a magnet for butterflies and hummingbirds.

From the parking area, pass around the gate and walk along a wide, easily followed path. The trees that grow here are representative of those that thrive in the rich bottomland soils of floodplains, including sycamore, maple, and ash. Black locust also grows here, the twisted trunks lending a spooky look to the forest. In late spring, the thick, sweet scent of locust flowers fills the air. After a short walk of about 0.3 mile, the path comes to an open area on the left where an old foundation hides in the weeds at the edge of the grass. The delicate magenta flowers of pink-eyed grass bloom here in summer. At the edge of the clearing are an apple tree, with soft, white-pink blossoms in May, and a magnolia, with lotus-shaped flowers in spring.

Proceed along the riverbank, crossing a shallow drainage that empties into the river. Growing among the rocks are coltsfoot, a low-growing plant with dandelion-like flowers in March; yellow flag, a water iris with bright, butter-yellow flowers in late May; black-eyed Susan; and Joe-Pye weed. Just beyond the small stream, the trail enters a picturesque stand of hemlock and white

The clear waters of the Housatonic River rush beside the Appalachian Trail river walk.

pine. The wide and shallow Housatonic River is a constant companion to the right, where Canada geese, mallards, wood ducks, and black ducks often feed. Another interesting water bird to look for here is the common merganser (see essay in this chapter).

The evergreens slowly yield to a collection of hardwoods, including sycamore and silver maple, a species that loves the occasional flooding that occurs along rivers. To the right is an open area with a short side trail that leads to the riverbank. Cedar waxwings like to gather on the branches of the snags that line the waterside. Hummingbirds sometimes zip along the water's edge looking for flowers, and crayfish hide in the muddy shallows. In fall, goldfinches flit among the seedheads of thistle like yellow sparks against the sky.

From the clearing, the AT continues north along the bank, the path wide and the terrain a series of easy ups and downs. In addition to the waterfowl, which are plentiful all year long, many animals visit the river. Deer come down the hillside to the left to drink, and raccoons love to scour the shoreline at night.

The path then enters a grove of sugar maple near a small stone foundation to the left before entering a massive plantation of red pine. The pines were planted in the 1930s, and decades later this grove became known as one of the most beautiful places along the Connecticut section of the AT. In the 1970s, however, the trees began to die from an insect-caused blight. Today all the trees in the original grove are dead, and they're slowly being

COMMON MERGANSERS

Common mergansers are commonly seen and uncommonly beautiful water birds. The word *merganser* has been in the English language since 1555, but the birds have been paddling along the Housatonic River since long before that. The male common merganser is a flashy dresser and can be recognized easily by his emerald-green head and snow-white body accented with a black racing stripe down his back. The female is more reserved, with a gray-plumed body and a rust-colored head.

Common mergansers gather in flocks of 20 to 30 birds in the warmer months. They can be recognized even from a distance by their habit of facing upstream and chasing each other over the water. They feed on small fish and dive frequently underwater in pursuit of a meal. Common mergansers are exceptionally strong swimmers, their bright orange-red bills lined with serrations to hold on to their slippery prey.

In late winter, usually early March, the flocks break up and the birds form mating pairs. They build their downy nests in a number of places, from hollow trees to unused raptor nests and sheltered spots on the ground. The birds lay about ten eggs, which hatch a month later, creating a flock of fuzzy little mergansers. Two months later the baby birds are on their own.

Common mergansers like the Housatonic River because it overlaps their traditional wintering and breeding ranges, allowing hikers to view these beautiful water birds from River Road virtually all year long.

replaced by a first-succession habitat of sapling black birch and brambles. Even in death the stately trees have a certain majesty—and usefulness. The Connecticut Chapter of the AMC has harvested some of the dead trees to build shelters along the trail.

From the pine plantation, the trail passes a long, narrow field to the left. The soil here is poor, sandy, and so well drained that the plants of the field need to be drought tolerant. Two plants that meet that criterion are knapweed and wild sensitive plant. Knapweed has an open habit and wiry stems topped with small, thistle-like flowers. Wild sensitive plant is small, reaching only about 6 inches high, with ferny leaves. Wild sensitive plant conserves moisture in an ingenious way: To reduce the leaf area exposed to drying winds, the plant simply folds up its leaves in windy weather. It will do the same if you touch it repeatedly with your finger. Kids love to watch this little plant do its thing.

From the field, the trail follows a stone wall into a forest of hornbeam, red oak, maple, hickory, tulip tree, and witch hazel. You also find specimens of linden, which bear sweetly scented flowers in summer; flowering dogwood, which blossoms in spring; and some very large sassafras trees. All parts of sassafras are wonderfully aromatic, with a spicy fragrance. Just scratch a twig and enjoy a scent that, in colonial times, European nobility paid huge sums of money to enjoy.

The trail then wanders closer to the river, and the land closes in a bit, with a steep hillside to the left. The river narrows, and the current is faster, producing sweet sounds as it tumbles over the rocks. After crossing Stewart Hollow Brook on a log bridge, a side trail leading to Stewart Brook Shelter leaves left. To return to the parking area, simply retrace your steps.

MORE INFORMATION

A privy is available at the shelter. Leashed dogs are permitted on the trail. This section of the AT is maintained by the Connecticut Chapter of the AMC; 860-742-8243; www.ct-amc.org.

—C. S.

TRIP 9
MALLARD MARSH AND LITTLE POND

Location: Litchfield
Rating: Moderate
Distance: 4.7 miles
Elevation Gain: 40 feet
Estimated Time: 2.5 hours
Map: USGS Litchfield, White Memorial Foundation Trail map available online

Abundant aquatic wildlife and wonderful birding await the hiker at this 4,000-acre multiuse property that features a 1.2-mile boardwalk leading through a biologically rich wetland ecosystem.

DIRECTIONS

From the intersection of Routes 202/63 in Litchfield, drive west on Route 202 for 2.1 miles and turn left onto Bissell Road. Almost immediately turn right onto Whitehall Road and drive 0.5 miles to the signed, large gravel parking area on the right.

TRAIL DESCRIPTION

From the parking area, walk toward the museum building, passing through a roofed-over structure with a large map of the property. Continue on the gravel roadway to the left of the museum, and turn left just before you reach two stone pillars. For 0.1 mile, follow along the meandering Bantam River, which flows south into Bantam Lake, the state's largest natural water body. To the left is a marsh showing signs of beaver activity; bluegill inhabit the shallows, from which clumps of tussock sedge sprout like soft stepping-stones. Northern pike inhabit the pond, too, feeding on the bluegills. In spring, the trilling toad chorus can be almost deafening. Look for the white, four-petaled blossoms of cuckooflower along the shore in May and June.

Pass the start of the Nature Interpretation Trail on the left and continue straight on the blue-rectangle-blazed Mattatuck Trail through a shady grove of eastern hemlock and white pine until you reach paved Bissell Road, where you'll find a map kiosk. Cross Bissell Road to examine the map and continue through more shaded evergreens where olive-green and yellow pine warblers utter sweet musical trills in spring and early summer. The marvelous aroma of

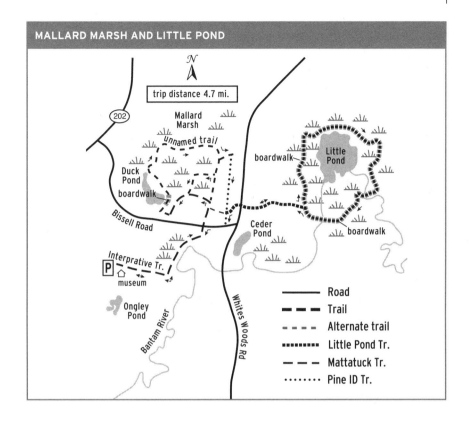

MALLARD MARSH AND LITTLE POND

N

trip distance 4.7 mi.

202

Mallard Marsh

Unnamed trail

boardwalk

Little Pond

Duck Pond

boardwalk

Bissell Road

Ceder Pond

boardwalk

Interprative Tr.

P

museum

Ongley Pond

Bantam River

Whites Woods Rd

———— Road

▬ ▬ ▬ Trail

- - - - Alternate trail

•••••••• Little Pond Tr.

— — — Mattatuck Tr.

········ Pine ID Tr.

pine resin fills the air in sunny openings. Where the Mattatuck Trail turns left, continue straight on the Pine Island Trail. In late spring and early summer, brown-and-white-striped northern waterthrushes nest in the wetland. Four hundred feet farther, turn left to continue on the red-triangle-blazed Pine Island Trail, open only to foot travel, through wet hemlock woods. Skunk cabbage, starflower, sphagnum moss, cinnamon fern, and wild calla are wetland indicators here. Wild calla belongs to the same family as jack-in-the-pulpit.

Come to a T-intersection (Pine Island Trail goes both directions), turn left, and walk 150 feet to another T-junction, this one returning you to the blue-blazed Mattatuck Trail. Turn right onto the Mattatuck Trail and cross an unnamed dark-flowing brook. The yellow blossoms of bullhead lilies protrude above the water in spring and summer. At Duck Pond turn sharply right onto the Pine Island Trail. Wood duck nest boxes are visible on posts in the pond. Alain White, who with his sister Mary W. White created the White Memorial Foundation in 1913, was responsible for reintroducing this stunning species of cavity-nesting waterfowl in 1924. Follow the trail for 0.1 mile along the southeastern shoreline and over a wooden boardwalk.

A boardwalk extends through the marsh on the Little Pond Trail.

To the right, a 6-inch-diameter American chestnut once stood protected from the sharp incisors of beavers by a fence. Sadly the fence could not protect it from Chestnut Blight to which it has now succumbed. Farther along (100 yards), stay straight where the red-blazed Pine Island Trail turns right. You are now on an unnamed, unblazed, but easy-to-follow path. Cross a wooden bridge near remnants of a former beaver dam. Turn right at the grassy un-named trail T-intersection and walk along a red maple swamp. Note another mass of sticks and soil that was once a beaver lodge. In spring, wild geranium blooms purplish pink along the grassy path, while foamflower has a frothy ap-pearance. Note, too, the green jointed stems of horsetails, holdovers from the Carboniferous era some 300 million years ago.

Cross a stream on a tiny wooden footbridge in the midst of an extensive cattail–red maple swamp known as Mallard Marsh. Cross a second small footbridge, enter a dimly lit hemlock-pine grove, join a wide old woods road, and turn right. After 200 feet, turn left at the first trail junction to follow the red arrow for the Pine Island Trail. After walking 300 feet, turn right (south) at the next old woods road, where toothwort, a mustard, flowers white in spring. The caterpillars of two uncommon native white butterflies depend upon it for food. Turn left when you reach the Little Pond Trail, just before Bissell Road. It is blazed with a black square on white. Amble through a young pine-oak woodland where Canada mayflower (also known as wild lily of the valley) carpets the forest floor. Clintonia, or blue-bead lily, is also exceedingly common.

Cross Whites Woods Road (paved), walk past the gate, and follow a wide old woods road through mixed woods. (To shorten this hike, park off Whites Woods Road at this point.) When you arrive at a Y in the road, stay straight. Japanese knotweed, or Japanese bamboo, grows profusely at the damp intersection; this non-native plant is aggressive and invasive. Just beyond this intersection lies a shrubby open area where Russian olive bushes were planted. Gray catbirds "meow" their catlike alarm calls from the thickets. A sandy clearing has been planted with tiny spruce and pine. Pass by boulders in the trail at the woodland edge and follow the path to the margin of the wetland that encompasses Little Pond. Reach a T-intersection of the Little Pond Trail; you can go in either direction to circumambulate the pond. Turn left and immediately pass the intersection for the Pine Island Trail. Continue straight on the Little Pond Trail, walk under power lines, and bear left. Water is visible past red maples to the right.

Arrive at the beginning of the Ralph T. Wadhams Memorial Boardwalk, which traverses more than 1.0 mile of this extensive and scenic swamp. This section provides a rather intimate wetland experience and offers wonderful glimpses of wildlife. The autumnal foliage spectacle alone makes a walk worthwhile. The boardwalk is very narrow and negotiating it on a busy weekend can provide an added challenge! Among the birds we saw in late May were nesting mute swans. These big aggressive birds are native to Eurasia and have become a nuisance in many parts of the eastern seaboard. Growing up out of the dark, tannin-stained water are meadowsweet, royal fern, tussock sedge, pickerelweed, and narrow-leafed arrowhead. Buttonbush forms a dense woody tangle that produces attractive 1-inch-diameter white flower heads (the buttons) in summer. Farther along are winterberry shrubs, which bear masses of bright red fruits in fall.

Muskrat lodges—mounds of cattail leaves and mud—are readily apparent in the marsh. Although mostly vegetarian, muskrats will eat animal food on occasion—something beaver will never do. Scent posts may be evident along the watercourse where beaver have rubbed scent from their castoreum gland onto the mud as a territorial sign. When you reach the junction at Tannery Brook with an unnamed boardwalk on the left, continue straight. The dangling yellow flowers of wild currant grace the edge of the boardwalk in late May. Skirt the edge of red maple and white pine woods. Interestingly, currants and gooseberries are alternate hosts for the destructive white pine blister rust, a fungal disease. Pass a huge, gnarled, and picturesque highbush blueberry, with

HATS TO HABITAT

North America's largest rodent, the beaver, thrives once again in Connecticut and the rest of New England, but that wasn't always the case. Beaver were reintroduced to the state in 1914 after a very long absence. In colonial times these semiaquatic mammals, which sometimes exceed 70 pounds, were trapped and hunted for their luxuriant, waterproof fur until they were literally extirpated from southern New England.

Beaver were, in a very real sense, responsible for the exploration of this continent. In the seventeenth and early-eighteenth centuries, both Britain and France established vast trading empires that saw beaver pelts exchanged for all manner of trade goods. The pelts were processed and used to manufacture beaver hats, which any self-respecting gentleman of that age felt compelled to wear. The demand for beaver hats thus created a great impetus for exploration and empire building among the colonial powers in North America.

Perhaps it is ironic, then, that the family of May and Alain White, the donors of this property, came to financial prominence as a direct result of its good fortune in the fur industry. For ultimately it enabled their heirs—a brother and sister who loved nature—to set aside this large piece of real estate in perpetuity for the benefit of both wildlife and people.

Today the loud slap of a beaver's tail on the water is once again a common sound in rural and even suburban New England. The animal's great resurgence has led to population increases for many other species of wildlife as well. Great blue herons, for instance, are becoming more common these days, due to the creation by beaver of wooded swamps as breeding habitat all over the region.

Wetlands are, after all, among our most productive ecosystems, and certainly among the most interesting. With the help of humans, beaver, those master builders, have contributed mightily not only to their own welfare but to the future welfare of much of New England's wildlife.

more than ten main stems. Olive-drab warbling vireos nest near water; listen for their pleasant, deliberate phrasing.

Come once again to a boardwalk, turn right, and cross the river on a wooden bridge. Emerge to open marsh, where colorful and sweet-singing yellow warblers are very common breeders. Watch too for fuzzy yellowish Canada goose goslings in spring. Cross the Bantam River again, on the Francis Howe Sutton Bridge. Tall, plumed common reed has invaded this end of the pond. Reenter deciduous woodland and complete the loop around Little Pond. Turn left and follow the wide pathway back toward Whites Woods Road. Cross it, continue on the Little Pond Trail to the woods road, and turn left. This leads south 200 feet to Bissell Road. Turn right, walk 100 yards on Bissell Road, and turn left onto the Mattatuck Trail, marked with blue blazes through the hemlock-pine stand and along the Bantam River where you began the hike. Reach the dirt road and turn right to return to the museum and parking area.

MORE INFORMATION

A nature museum is located in the White Memorial Conservation Center. Exhibits (accessible to the visually impaired) focus on local natural history, conservation, and ecology. Restrooms are located here, with pit toilets at the picnic area and at several other points near the heart of the property. The museum is open Monday through Saturday 9:00 A.M. to 5:00 P.M., Sunday noon to 5:00 P.M. There is no fee for using the trails. Pets must be leashed at all times. White Memorial Conservation Center, Inc., 80 Whitehall Road, P.O. Box 368, Litchfield, CT 06759; 860-567-0857; http://www.whitememorialcc.org/index.html.

—R. L.

TRIP 10
MACEDONIA RIDGE TRAIL

Location: Kent
Rating: Difficult
Distance: 6.4 miles
Elevation Gain: 761 feet
Estimated Time: 4.0–5.0 hours
Maps: USGS Ellsworth, Amenia—NY, CT; Macedonia Brook State Park Trail map (available online)

The Macedonia Ridge Trail, in 2,300-acre Macedonia Brook State Park, presents the hiker with a formidable section requiring rock scrambling. But the views from Cobble Mountain are superb, and the fall foliage spectacle, as seen from these rocky heights, is splendid.

DIRECTIONS
From the intersection of Routes 7/341 in Kent, follow Route 341 west for 1.75 miles. Turn right onto Macedonia Brook Road and follow it for 1.5 miles (passing the Fuller Mountain Road turnoff on the right after 0.8 miles) to a small parking area on the left (immediately after crossing a bridge over Macedonia Brook).

TRAIL DESCRIPTION
The blue-blazed Macedonia Ridge Trail begins on the east side of Macedonia Brook Road. To reach the trailhead, cross the bridge over the gushing brook, stocked with fingerling trout, and walk 200 feet back down the way you drove in to a trailhead sign on the left. **Caution!** Be sure to follow the loop trail in this counterclockwise fashion in order to avoid having to descend from very steep ledges on the northeast slope of Cobble Mountain!

Begin by climbing the southwest-facing slope under a canopy of red, black, and chestnut oaks, and enter hemlocks as you level out. The shrub or small tree witch hazel blooms in the understory in fall, while lowbush blueberry produces familiar and sought after fruits in late summer. On your way up to the ridgeline you have already passed gneiss (pronounced *nice*) outcrops. Continue climbing gently and note the remnants of four strands of rusty barbed wire engulfed by oak trees along the footpath. It is difficult to imagine livestock grazing here in what is now woodland. The acidic soils under the low chestnut

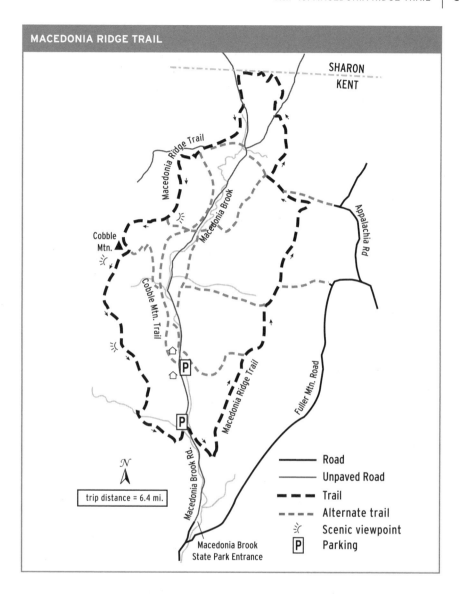

MACEDONIA RIDGE TRAIL

SHARON
KENT

Macedonia Ridge Trail

Macedonia Brook

Cobble
Mtn.

Cobble Mtn. Trail

Appalachia Rd

Macedonia Ridge Trail

Fuller Mtn. Road

P

P

$\mathcal{N}$

trip distance = 6.4 mi.

Macedonia Brook Rd.

Macedonia Brook
State Park Entrance

	Road
	Unpaved Road
	Trail
	Alternate trail
	Scenic viewpoint
P	Parking

oaks, characterized by blocky bark, provide suitable conditions for a thick growth of huckleberry.

The trail turns sharply north and then levels out. Watch for very erosion-resistant milky quartz veins in some gneiss boulders. Pass a collection of stacked stones to your left and then begin climbing steadily. Granitic gneiss boulders contorted by tremendous heat and pressure lie left of the trail. Listen for denizens of the oak woods—tufted titmice, blue jays, and red-bellied woodpeckers—and watch for fleeing white-tailed deer with their "flags" held high as they bound away. Acorns form an important part of their diets. After 0.85 mile reach the yellow-blazed trail on the left; continue straight on the blue-blazed trail, once a part of the Appalachian Trail (AT). The oaks stand taller here, and young black birches are common. One late March day I happened upon millions of tiny charcoal gray "snow fleas" catapulting themselves above the snow-covered ground.

Shade-tolerant, smooth-trunked American beech trees now become common in this rocky, rolling woodland. Descend easily into a gray birch grove where old rectangular excavations made by crow-sized pileated woodpeckers are numerous. Similar white birches appear on the left (but note the thin, peeling bark of this "paper birch"). Amid the increasing undergrowth are the green-and-white striped trunks of sapling striped maples. Soon arrive at the intersection on the left with the green-blazed trail. Bear right to continue on the blue-blazed Macedonia Ridge Trail. Notice the appearance of brassy-barked yellow birches just before passing through a stone wall gap. The mostly level trail is marked by dual blue and green blazes for a short stretch, until you reach a Y intersection where the two split. Bear left on the blue trail (note the arrow on the tree).

The trail becomes a flowing brook during snowmelt and after heavy rains. Sugar maple, black cherry, hickory, and ironwood with gray sinewy trunks appear in the rocky woodland. Pass a ring of stones on the left—perhaps an old foundation. The understory in this shallow valley is bedecked with ropelike grapevines. You'll soon climb out of the valley and up to the rim of the bowl. This is still predominantly oak forest, and some chestnut oaks are sizable. Descend from the rim through an area with fewer blue blazes and then level out. Bear right, then left, and reach a flowing spring on the right. At 2.0 miles reach the T intersection with Appalachian Road. Turn left to follow the old roadway, worn into a "trench" and bordered by a rock wall on the left; a gurgling brook parallels the road to the right. Appreciate the large oaks, especially one monumental specimen with five trunks!

Just before reaching a clearing studded with picnic tables, turn right to continue on the blue trail. It descends gradually to the brook you've been paralleling and which you cross on stepping-stones. Follow the trail up the boulder-strewn slope marked by a low, snaking stone wall. These slopes provided an unlimited supply of building material for stone walls to eighteenth- and nineteenth-century pasturalists. In one spot on the right, the gneiss rocks appear as a pile of large, gray dominoes. In spring, the cold, rushing flow of Macedonia Brook becomes audible as you approach Keeler Road. Watch for two large gneiss boulders on the left softened by emerald green mosses. What

This imposing cliff ledge looms above you as you make your way up the steepest and most challenging trail section of the Macedonia Ridge Trail.

is now state park was by the mid-nineteenth century devoid of trees due to the insatiable need for charcoal. Charcoal was produced to power iron furnaces because it was cheaper than coal and burned much hotter than wood. Until 1865, iron represented the major industry in these parts.

At the road, turn left, cross the brook via the road bridge, and turn right just past the end of the right guardrail (at the sign) to follow the blue-blazed trail through a stone wall gap. The floodplain woodland is composed predominately of red maple and white ash. More stone fences wind along the slope to your left. Watch for the tracks of gray squirrel and wild turkey, which both rely heavily on acorns. Bear left away from the brook and begin a gradual climb. Clumps of evergreen Christmas fern decorate the woodland, even in winter. Reach a posted private property boundary on the right at the edge of a mowed field; bear left and continue the gradual ascent. Hop hornbeam joins oaks, hickories, and black birch on this slope. Note an 8-inch diameter specimen, marked by a blue blaze. Coyote scat placed on a rock contained cottontail fur and bones.

Now turn left and climb more steeply to the rocky ridge top, covered with a low stand of hickory. A tiny gap permits enough sunlight to foster a stand of little bluestem grass. Start heading downhill, bearing left, and reach a mature hemlock grove on a steep slope often bathed in breezes. Follow the contour downhill 50 feet, turn right at an arrow, and continue descending,

The bony summit of Cobble Mountain offers expansive views in three directions and beckons hikers to linger awhile.

following slope contours in the perpetual shade of the evergreens. Numerous switchbacks are designated by light blue arrows on this steep and rocky hillside. Fallen trees make route finding more challenging, and wet or icy conditions require proceeding slowly with caution! Evergreen wood fern thrives in the thick shade here.

After leaf fall, Hilltop Pond is visible ahead through the trees. Shortly arrive at gravel Weber Road. The earthen dam and spillway at the southern end of the pond are visible beyond the road. Follow the road to the left almost to a large brown and yellow state park sign and turn right to follow a wood road past a metal barway and over Macedonia Brook which outflows from Hilltop Pond just upstream. The wide, level roadway, built by the Civilian Conservation Corps (CCC), is marked by few blue blazes, but it is very easy to follow. A fine dry masonry wall graces the left margin of the road. A dramatic rock cut topped by young woody growth borders the roadway on the opposite side. Ash, black birch, black cherry with scaly black bark, and maple populate the forest. Spring finds male ruffed grouse (or partridge if you prefer) beating their stubby wings furiously against the air in an age-old effort to attract mates.

Reach paved Chippewalla Road at a wooden barway; bear right and cross it to continue on the old roadway. It is blazed both orange (closer to red) and blue for a short distance. Soon the blue trail splits off and proceeds up a gentle slope at a sign to the right (be watchful since this intersection can be missed). The trail zigzags up the rocky slope under a canopy of oaks. Trailing arbutus or mayflower (the state flower of neighboring Massachusetts) creeps along adjacent to the treadway. A white pine on the left announces the first mountain laurel stand so far. Cross flat bedrock to a dry, oak-studded ridge top where the shallow soil grows shorter trees. Once the leaves have fallen, ridges are visible all around. Reach another bedrock clearing crowned with little bluestem and hickories.

As you begin a gradual descent from the top of the summit, a lovely vista of distant knobby hills and ridges unfolds to the southwest. During wet conditions the bedrock underfoot can be slippery, so be careful, especially as the aspect of the slope increases. A sentinel red cedar (juniper) pokes out on the right just before you turn in that direction (note the blue arrow on bedrock). Descend fairly steeply over rocks, where trekking poles may be of assistance. The gneiss bedrock exhibits ribbed bands of harder minerals—a fine example of differential weathering.

Reach the intersection with the green-blazed trail at 4.3 miles on the left. Bear right on the blue trail in the direction of the arrow through mostly oak woodland with red maples, black birch, and a few hickories. Enter a narrow ravine and cross a little brook; bear right and begin climbing the rocky slope. Note the boulder on the right bearing a 10- or 12-inch wide quartz intrusion. Soon reach a very steep ledge cliff. Continuing requires scrambling over rock, tight, steep "hoist ups," and a reliance on small trees for handholds. If this is more challenging than you or a member of your party wish to undertake, backtrack to the green-blazed trail, turn right, and follow it 0.16 mile to the orange-blazed trail. From there it is 0.9 mile right (south) to the park office and an additional 0.5 mile down Macedonia Brook Road to where you parked your vehicle.

As you prepare to ascend the ledge, observe the brown leafy rock tripe lichen clinging to the cliff face. **Caution!** Be sure to use great care in making the ascent, which is not recommended during wet or icy conditions. The slope is clothed in oaks with mountain laurel shrubs beneath. Scattered white pines appear as you approach the summit of Cobble Mountain. From a grassy bald vegetated with grasses, sedges, and scrub oaks, you'll appreciate the view to the west, but it gets better. Continue over bedrock near the cliff edge with nice views to the west. Reindeer lichen and little common polypody fern also decorate the ridgeline. You soon reach an excellent vista point with wonderful views to the south, west (the next ridgeline is in New York), and north. You'll want to linger here; it's a great place for lunch or a snack. When you are ready

A lovely vista southward of distant knobby hills and ridges unfolds as you descend toward an old burn area.

to resume walking, continue skirting the cliff face past a lone pitch pine and then bear left away from the precipice.

Now begin a descent over bedrock and soon reach the white-blazed Cobble Mountain trail descending on the left. This trail's steep angle argues against descent. Instead bear right on the blue-blazed Macedonia Ridge Trail and walk down a moderate and rocky slope under oaks. Under taller oaks—some quite large—the trail levels out. A straight and tall tulip tree stands nobly on the left. Huckleberry shrubs, which produce sweet blue fruits in late summer, form a near monoculture under the trees, and mountain laurel shrubs are scattered throughout. Turn right at the double blue blaze and proceed uphill a short distance; then turn left and head downhill past a ledge outcrop on the right. Here you'll enter an old burn as evidenced by a few charred chestnut oak trunks and an abundance of sweet fern, which requires full sun. A shade-loving, pioneer big tooth aspen is invading as well. The rust-colored path, stained by the iron ore limonite, skirts the area burned by the forest fire. Bees gather pollen and nectar from goldenrods and asters in autumn. One early October day I was fortunate to see a basking northern redbelly snake, an irregularly distributed species in Connecticut.

A very nice vista down the valley opens up as you make your way past craggy chestnut oaks and openings with bluestem grass. Teetering turkey vultures, sometimes only feet away, ride the updrafts created when westerly winds strike the cliff. Soon a tributary brook comes into view (at certain seasons you will hear it first). Bear right at the triple-blazed tree, then right again. The trail turns sharply left and descends toward the rushing stream, narrow enough to jump across. You'll cross it again shortly. On an early October outing a thick, 2-foot-long northern water snake caught my eye as it eyed a nearby green frog.

Enter a mixed oak/hemlock stand and continue downhill along the contour of the slope, sometimes moderately steeply. Turn sharp left (note the triple blaze ahead) and proceed downward toward your parked vehicle. Cross the brook on stepping-stones. An outhouse and picnic tables are situated ahead near Macedonia Brook Road.

MORE INFORMATION

Macedonia Brook State Park is open from 8 A.M. to sunset daily. Leashed pets are permitted on trails and in picnic areas, but not in the campground. There is no fee to use the trails. A camping fee is charged. The trail is maintained by Connecticut Forest & Parks Association trail maintainers. Macedonia Brook State Park, 159 Macedonia Brook Road, Kent, CT 06757; 860-927-3238; http://www.ct.gov/dep.

—R. L.

TRIP 11
MOUNT ALGO AND INDIAN ROCK

Location: Kent
Rating: Difficult
Distance: 7.6 miles
Elevation Gain: 900 feet
Estimated Time: 5.0 hours
Maps: USGS Kent, CT; Dover Plains—NY, CT

This hike takes you from the Housatonic River Valley, up fairly steeply over the wooded summit of Mt. Algo, down to cascading Thayer Brook, then up again over forested Schaghticoke Mountain, along a rocky ridge top to several fine vista points high above the valley, and finally reaches Indian Rock with expansive views, before returning along the same route.

DIRECTIONS
From the intersection of Routes 7/341 in the center of Kent, follow Route 341 west for 0.8 mile (crossing the Housatonic River) to the Appalachian Trail (AT) trailhead on the left. Park on the left, well off the pavement.

TRAIL DESCRIPTION
Enter the forest; veer left up the slope under the dense shade of eastern hemlocks (some large) on the white-blazed AT, and cross Old Barn Road after 100 yards. Soon come to a small wooden box containing trail maps attached to a tree on your right. Follow a switchback and ascend stone steps for a moderately steep ascent. Diagonally placed rock water bars shunt water off the footpath. Large red oaks dot this slope marked by car-sized boulders. Follow the contour lines along the slope, and watch for a colony of delicate maidenhair fern that delights the eye after you pass through the remnants of a rock wall. Indian cucumber-root produces greenish-yellow pendant flowers here in late spring. This lily's root is edible, but please don't dig it up.

A blue-blazed side trail on the right leads 200 yards gently down to the Mt. Algo shelter built in 1986. It's worth a brief detour. En route you'll cross a small brook over stepping-stones. A privy is located behind the shelter. This is a delightful venue above the babbling brook. I discovered the remnants of two moss-covered eastern phoebe nests attached to support beams. After

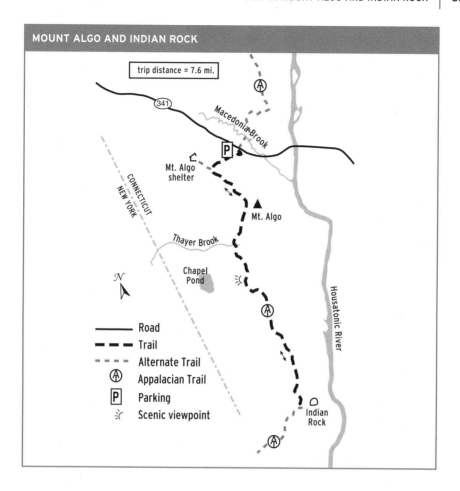

MOUNT ALGO AND INDIAN ROCK

trip distance = 7.6 mi.

341

Macedonia Brook

P

Mt. Algo
shelter

Mt. Algo

Thayer Brook

CONNECTICUT
NEW YORK

Chapel
Pond

N

Housatonic River

Indian
Rock

——— Road
━ ━ ━ Trail
- - - - Alternate Trail
Ⓐ Appalacian Trail
P Parking
☀ Scenic viewpoint

returning to the AT, begin a gradual climb under oaks, big tooth aspen, yellow and black birches, and red maple. Soon a fairly dense mountain laurel thicket of 8–10 feet high shrubs surrounds you. You'll enter a shallow basin and proceed up the far side. Lower stature woodland of wavy-leaved chestnut oak with a shrub layer of huckleberry dominates this dry slope. A boulder to the right of the trail makes a convenient seat, if you are so inclined.

Along this section of the route you'll find both the state flower of Connecticut—mountain laurel—and that of Massachusetts—trailing arbutus or mayflower. Both are evergreen heaths, but light-pink blossoming mayflower attains a height of only a few inches. As you level out amid American chestnut sprouts and pass between two gneiss (pronounced *nice*) boulders—the left one covered with rock tripe lichen—you are nearing the wooded summit of Mt. Algo (1,152 feet), although you won't cross the actual summit.

An abundant acorn crop provided a wildlife bounty during 2006. The constant patter of falling acorns produced a soothing percussion for an October outing that year. Following the same trail the next April revealed that many acorns had begun to send down taproots.

Watch for rattlesnake plantain; its rosette of lacy white-veined green leaves becomes noticeable against the subdued shades of the autumnal forest floor. This orchid's spike of modest white flowers blooms in summer. As you descend more steeply, the soothing sound of flowing water becomes audible. Soon reach fast-flowing Thayer Brook, a lovely refreshing spot. Its cold waters cascade over mossy emerald-hued rocks that provide seats for green frogs seeking insects. Cross the 30-foot-wide stream on stepping-stones. Note the three-trunked tulip tree on the far side (right) and begin a gradual ascent over a rocky path.

Ledge outcrops and boulders predominate and poke out amid a veritable "forest" of huckleberry shrubs that do well on dry, rather infertile slopes like this one. In summer they produce a sweet feast for wildlife. Hickories are present as well as you follow the contour lines and gain a screened view to the left of wooded ridges across the Housatonic Valley. Witch hazel, a small tree or large shrub, is quite common, as is red maple. Golden hickory and scarlet maple leaves illuminate these woodlands in fall. Soon you'll reach the trail's highest point at about 1,370 feet. The wooded summit of Schaghticoke Mountain (named for the tribe) is just to your right at 1,403 feet elevation.

Just a bit farther, at 2.2 miles, is a small clearing that offers a nice view of the Housatonic to the southeast. You'll have to walk about 35 feet to the right of the trail here to gain the best vantage point. Sitting on the ledge rock amid scrub oak, black cherry, and little bluestem grass to the left of the path is relaxing, and you may find yourself distracted by soaring turkey vultures, croaking ravens, or dragonflies. The rock contains milky white quartz intrusions that are harder than the surrounding rock.

From here, descend moderately over bedrock outcrops, and arrive at another scenic view ahead marked by two red cedars. The view from both this and the previous location improve after leaf fall. At your feet meanwhile, a 9-inch thick quartz intrusion runs for 20 feet or more through the exposed rock. Bear right, around a ledge capped by a cabin-sized boulder festooned with brown rock tripe, and reach a shallow valley. The maniacal call of a red-crested pileated woodpecker resounded through the oak woodland one early April day. From here you'll cross three small brooks in fairly short order that pour down the slope. Lowbush blueberry and huckleberry thrive in the tannin-rich soils at the foot of the oaks.

Indian Rock, on the Schaghticoke Indian Reservation, provides a lofty perch from which to survey the bucolic Housatonic Valley and beyond.

Arrive at a vista point where bucolic views of the river valley dotted with tidy New England homesteads are to be had. I was thrilled when an immature red-tailed hawk suddenly came in for a landing and even happier when it allowed a fairly close approach. This is a nice spot for lunch or a snack. From here the trail parallels the rock face and the river for some distance. A flock of half a dozen golden-crowned kinglets flitted frenetically from limb to limb, seeking tiny insects, all the while uttering high-pitched calls. The AT contours along the slope through stands of mountain laurel and reaches a gushing brook just before a blue-blazed path leads right, up to the Schaghticoke Mountain Camping Area, at 3.2 miles. Continue on the white-blazed AT, ambling among mountain laurel and a tiny relative—wintergreen. Reach another bedrock vista point that offers an idyllic view up the Housatonic Valley to Kent and beyond.

You may be a bit surprised, as I was, to look down into a small ravine, known locally as Dry Gulch. After passing some very angular gneiss boulders, the path leads into the "trough" hemmed in by parallel gneiss ledges, turns right, then left, and switchbacks rather steeply, partly over stone steps. Just below Indian Rock, cross pegmatite bedrock that sports jutting crystals. These larger crystals formed deep underground where they cooled slowly. Finally, reach Indian Rock (at 3.8 miles), a protruding outcrop flanked slightly downslope by a sparse row of straggly red cedars. It affords a fabulous lofty perch from which to survey the valley and ridge upon forested ridge beyond. As you gaze east and south, watch for both turkey vultures and their more southern cousin, black vulture, gliding by. The latter, with shorter tails and white near the wing tips, are near the northern limit of their range here. This is the end point for the hike, so when ready, retrace your steps back to Route 341.

MORE INFORMATION

Volunteers of the Appalachian Mountain Club Connecticut Chapter maintain the more than 50 miles of the AT (and many side trails) in the state. Hikers should take precautions during the fall deer-hunting season by wearing blaze orange; hunting is prohibited on Sundays. Fires are not permitted on the AT in Connecticut. Pets must be under control. For more information or to report problems, contact Appalachian Mountain Club, 404 LeGeyt Road, Sheffield, MA 01257; 413-229-9147; http://www.appalachiantrail.org.

—R. L.

TRIP 12
CANDLEWOOD MOUNTAIN

Location: New Milford
Rating: Moderate, with steep rocky sections
Distance: 3.0 miles
Elevation Gain: 640 feet
Estimated Time: 3.0 hours
Maps: New Milford

This hike will take you along and over a hard granite spine, topping two promontories in the process. Although an out-and-back hike, interesting geologic features and rich fauna and flora combine to make the return walk along Kelly Slide, on the flank of Candlewood Mountain, even more noteworthy than the ascent.

DIRECTIONS

From the junction of Routes 202/67 in New Milford, follow Route 202 west for 0.5 mile across the Housatonic River to its junction with Route 7. Turn right onto Route 7 and drive northward for 2.8 miles to Route 37 on the left. Follow Route 37 for just over 0.1 mile to its junction with Candlewood Mountain Road on the left. Park on the wide shoulder to the left of the intersection of the two roads.

TRAIL DESCRIPTION

Note that this trail is located entirely on private property.

Enter the woods, walking gradually uphill within a shaded, cool hemlock stand. As a precursor of much more to come, cross over bedrock and boulders of gray granite. Follow blue triangular blazes to a sign for the Housatonic Range Trail System, where you can pick up a leaflet. You find little undergrowth in the hemlock's deep shade, although red, black, and white oaks do appear, as well as a few yellow birch. The first outcropping appears on the right, and to your left, just beyond the forest edge, are several houses. The trail swings right and goes up over rocks.

In summer, gaudy scarlet tanagers, blue-headed vireos, and black-and-white warblers sing and nest in these woodlands. The eastern hemlock increase in girth just before you pass through a boulder field and reach the linear clearing of the Iroquois Gas pipeline. In summer you'll notice the dramatic

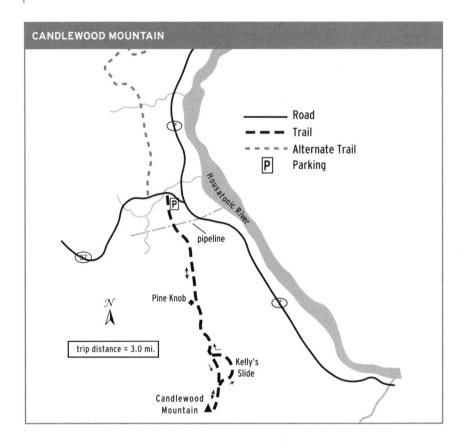

CANDLEWOOD MOUNTAIN

Road
Trail
Alternate Trail
P Parking

Housatonic River

pipeline

87

N

Pine Knob

trip distance = 3.0 mi.

Kelly's Slide

Candlewood Mountain

temperature difference as you step out of the shade and into the warmth of the sunny gas-line cut. The odors are different, too. Brilliant blue indigo buntings build their nests in trees along the edge of clearings like this, and butterflies draw nectar with their coiled, tubular tongues from the abundance of blooming flowers that thrive in sunny openings. Below to your left, well beyond the roadway, is a quarried cliff face. As you continue walking uphill, cross gray bedrock and reenter hemlock woods, where a gray squirrel may scold your unwanted arrival. The path leads gradually upward across the surface roots of hemlock. White pine and chestnut oak are also present. Chestnut oak trunks are characterized by their rough, blocky bark. You now pass through quarried granite on the small hillside, jumbled and angular, in the shade of hemlocks.

Soon a picturesque, 25-foot-high rock wall, topped by pine and hemlock, rises up to the right. Make a sharp left turn here, stepping down along the outcrop. Turn right, then almost immediately left, and be sure to watch closely for blue blazes in this area. Follow along the outcrop wall on the left and then swing right in a small grove of impressively large white pine and hemlock.

The path now bears right and leads you gradually up the rocky slope and over a granite ledge to the left. The short green fronds of common polypody fern create a soft cap for the gray stone, while chestnut oak is now common. Walk up over bedrock and swing right, continuing up the slope. This section is a bit tricky; the trail becomes more challenging, although hemlock roots provide some grip for your feet. The sweet trills of olive-green and yellow pine warblers may fill the late spring and early summer air as you make your way up the steep slope. Soon you arrive at a small bedrock clearing surrounded by oak, white pine, hemlock, and black birch, all of short stature. Spongy (when moist) reindeer lichen, soft haircap moss, lowbush blueberry, pink lady's slipper orchids, mountain laurel, and even some wintergreen in shaded spots grow on the thin, acidic soil along the perimeter of the clearing. Oaks notwithstanding, the combination of exposed granite bedrock and acid-tolerant vegetation harkens to thoughts of northern New England.

The first pitch pines, certainly not a plant of northern New England, make their appearance here also. The name Candlewood actually refers to this species. The high resin content of its soft wood causes it to burn with a bright, illuminating flame. Few pitch pines remain on the mountain named for it; instead, white pine is by far the most numerous pine here today. Some views, albeit screened, also are possible. Continue walking and reenter the shaded hemlock–white pine forest. Strikingly beautiful orange, black, and white Blackburnian warblers sing loudly and continually from evergreen boughs during their breeding season. Catching a glimpse of the striking males through binoculars may not be easy, however, as you make your way up this hillside shelf trail. From below to the left, the enthusiastic bubbling song of the tiny winter wren reached my ears during a late June outing. Few songs are more beautiful and sustained than this one, in my opinion.

While passing through another granite boulder field, note that the dark, damp soil beneath the hemlock is springy and peatlike.

As you continue upward, reach a small sheer cliff on the right perhaps 13 feet high. The trail bears left and then right, passing through two very large diameter evergreen trees—a hemlock on the left and a white pine to the right. Listen in summer for the songs of interior woodland nesters such as wood thrush and ovenbird, as you pause among the granite chunks of another boulder field and then continue along the rock outcrop. Small, smooth-skinned black birch hold fast amid the rock slabs. The vertical, unyielding granite surface is partially covered with rock tripe, a leafy lichen (tan above, black below) whose algal component turns green and begins producing nutrients after it absorbs moisture. The waste acids the lichens produce eventually etch even this hard rock.

The trail now turns sharply right, demanding that you scramble up the multitiered granite outcrop. You'll need both hands in some places, and exercise caution, as dead leaves underfoot can be slippery. Turn left after you reach the top. As I caught my breath there, I enjoyed listening to the ethereal music of a hermit thrush drifting down the slope. Short chestnut oak, white pine, black birch, and lowbush blueberry vegetate the slope above the outcrop. Soon come to a fork in the trail, and continue straight on the blue-blazed trail (the unblazed trail goes downhill). These rather open pine-oak woodlands remind me of Cape Cod, with the very notable exception of the rocky slopes. Soon reach the fairly level summit of Pine Knob (700 feet). A screened view is possible to the left.

The trail now winds first moderately and then steeply downhill through dry oak woodland. Some of the oak trunks are decorated with gray-green lichens. As you descend, reach shaded and cooler forest where hemlocks again thrive. Continue past rock outcrops and a jumble of boulders, then turn right. Note the 1-foot diameter black birch that has forced its way up through a crevice in the granite. The level path swings left and then leads through cutover and re-sprouting red maple woods. Bear left again and walk down over boulders and ledges. Virginia creeper vines, whose leaves turn scarlet in fall, stretch across some slabs. Walk downhill rather steeply for a short distance and enter hemlock woods again. An overhanging ledge on the right, opposite a large black oak, could provide shelter during a downpour.

The trail swings right and leads over granite slabs. Striped maple, with attractive, tight-fitting, green-and-white bark, dot the woods; some are decorated with winged seeds. The roots of a large wind-thrown oak on the right still hold a lot of soil in their grasp. As you climb gradually through rocky oak, pine, and birch woodland and bear right, come to a trail junction. The blue-blazed trail goes left; stay right and scramble up over rocks to a horseshoe-shaped granite bowl. Blooming mountain laurel shrubs ahead add to the beauty of the scene. The blossoms of Connecticut's state flower are more white than pink here on Candlewood Mountain. Continue up through rock outcrops brightened by mountain laurel. Chestnut oak is now the dominant tree, as a few sassafras trees appear. Here I inadvertently flushed my first ruffed grouse of the day, which burst from the forest floor in a heart-stopping explosion of feathers. Soon reach the lower end of the Kelly Slide side trail, which is marked with a sign. Stay right and walk past lady slippers, Canada mayflower, lowbush blueberry, and wintergreen, all acid-tolerant plants.

Swing gradually right and walk uphill through sunny patches of dry oak-pine woodland with a fairly thick growth of huckleberry and lowbush blueberry

A limited, but pleasant, view of the Housatonic River can be enjoyed from the steep slope known as Kelly Slide.

below the oak. Huckleberry resembles blueberry, but huckleberry leaves, both top and bottom surfaces, are flecked with tiny resin dots. At a fork in the trail another sign on the left indicates the direction to Kelly Slide; this is the upper end of the Kelly Slide side trail (both are blazed blue). Pass it up for now, staying right and continuing fairly steeply uphill. Below the 30-foot-tall oak, huckleberry and lowbush blueberry—both with green fruit in late June—grow in profusion. A few smooth, gray-trunked Juneberry (shad) trees supply red fruits to grouse and other wildlife. Here I flushed my second grouse of the day. The trail levels off on bedrock and continues through low pine-oak woods. The tiny male "cones" of white pine, empty now of their yellow pollen, may pile up on the ground below the pines in spring.

A few sunny openings come into view as the summit is neared. Scrub oak, also known as bear oak, and red cedar, both light-loving species, make their first appearance. Eastern towhees give their distinctive chewink call and scratch in the leaf litter. Emerge into a level clearing on granite bedrock. Swing right through scrub oak, white pine, red cedar, and pitch pine, which has relatively short, stiff needles, some of which poke out directly from the trunk. Coyotes leave telltale scat composed of cottontail fur and bone on the rock. Arrive soon at a stone bench where you can sit and enjoy your lunch. You are now on the 991-foot-high summit of Candlewood Mountain. Unless you

PARTRIDGE IN A SHAD TREE

Ruffed grouse are somewhat chicken-like, but far more interesting. Normally they rely upon their excellent camouflage to aid them in melting into the background. If that fails, grouse take wing with an explosive blast that leaves most potential predators, including humans, stunned. Swift fliers for short distances, grouse spend much of their time on the ground. They are also rather able climbers, clambering about on surprisingly spindly limbs and nimbly plucking ripe fruits such as Juneberry (a.k.a. shad or serviceberry) in summer and fall or buds in winter.

In spring male grouse court by selecting or returning to a favorite fallen tree to make music. Grouse "drum" the air by very rapidly beating their cupped wings forward and upward until they are but a blur to the eye. The drumming begins slowly and then builds to a crescendo of whirring wing beats. This action creates a very deeply resonant sound reminiscent of a distant lawn-mower engine starting up and then sputtering out. Such very low frequency sounds are capable of traveling up to a quarter mile, even in densely wooded areas. Males also drum to protect their territories from other males. In addition, males raise their crests and dark shoulder ruffs, fan their tails, and strut. It is a quite a show, certain to impress hen grouse and hiker alike.

For their part, female grouse with chicks are among the most brazen of creatures in the forest. Should your path happen to come too close to a grouse hen and her brood, you will probably suffer her wrath. This can be exemplified by several levels of intensity, but usually begins with the female making odd mewing sounds that may have you wondering what you are listening to. She may then walk boldly, wings partially extended, and crouch low. In extreme cases, a female grouse will actually attack an intruder in a valiant effort to drive them away from her offspring. It is an amusing but intimidating display that usually succeeds.

In fall, grouse develop rows of fringe along the edges of their toes, providing them with a type of home-grown snowshoes. And to escape the subfreezing cold of winter nights, grouse burrow deep into the snow, relying upon its insulating properties to help keep them warm. When you're in the winter woods, look for their single-file tracks in the snow, about 3 inches apart.

climb a tree no views exist here, except perhaps in winter. The blue-blazed Housatonic Mountain Trail turns left just to the left of the bench and continues south down the mountain.

When ready, retrace your steps back to Kelly Slide side trail on the right. Even if you don't make the full Kelly Slide loop, which can be tough going over downed trees and boulders, walk the short distance downslope to where a fine view of the Housatonic Valley can be had. In this area the Housatonic has done a very strange thing: It has cut directly across the billion-year-old granitic mass of the highlands rather than follow the course of lesser resistance—the relatively soft marble valley. Geologists are still puzzled by this seeming contradiction to the laws of earth science. **Caution!** Walking this section of the trail under wet or icy conditions is not recommended, however. The trail enters oak, hemlock, and white pine woods, descending over rocks. The hillside drops away to your left and then you descend more steeply, going down the slanting ledges as one might a staircase with the path skirting the perimeter of the slide area. With granite bedrock so close to the surface on this tilted slope, deep soils could never develop. When waterlogged, the thin soil holding the root systems literally slides right off the mountainside, exposing the bedrock. In some places the shallow root systems of hemlock and other trees are evident above the clean light-gray stone.

You may want to go no farther along the hillside, instead retracing your steps to the main trail, turning right to follow it back to your car. Or you can continue following the trail as it skirts the mountainside. At the end of the horizontal ledges, follow the trail down to the right; a small downed hemlock obscures this turn. Watch your footing. Numerous young wind-thrown hemlocks along this portion of the trail may make walking difficult. On a hot summer day though, you'll appreciate the natural air conditioning emanating from the granite ledges. Pass under a big, lengthy fallen tree where a long, tapered black wing feather belonging to a turkey vulture caught my eye. Perhaps the big black carrion eaters nest among these rugged ledges.

The trail continues down over massive chunks of granite strewn along the slope and then scrambles up the slope over a boulder field after swinging left. Continue bearing left and pass several ledge crevices large enough to shelter a bent-over person. A luxuriant growth of evergreen fern caps the ledge. More small "caves" come into view as you walk up, finally joining the main trail. Turn right and follow the main trail back to your vehicle. Be sure to stay straight (left) at the trail junction, and be careful also not to miss the sharp right where you make the short but steep descent down the ledge.

MORE INFORMATION

Camping and fires are not permitted. The Housatonic Range Trail is maintained by a dedicated group of volunteers.

—R. L.

TRIP 13
MOUNT TOM STATE PARK

Location: Litchfield
Rating: Easy to Moderate
Distance: 1.1 miles
Elevation Gain: 360 feet (395 feet if you climb tower)
Estimated Time: 1.0 hour
Maps: USGS New Preston, Mount Tom State Park map available online

This is a wonderful destination for families with children, featuring excellent panoramic views from a stone tower perched atop an easy to reach summit.

DIRECTIONS
From the intersection of Routes 202/63 in the center of Litchfield, follow Route 202 west for 6.3 miles. Watch for the brown-and-white state park sign on the left, turn and drive 0.2 mile to the gatehouse (note that the roadway splits and becomes one-way here; take right fork). Continue another 0.2 mile to a sign on the right identifying the Hillside Picnic Area and Tower Trail.

TRAIL DESCRIPTION
If you seek lofty views with minimal effort, this short hike is for you. At 232 acres, this state park—one of Connecticut's oldest—has plenty to offer. Moderately deep and clear, Mount Tom Pond is spring-fed and a great place to cool off after your trek. But primarily, it is a wonderful place to introduce young children to the joys of summiting. For the most part, the climb is gradual, with one short, steep stretch on the descent. A medieval-looking stone observation tower, interesting geology, and remnants of past human use add additional spice. One brilliant fall day, the sight of a red fox crossing the park road thrilled me.

From the gravel parking area (a pit toilet is located here; flush toilets available in season at the beach), follow the wide pathway a short distance to a fork in the trail where a sign points uphill; follow the right fork passing a wooden barway. Yellow paint blazes mark the trail as it bears left over a cobbled, eroded old roadbed and through oak-dominated woodland. Look down as you tread

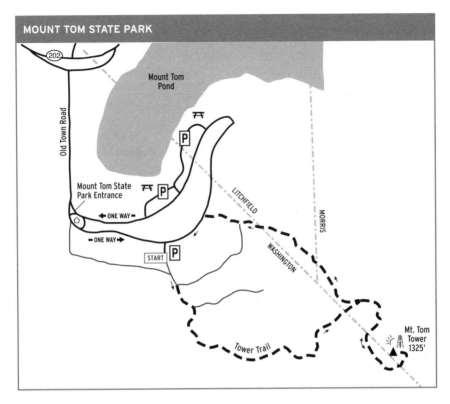

MOUNT TOM STATE PARK

over a shiny gneiss (pronounced *nice*) outcrop, polished by mile-thick ice some 25,000 years ago.

Soon you'll reach another split in the trail. Follow the left path up to a junction with a level wood road. Here note the outcrop of schist (a mica-rich rock) with nearly vertical bedding. Both schist and gneiss are metamorphic rocks altered by intense heat and pressure deep underground. Turn left and walk through a rolling, rocky landscape, where oaks, lowbush blueberry, and mountain laurel thrive in the acidic soil. Large saw-cut logs and decaying stumps attest to logging decades earlier. On sunny days, waxy, dark green mountain laurel leaves reflect sunlight like glass. Many oaks here are multi-trunked. Black birch, a tree that regenerates well after fires, is also common. Young trees have smooth, almost black bark.

Watch for a large rounded boulder on the right studded with hard, angular feldspar crystals—a key component of granite. One such rock nearer the summit is reminiscent of a whale encrusted with barnacles. On your left at the top of a rise, a black birch is in the process of splitting apart a nearly vertical chunk of gneiss with its octopus-like roots. Another oak—chestnut oak—is characterized by deeply furrowed bark and generally colonizes drier sites than the

Evergreen Woodfern thrives among gneiss outcrops and reproduces like other ferns from minute spores released by sori located beneath the subleaflets.

oaks you've passed by previously. A tiny pool left of the trail marks the junction of the yellow-blazed return trail (immediately after the pool). This may well be a vernal pool where wood frogs and mole salamanders breed in early spring. Continue straight—toward the summit. As the path curves right, note the 60-foot-high gneiss outcrop. Glacial movement, followed by freezing and thawing, is responsible for the jumble of angular boulders on the left.

Verdant evergreen wood fern and smaller common polypody fern soften the gray boulders with their luxuriant growth where the path briefly splits; here an alternate route has been created to avoid flowing water. Walking continues to be rather easy over the old road's rocky surface. When you reach the final left turn, just below the summit, explore a short trail to the right that ends on the top of a high ledge, affording great views of the wooded ridges to the west. **Caution!** Be extremely careful here due to the sudden drop-off, especially with children! On a crystal clear fall day two adult red-tailed hawks rode the updrafts created by the cliff face. Huckleberry (with bright red autumn foliage), scrub oak, and a bit of little bluestem grass cling to this exposed ledge.

Continue up to the blackish stone tower at 1,291 feet elevation. The tower was built of very dark local rocks containing the mineral hornblende. You passed chunks of it on your way up the trail. The summit is vegetated mostly with low chestnut oaks. You'll want to ascend the wooden steps approximately

For a wonderful 360-degree view of the forested countryside, climb the tower steps to the observation deck.

35 feet for a 360-degree view of the forested countryside, but watch your head (I bumped mine) as you emerge onto the observation deck! You'll be treated to a fine view of Mount Tom Pond to the north and woodland, with interspersed homesteads here and there in every direction, as far as the eye can see.

After enjoying the view, follow the same route back to the small pond (which may well be dry in summer) and watch for the yellow-blazed trail that leads off to the right. The ground-hugging evergreen leaves of trailing arbutus or mayflower, the state flower of neighboring Massachusetts, border the path. Its delicate light-pink blossoms are a delight in May. Soon you will encounter the steepest section of the hike. This short descent can be tricky, especially if the rocks are wet, so use caution. If your sense of balance isn't the best, trekking poles could be helpful here. The slope is especially green with ferns. A bit farther, a chunk of moss-covered milky-white quartz lies near the base of an impressive four-trunked red oak left of the trail.

Continue an easy descent through a forest that boasts four species of birches—black, gray, yellow, and white. White or paper birch exhibits finely peeling bark strips that vireos gather to weave into their nests. Follow the path straight ahead and soon you reach a cemented stone chimney and adjacent

Eastern chipmunks are among the most charming and abundant creatures of Connecticut's signature oak woodlands.

concrete foundation on the right. This is all that remains of a Boy Scout camp. Winged euonymus (burning bush)—an invasive, exotic shrub—thrives within the foundation. Soon a picnic area comes into view ahead through the trees. Turn left at the asphalted park road and walk past eastern hemlocks approximately 300 feet back to your vehicle.

MORE INFORMATION

Mount Tom State Park is open 8 A.M. to sunset. Leashed pets are permitted in picnic areas and trails. Fee for resident vehicle $7, $10 nonresident vehicle weekends/holidays; $6 resident vehicle, $7 nonresident vehicle weekdays. Park Office (Memorial Day to Labor Day), 860-567-8870; September–May, 860-868-2592 (Lake Waramaug State Park); http://www.ct.gov/dep.

—R. L.

TRIP 14
SUNNY VALLEY PRESERVE

Location: Bridgewater, New Milford
Rating: Moderate
Distance: 3.4 miles
Elevation Gain: 350 feet
Estimated Time: 2.0 hours
Maps: USGS New Milford, Sunny Valley Preserve map

This loop trail on a 1,850-acre Nature Conservancy composite of parcels wends through forest with a primeval feel, attractive fern glades, along Lake Lillinonah, and to a ledge vista—an unusual but pleasing juxtaposition.

DIRECTIONS

From the junction of Routes 202/67 in New Milford, take Route 67 east for 3.1 miles to where Route 133 merges on the right. Follow Route 133 south for 0.8 mile and turn right at the stop sign onto Hat Shop Hill Road. Drive down Hat Shop Hill Road for 0.6 mile to a triangle. Turn left, then immediately right around the triangle and drive straight on Hemlock Road for 1.8 miles to the gravel parking area on the left at the end of the road. The small lot has room for four to five vehicles.

TRAIL DESCRIPTION

From the kiosk at the trailhead, follow the light blue-blazed Silica Mine Trail into the forest of black birch, sugar maple, red oak, and American beech and up a gentle slope along a metamorphic schist outcrop on the left. Private property borders the preserve to the right. The path then levels out. In late spring and early summer the forest is alive with the songs of tufted titmice, scarlet tanagers, and red-eyed vireos. Schist rocks, with a high content of the mineral mica, glisten. Large white oaks and tulip trees are visible in the forest, and below them Christmas, New York, and hay-scented ferns. You also find hemlocks and black oaks. More dark gray outcrops protrude on the left. The trail swings in that direction and climbs steadily now, crossing a tiny trickle of water green with skunk cabbage. White ash and shagbark hickory join rather large black birch trees in the forest. Cross a dry rill.

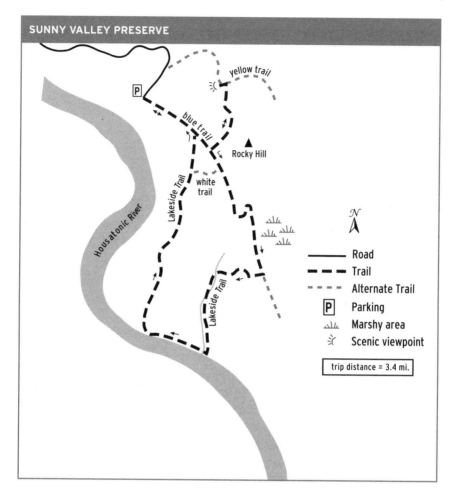

SUNNY VALLEY PRESERVE

yellow trail

P

blue trail

▲
Rocky Hill

Lakeside Trail

white
trail

Housatonic River

Lakeside Trail

𝒩
Λ

——— Road
▬ ▬ ▬ Trail
- - - - Alternate Trail
P Parking
⎯ Marshy area
⋇ Scenic viewpoint

trip distance = 3.4 mi.

Climb through shady hemlocks and reach the red-blazed Lakeside Trail on the right. Continue straight uphill on the blue-blazed trail. Shards of milky-white quartz (silica) appear underfoot. Silica, the most abundant mineral on the planet, was once mined here and used to make glass. Note a small field-stone foundation on the left. The slope rises steeply on the left as you pass another rock outcrop and drops off to your right. Hermit thrushes sing their incomparable ethereal tunes from the shaded woods. Mountain laurel and witch hazel shrubs appear, and then the trail levels out under hemlocks where gray slabs of rock, uptilted at 45 degrees, rise out of the forest floor above you to the left.

Just before the crest of the hill, come to the white-blazed connector trail on the left (this trail is easy to miss and a second goes right, after the crest), which winds up fairly steeply through outcrops to a vista point. Turn left onto the first white-blazed trail and walk up the rather steep hillside. Black-throated green warblers nest in the evergreens. Crest the hill shortly, treading on a duff-cushioned trail under hemlocks, oaks, and hickories. You are walking on the shoulder of Rocky Hill. Walk downhill briefly under dead and dying hemlocks, killed by the woolly adelgid. Start climbing gradually again through hemlocks, black birches, and oaks with notably straight trunks. Copious amounts of glittering mica schist rocks litter the trail. Level off briefly, note the sharp drop on the left, then swing left, and descend easily. Chestnut oak joins red oak on this drier, rock-littered slope.

Follow the trail right, along the hillside. Listen for the *ee-o-lay* refrain of the wood thrush here. Begin climbing at a moderate incline and then level off again. Schist slabs, set at the now familiar 45 degree angle, sit exposed on the right. This rock was formed about 400 million years ago and later distorted by great heat and pressure well below the earth's surface. Solomon's seal, so named because the root purportedly resembles King Solomon's royal seal, grows on the outcrop. Striped wintergreen blooms in summer along this trail, while lowbush blueberry and little oak fern indicate acidic soils. The trail undulates on this rather sheer hillside with a fairly dramatic dropoff to the left. Black oak, distinguished from red oak by its darker, more fissured bark, joins white oak, red maple, quite a bit of mountain laurel, and sassafras. Silvery cushion moss softens the margins of the path.

Eastern wood pewees whistle their melancholy *pee-a-wee* from the treetops, while through the leaf litter the twin green leaves of pink lady's slipper are evident. This orchid blooms in June. It is definitely sunnier now, due to decreasing hemlocks on this drier slope. White oak, red maple, black oak, and small black birch are now common. Come to a very short side trail on the left that leads to the vista point atop the ledge (at the junction with the yellow-blazed trail). If you visit on a summer weekend, the roar of invisible motorboats far below will be in the air. A screened view offers rolling forested ridges laid out to the west, while at your feet a 9-inch-diameter pool formed in the outcrop serves as a tiny reservoir for rainwater. Close inspection may reveal mosquito larvae wriggling about. Rock tripe lichen clings to the outcrop. The rocky spot is a great place for snakes.

While I was maneuvering into position for panoramic photos from the ledge, the loud scolding of titmice and chickadees suddenly distracted me. Following the racket led me to a black oak nearby. I searched the site of the commotion with my binoculars. Focusing upon one particularly agitated titmouse, I saw a medium-sized shiny black rat snake resting on a horizontal limb. It appeared to be looking right at me. Running for my pack and the longer lens it contained, I returned just seconds later to find the snake gone. I searched for it, but to no avail. It apparently had slid into a large knothole situated just below the limb it had been basking on. Disturbed first by a flock of agitated birds and then by a nosy human, it had decided to take its leave. After the snake's retreat, the birds' noisy jeering stopped almost as if on cue.

Black rat snakes are very adept climbers and are known to prey upon birds and their eggs and nestlings. The frantic alarm calls of the titmice had enlisted the aid of chickadees, a downy woodpecker, and even a black-throated green warbler in the campaign against this shiny black threat in the trees. I had seen instances of "mobbing" before, directed mostly at hawks, owls, and even myself on occasion, but never at a snake. It was something I had read about, but, since black rat snakes are rather uncommon in most of southern New England, I had never witnessed such a thing until now. The incident stayed with me all day and well beyond; it certainly made my day that mid-July.

Turn right after leaving the lookout and retrace your steps downhill back to the junction of the white- and blue-blazed trails and turn left onto the blue trail to continue. Walk through the shade cast by hemlocks immediately to a small foundation made of schist immediately left of the trail. Bits of quartz are piled along the foundation's edge. Continue walking through slanting schist ledges on both sides; some form natural overhangs that can shelter small creatures like chipmunks. Proceed easily downhill under oaks and hemlocks to a second intersection with the white-blazed trail, this time on the right, where you should continue straight and gradually downward past more jumbled outcrops. Soon bear left. More quartz litters the trail, and then a very massive, straight, and tall tulip tree appears on the right. Its lowest limb exits the columnar trunk nearly 50 feet above the ground! It has reached this size in a small dip between hillsides, probably because moisture and nutrients tend to collect here. A little farther on, pass a small mining pit that has chunks of quartz lying about on top along the edge. The trail swings left to cross a seep area on bog bridges. Note the wetland indicator plants—sensitive and cinnamon ferns, jewelweed, nettles, and skunk cabbage.

Regain drier ground and bear right along the base of the slope. A brilliant male scarlet tanager sang his burry, robin-like song from a hickory during a summer visit. Pass through a small fern glade, begin ascending, and then bear sharply left. If it has rained recently listen for the soothing trickle of water flowing over moss-covered boulders to your right. The trail swings right, up a moderately steep but short slope held in place by shallow, exposed hemlock roots. Soon you are walking on more-level ground along a tiny intermittent

Lakeside Trail leads to the wooded shores of Lake Lillinonah, a wide section of the Housatonic River.

stream flowing down on the right under young hemlocks. Bear right and amble up through a jumble of schist boulders on the oak-and-birch-covered slope. Common polypody fern caps some slabs. During wet periods, cross a flowing rivulet on rocks.

Upstream a few feet is a small wetland dominated by the broad leaves of skunk cabbage, sensitive and cinnamon ferns, and sphagnum moss. The moss is yellowish green and spongy, fine habitat for green frogs. You know they are present when you hear their single or double twang, often compared to the sound made by a plucked banjo string. A group of males in chorus sounds as though they are all gulping for air. Pass an 18-inch-diameter, rough-barked tupelo tree growing along the flowage on the left—that's right, a tupelo (a.k.a. black gum)! This species is more common in the southeastern United States, thriving in moist soils everywhere there; it's odd to find it here on the flank of Rocky Hill. A passing bird probably dropped the seed into this fortuitously damp spot decades ago.

Follow the trail as it turns left under red maple and white and chestnut oaks. Clumps of tussock sedge, swamp white azalea, sweet pepperbush, but-tonbush, and a film of bright green algae are visible in the "perched" wetland below on the left, while beeches grow above it. Continue through hemlock-oak woods on a level path parallel with the wet area. Oak seedlings are fairly numerous on the forest floor, and cinnamon ferns crowd the wetland shore. At a T intersection (unblazed) at the end of the wetland, turn right. Shortly come to a Y; stay left on the narrower trail that swings left. Blue-headed vireos sing their measured phrases of dialogue from the trees above. Where openings in the forest canopy allow sunlight to penetrate, lacy ferns thrive in yellowish-green gardens. Enter shaded and rocky hemlock woods. Black and chestnut oaks join the hemlocks, and the slope drops away to a small hemlock ravine on the left filled with attractive hay-scented ferns.

Reach another Y intersection; bear left and descend (the right fork enters private property and is closed). Proceed downhill. Although the trees are not particularly large, the forest has a primeval feel here. Perhaps it's the lacy green garden of hay-scented ferns from which straight trunks of hemlocks rise up like Greek columns. An abandoned cabin is perched on the hilltop to your left. Pass a large black birch immediately left of the trail. Parallel a small hemlock ravine located on the right. Hemlocks cast a perpetual shade, but some oaks and black birch hang on in these rocky woods.

Behold the many dead and dying hemlocks killed by the tiny sap-sucking woolly adelgids. Tread over a duff-cushioned path. Bear right and walk gradually downhill among a multitude of oak seedlings. Cross a seep where silica rock glistens in the sun. Continue downslope; a blue arrow points the way. Pass the preserve boundary marked by small diamond signs and red blazes on the right. Curve right at a very large double oak on the right. Pass a 2-foot diameter American beech and then a large tulip tree on the left. Walk past a hemlock snag riddled by angular pileated woodpecker excavations and bear right around it, continuing downhill and following blue blazes.

At two fallen trees on the left, the path swings in that direction; climb between the trunks. Continue on an undulating trail through hemlock and black birch forest. Bear right; a paved Rocky Hill Road is visible through the foliage on the left. Now bear left, walk downhill, and cross the road. Reenter forest on the left after about 80 feet. Continue walking under a canopy of oak, hemlock, and black birch. The pleasing sound of running water drifts to your ear from the ravine ahead. On the left 30 feet below is a lovely, gurgling stream. Now bear right sharply, and head down closer to the brook. Remnant scraps of lumber and plastic pipe are all that remains of a structure that once stood among sizable hemlock trees. In the cool shade of the conifers along the stream, you may want to stop for lunch, especially on a hot day.

MOB MENTALITY

An old saying notes that you find safety in numbers. Small birds certainly find truth in this axiom when confronted by a potential predator. The presence of the black rat snake in the oak tree was quickly telegraphed to other nearby avian residents by the first tufted titmouse to discover the snake. And although the snake couldn't hear the screams of the excited birds, it certainly saw them jumping about, just out of reach. And that is the key: The birds doing the mobbing are generally smaller and faster than the predator being mobbed. But rat snakes, when sufficiently warm, possess the ability to move with great speed. Reason enough for the birds to remain just out of harm's reach.

When chickadees mob screech owls, crows dive upon red-tailed hawks, or crows themselves are set upon by any number of smaller species, the mobber has always chosen a larger and slower target—something akin to fast fighter planes flying circles around a cumbersome bomber. Usually this kind of harassment succeeds in driving away the potential predator. Perhaps this is because without the element of surprise working in its behalf, the predator's chance of procuring an easy meal is greatly reduced.

In reality some conjecture still exists among bird behaviorists about the true role or roles that mobbing may play. But whatever its advantages, birds continue to rely upon it as an apparently effective predator-deterrent device.

Birders often use to their advantage the knowledge that small birds will mob a potential predator. By whistling an imitation of the screech owl's call (even a poor approximation will often do), the birder can usually attract a number of birds, often of a variety of species, to his or her location. The agitated birds flit about, attempting to locate the source of the quavering owl call, but to no avail. It is a popular ruse that sometimes works amazingly well; still, other times it doesn't work at all. It can be overdone, however, especially when birds are nesting, and because it could expose them to a real predator, this tactic should be used sparingly and only in the proper situations.

Check the mud for the impressions of deer hooves. Crayfish scoot about on the brook bed, and dusky salamanders favor the moist recesses under protective rocks and logs in the water.

Proceed up into the forest when ready and marvel at several gigantic tulip trees situated on both sides of the trail. One forest patriarch is fully 3 feet in diameter. Catch a glimpse of Lake Lillinonah (actually the Housatonic River) through the foliage beyond the brook. The road is just to your right. Another huge tulip tree stands at the switchback leading down to the brook again. At the brook turn right and follow along it to the lake. You'll soon cross the stream on a wooden span. A sign affixed to a tree at near end reads "Trail Closed Private Property." Turn left and begin a gradual ascent through the familiar hemlock, oak, black birch woodland. Mountain bike tires have gouged the footpath here, and a stone wall stands mute on the left.

Come to a Y intersection in a thick patch of Christmas fern. The red-blazed trail goes straight, while the blue-blazed trail turns left, uphill. Turn left and walk up through red maple, oak, tulip tree, and hemlock forest. Bear right to walk through a stone wall gap and reach another Y intersection with the white trail on the right. Bear left on the blue trail through open woodland with a fine stone wall on the right that once framed a sheep-filled pasture. Pass a rock outcrop on the right where a dead spreading white oak stands guard. The path undulates, reaches another stone wall made of schist, which it closely parallels, then bears left around the end of it. A forest opening filled with ferns, grasses, and sedges provides a welcome contrast to the eye here.

Now enter deciduous woods of sugar maple, white ash, and black birch. Cross a seep on stepping-stones, and then pass a large sugar maple on the right and just beyond it on the left an unusually large black birch. Pass through another stone fence. Canada mayflower thrives under the trees and lights up the forest floor with their frothy white flowers in May. The paved road lies ahead. Ore Hill Management Area lies beyond the pavement. This is a forest management study area. Turn back and retrace your steps back to your vehicle.

MORE INFORMATION

Open dawn to dusk. Trail maps can be obtained by calling 860-355-3716. Dogs are not permitted. Hunting, fishing, and camping are not allowed.

—R. L.

TRIP 15
KETTLETOWN STATE PARK

Location: Southbury
Rating: Moderate
Distance: 3.5 miles
Elevation Gain: 400 feet
Estimated Time: 2.0 hours
Maps: USGS Southbury; Kettletown State Park map available online

From a short walk through a hemlock gorge that cradles Kettletown Brook to a wonderful hilltop view of Lake Zoar, this loop trail has much to recommend it.

DIRECTIONS

From I-84, take exit 15 to Route 67 south. Very soon—at the second traffic light—turn right onto Kettletown Road. Follow Kettletown Road for 3.5 miles and take a right onto George's Hill Road. Follow George's Hill Road for 0.7 mile to the park entrance on the left. The entrance station is 0.1 mile ahead; park on the wide gravel shoulder left of the gatehouse where the road splits.

TRAIL DESCRIPTION

Just past the gatehouse, turn left and walk downhill on the paved surface over a bridge across Kettletown Brook. You'll soon reach the start of Brook Trail (blazed blue over yellow) on your right. Brook Trail descends into an idyllic hemlock-shaded rocky chasm. The highly oxygenated waters of Kettletown Brook, hemmed in on the far side by a 30-foot high gneiss (pronounced *nice*) rock wall, tumble over a boulder-littered brook bed. Partridgeberry, Christmas fern, common polypody—the latter on rounded glacial boulders—and spinulose wood fern are among the few plants able to thrive in the subdued light. Follow the trail for 0.2 miles and then cross the paved park road.

Re-enter shaded woodland, and after passing a large white oak on the right, proceed up the slope on railroad-tie steps. After two additional sets of stairs, the trail goes right, passing a massive 3.5-foot diameter black oak. Black birch and red maple as well as oaks and hemlock clothe the slope. Here I watched as a blue-headed vireo snatched and just as quickly dropped a foul-tasting, brown stinkbug. After a couple more sets of steps, you'll reach a split in the trail. Wooden steps descend to the right, but continue straight (curving left)

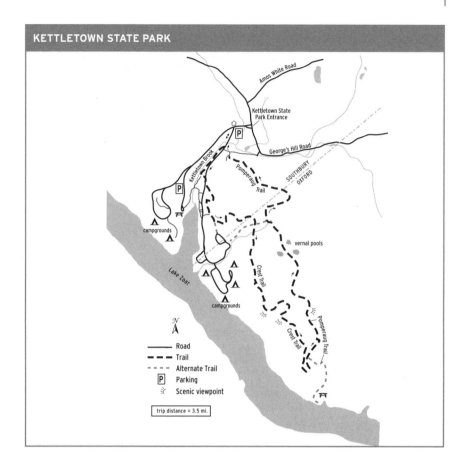

KETTLETOWN STATE PARK

Amos White Road

Kettletown State
Park Entrance

P

George's Hill Road

Kettletown Brook

Pomperaug Trail

SOUTHBURY
OXFORD

P

campgrounds

Lake Zoar

vernal pools

Crest Trail

campgrounds

Pomperaug Trail

Crest Trail

N

Road

Trail

Alternate Trail

P Parking

Scenic viewpoint

trip distance = 3.5 mi.

on the blue-over-yellow-blazed path. Just before reaching the camping area restroom building, the trail turns left and climbs more steadily before leveling out through lovely mixed woodland of eastern hemlock, black birch, white oak, and a few understory hop hornbeams.

A dump truck-sized angular gneiss (pronounced *nice*) boulder soon catches your eye, while the forest has changed character and is now drier. As a result, oaks and hickories become dominant with shadbush (Juneberry) below. Both eastern chipmunks and red-bellied woodpeckers collect the abundant acorns and store them for later consumption. The woodpecker, steadily expanding its range northward—perhaps due to global climate change—didn't nest in Connecticut until 1971. You're now standing on top of a low ledge that drops off sharply on the right. In autumn the golden mittens of sassafras trees enliven the scene. When you reach the intersection with the trail leading to the campground on the right, continue straight. A sign indicates that you are now on Crest Trail. As you pass through a gap in a stone wall, note the flowing spring

You may wish to contemplate construction of the state's 5th largest water body from this vantage point 400 feet above the waters of Lake Zoar.

at your feet. The blue-over-white-blazed path undulates for a distance and passes through a rocky area. After about a half mile on the Crest Trail, Lake Zoar comes into view. When Connecticut Light and Power constructed Stevenson Dam across the Housatonic River to produce hydroelectric power in 1919, the state's fifth largest freshwater body was the result.

The rising waters also inundated a Pootatuck Indian village. It is said that European colonists traded a brass kettle to these Native Americans for hunting and fishing rights to the area—hence "Kettletown." That's an interesting bit of history to contemplate as you enjoy lunch or a snack from this sunny perch 400 feet above the lake, but be mindful of the sheer dropoff! This is the only location that offers an unobstructed view when trees are clothed with leaves. Ascend over ledge to continue. In autumn, fiery yellow/orange sugar maple and red/orange red maple foliage illuminates the woodland. After passing through mountain laurel growing over your head, you'll reach a screened view of Lake Zoar. On one fine fall day, the raucous screams of common ravens filled the sky. Ravens are considered the world's most intelligent birds.

When you reach a tree on the right with double blue-over-white blazes (only 25 feet beyond a very short blue-over-white-blazed cross trail on the left), you have reached the end of the Crest Trail. The blue-blazed Pomper-

Red Maple leaves are illuminated from above by the intense sunshine of an October day, creating a feast for the eyes.

aug Trail turns right and also goes straight ahead. Continue walking straight, ascending slightly (the other trail leads down approximately one-third mile to the lake). The treadway leads through a natural gap in the gneiss outcrop and then appears to split; stay right through a thick growth of laurel. You'll reach another screened viewpoint as you ascend the ledge (blue blazes on bedrock) to its chestnut oak topped crest. A possible vernal pool may be glimpsed on the forest floor below. Watch for an unusual 18- to 20-inch-diameter pin oak to the right of the trail, and later a round pegmatite boulder showing lots of large pink feldspar crystals. The big crystals indicate it cooled very slowly, far underground. More vernal pools are situated here.

After descending gradually you reach a shrubby clearing filled with sweet pepperbush and highbush blueberry in a low bowl 100 feet to your right. Pepperbush, which produces frothy white flower spikes in summer, is more often found at coastal locations. About 150 feet past the bowl is a trail junction on the left. This spur leads to the campground. Continue straight uphill and past a gneiss boulder on the left with a tunnel through it stands a 5-inch diameter red maple, the base of which is intriguingly softened by a slipper of silvery mound moss. Bear right here and reach a private property boundary as indicated by a No Trespassing sign. During this last leg of the route, you'll pass over a once formidable 6-foot-wide stone wall. After leaf fall, houses along George's Hill Road come into view. Note the Lilliputian forest of non-flowering princess pine club mosses left of the path.

At a T intersection in the midst of a young hemlock stand, turn right and walk downhill on a wide trail. You'll reach another T intersection, this one with a wood road, after passing through a gap in another sign of former pastureland—a stone wall. Turn left and walk 125 feet to the paved road. Turn right to reach your vehicle after 100 yards.

MORE INFORMATION

Kettletown State Park is open 8 A.M. to sunset. Leashed pets permitted in picnic areas and on trails. Pets not allowed on beach or in campground. Resident vehicle fee weekends/holidays $7, $10 nonresident vehicle. No fee weekdays. There is a camping fee. Kettletown State Park, c/o Southford Falls State Park, 175 Quaker Farms Road, Southbury, CT 06488; May–September, 203-264-5678; October–April, 203-938-2285 (Putnam Memorial State Park); http://www.ct.gov/dep.

—R. L.

TRIP 16
DEVIL'S DEN PRESERVE

Location: Weston, Redding
Rating: Easy
Distance: 3.3 miles
Elevation Gain: 230 feet
Estimated Time: 2.0 hours
Map: USGS Norwalk North, Devil's Den trail map

Established in 1966 by Weston resident Katherine Ordway, the Nature Conservancy protects these 1,756 acres of crucial forested habitat for wildlife and a place of solitude for humanity. Enjoy this loop hike as you walk over rocky ridges to a scenic overlook.

DIRECTIONS
From Exit 42 off the Merritt Parkway (Route 15), travel north on Route 57 for 5.0 miles. Turn right (east) onto Godfrey Road and drive for 0.5 miles to Pent Road. Turn left onto Pent Road, following it for 0.35 miles to its terminus at the preserve's large gravel parking area.

TRAIL DESCRIPTION
Follow the red-and-white-blazed Laurel Trail past the wooden gate toward Godfrey Pond. White oaks are very numerous, and chestnut oaks, black birches, and red maples are common, too, with a dense shrub layer of mountain laurel and some witch hazel. The wide, chipped path leads uphill and bears left. Red oak becomes dominant; among these acorn-bearing trees, blue jays and tufted titmice are year-round residents. In late summer, dog-day cicadas fill the warm air with their mechanical buzzing. Walk downhill amid gneiss (pronounced *nice*) boulders. The reference to Satan in the preserve's name is based upon what was once thought to be the imprint of his cloven hoof in a rock on the property.

Pinesap, a plant that lacks chlorophyll and draws its nourishment from oak and pine roots, pokes from the leaf litter. It resembles Indian pipes, another saprophyte. Fittingly, this was once the site of ancient Native American encampments. The trail swings left at American beech trees scarred by graffiti. In damp soil, tulip tree, cinnamon fern, and sweet pepperbush, producing dense spikes of frothy white flowers in summer, thrive. Scarlet tanager, red-bellied

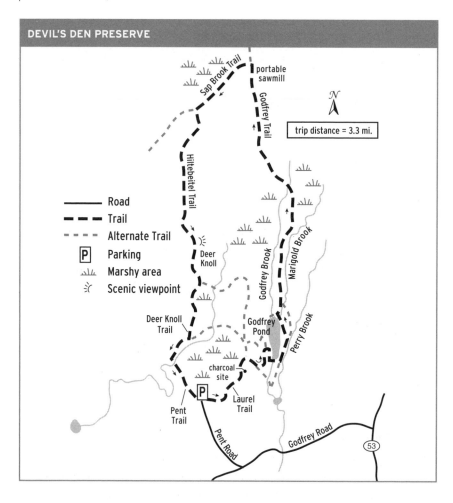

DEVIL'S DEN PRESERVE

Sap Brook Trail

portable sawmill

Godfrey Trail

N

trip distance = 3.3 mi.

Hiltebeitel Trail

Road
Trail
Alternate Trail
P Parking
Marshy area
Scenic viewpoint

Deer Knoll

Marigold Brook

Godfrey Brook

Deer Knoll Trail

Godfrey Pond

Perry Brook

charcoal site

P

Pent Trail

Laurel Trail

Pent Road

Godfrey Road

53

woodpecker, American robin, and Baltimore oriole are among the summer resident birds. Many red oaks are column-straight and tall, indicating that they grew up in a forest rather than an open field. The trail bears right and reaches a stone wall. Sassafras, with its mitten-like leaves, joins witch hazel beneath the big trees of these dry woods. Start downhill, bear left, and pass gneiss boulders just before reaching the 1800s charcoal burner's site replica—logs piled into a wigwam form. Back then, there were 40 active sites here.

A short distance past the charcoal site, bear right and pass a big gneiss boulder on the right. Striped wintergreen, sporting bold dark-green-and-white leaves, grows low along the trail. Pass through a stone wall and, at 0.3 mile, arrive at a T junction and marker 22. A rock outcrop and the Cub Scout Trail are to the left. Turn right and walk gradually downhill toward Godfrey Pond. The trail is now blazed red, white, and yellow. Ironwood saplings appear, as do maple-leaf viburnum and greenbrier. Soon reach an unnamed fork at marker 23 and turn left. This trail is blazed yellow and white. Pass through a boulder field and down through black birch and some hickory. Gray squirrels thrive amid the nut bounty. Ferns, mostly lacy hay-scented, as well as a patch of ever-green Christmas fern, enliven the slope.

Rock walls intersect at a boulder-studded, nameless brook, which you cross on a small wooden bridge. Keep alert for green frogs, identified by parallel pleats down their backs, on the damp rocks. Fountain mosses give the rocks a furry appearance. To the left, another wall sits atop a rock ledge, while at the end of the bridge, at marker 24, is a T junction. Bear left onto the unnamed yellow-and-white-blazed trail and parallel the brook bed. Note the appearance of yellow birch, a brassy member of the northern hardwood forest community. Mountain laurel borders the path. At marker 26, bear right and walk slightly uphill for a view of Godfrey Pond, built as a millpond in the 1700s. A wooden bench sits at the end of a level old stone-and-concrete dam with a center sluiceway. You'll enjoy the nice view of the pond's root-beer-colored, tannin-stained water from this vantage point. Pond inhabitants include snapping turtles, green frogs, gray tree frogs, and patrolling dragonflies.

The trail now turns right and leads to an intersection at marker 25. Turn left and cross the pond outlet. In late summer and fall, search the pond shallows for globular, gelatinous bryozoan colonies. These minute colonial animals are embedded in the surface of the sphere and wave tentacles to direct diatoms and other single-celled plants into their mouths. Below the dam, rusting machinery is all that remains of the former mill. On the far side, at marker 33, is another T intersection. Turn left and follow the red-and-white-blazed Laurel Trail through rocky oak, beech, birch, and laurel as it parallels Godfrey Pond. At marker 34 is a Y intersection. Follow the left fork (Godfrey Trail) downhill gradually through white, black, and red oaks, laurel, and witch hazel. Velvety cushions of silver mound moss border the yellow-blazed path. Cross a mostly flat rocky area just above the pond, where buttonbush and lilies grow, and enter a shaded forest. The slope to the right and Marigold Brook are punctuated by many large granite boulders. Swing left to cross the brook on a wooden bridge and continue along the pond shore. Some rocks glisten with large crystals of dusky mica, glassy quartz, and pinkish feldspar—the three constituents of granite.

An unnamed path soon merges from the right at marker 30. Turn right onto the now yellow-and-white-blazed Godfrey Trail and walk gradually uphill away from the pond in the midst of some fairly large beeches. Then descend easily to approach the edge of the brook, where sugar maple, yellow birch, tulip tree, and pole-straight black birch are common. Swing left and reach a T junction at marker 36. Turn left to continue on the Godfrey Trail, blazed red and white in this section. To distinguish between the New York and hay-scented ferns here, notice that New York fern is tapered at both ends. Pass by a sizable twin red oak on the left, its two pillarlike trunks diverging near its base. This forest patriarch bears no branches for 40 feet up. A bit farther, a twin tulip tree rises on the left, with a large old beech nearby. Swing right, proceed through low rock outcrops, bear left almost immediately, and cross Godfrey Brook via a wide wooden bridge. In a rock to the right is a miniature natural pool; it serves as a water source for forest dwellers. Moisture-loving cardinal flower blooms along the brook in summer with a red so intense it glows in the subdued light.

The brook veers off to the right as you continue to follow the old woods road straight ahead through oak-beech woodland. Tulip tree, yellow birch, and shagbark and pignut hickories are also well established. Reach a low-lying spot with red maple and cinnamon and New York ferns as the trail curves right. Red maple is extremely tolerant of both dry and saturated soils. Walk upslope gradually, bearing left through a boulder field. Eastern chipmunks use the boulders as observation posts and escape from enemies by dashing beneath their cover. Tumbled remnants of rock walls lie on the right as you climb gradually, then descend gently and curve left. Pass gneiss boulders where light gray, flaky-barked white oaks are numerous, and then level out as you pass through hay-scented and New York ferns. Many muscular-trunked ironwood trees thrive in the understory of these open, easy-to-walk-through woods.

The path undulates, then rises, and swings right. Numerous boulders dot the forest floor—the reason why this land was never suitable for crops. Cross through a damp area on corduroy and then over a tiny brook bed that is dry in summer. Incredibly absorbent sphagnum moss pads some stones, while pink knotweed, which blooms in summer, grows in the moist soil at your feet. Look for delicate and beautiful maidenhair fern along both sides of the trail. Note the magnificent two- and three-trunked tulip trees—the tallest species of our eastern forests, also known as tulip poplar—and the big red oak on the right. Through the trees to the right, you'll glimpse the rusting hulk of a portable sawmill that operated during the late 1800s and early 1900s. The steam boiler and large flywheel are most obvious. Red and white oaks, American chestnut, and tulip tree were harvested. The sawmill shut down for good in 1922. The trail proceeds gradually left and up past stone walls and ledge outcrops. At 1.75 miles, reach the Sap Brook Trail intersection at marker 39.

More than 90 years after this portable sawmill processed its last hardwood logs, the rusting machinery is still visible from Godfrey Trail.

Turn left onto this relatively narrow, yellow-and-white-blazed path and pass an outcrop on the right. Then curve right and into young oak, maple, and birch woods with mountain laurel, huckleberry, and sweet pepperbush beneath. Big chestnut oaks with deeply furrowed brown bark stand near the undulating trail. Ovenbirds—heavily streaked, ground-nesting warblers—inhabit the woodlands in spring and summer, preferring to spend the "off-season" in the Tropics. Gain ground gradually, swinging left through rocky woods where yellow and black birches are quite common. The sap of both contains oil of wintergreen. You'll find huckleberry, sometimes confused with blueberry, in rocky, acidic woodlands like these. Huckleberry leaves, unlike those of blueberry, are peppered with minute yellowish resin dots on both surfaces. In summer, its edible blue-black fruits are tasty. The trail bears left and descends gently to a T intersection at marker 38. Turn left onto the Hiltebeitel Trail and cross a tiny flow on rocks as the path bears left by a low-lying, seasonally wet area of sweet pepperbush, mountain laurel, highbush blueberry, and sphagnum moss.

Step over a living fallen beech that has transformed three side branches into surrogate vertical trunks, testimony to the species' prolific sprouting ability. Bear left and continue through rocky oak, birch, and maple woods with many old fallen trunks on a sinuous but level trail. Generally the forest seems young, with many slender stems. Cross over a flat bedrock outcrop amid mountain laurel, witch hazel, and chestnut oak, and pass the rusted remains of a cast-iron stove on the right. Here I came across a long column of red and black ants carrying ant larvae in their pincers. Perhaps this was a victorious raiding party returning with the spoils of war. At a rock outcrop on the left, the yellow-blazed (hiking only) trail swings in the other direction. Cross the bedrock floor of a small, sunny opening where only stunted oak and a few other species such as shadbush and mountain laurel eke out an existence. Chestnut oak, which does well on dry sites, remains the dominant large tree. Its sweet acorns mature in one year. Silver mound moss is common on the sandy soil as you weave through oak and laurel.

Cross another small bedrock clearing and then pass an outcrop covered with rock tripe lichens. Follow the path gradually up over the outcrop, which is decorated with the gray-green doilies of other lichens. Following the top of the low outcrop brings you to a T intersection. The trail to the right is blocked; turn left. Cross a seasonally damp swale on a single split log. The trail continues to be blazed yellow only as it bears right, then left, and gradually climbs past a rock ledge on both sides. Descend fairly steeply for a short distance and swing right. These outcrops were contorted as the rock melted and later resolidified deep within the earth under great pressure and heat. With the aid of a log ladder climb to the top of the outcrop and gain the vista point on Deer Knoll. The open granite prominence, studded with a few pitch pines, affords a pleasant view to the east of low, rolling, tree-clad ridges. The rock isn't totally naked; haircap moss and reindeer lichen have colonized it. Lichens produce acids as metabolic by-products, igniting the slow process of turning rock into rock flour and finally soil. In pockets where soil has collected, small oaks, including scrub oak, have gained a foothold.

Continue on the trail and notice the rock with prominent quartz veins turned on end. Quartz is extremely durable and makes granite highly resistant to erosion. Proceed down the rocks and off the outcrop, entering oak woods and bearing left down the rocky path through laurel. A few small oak ferns, miniature versions of bracken fern, grow here. The trail swings this way and that and reaches a T junction at marker 20 after 2.8 miles. Turn right onto the Deer Knoll Trail—an old rocky woods road—and step over characteristically shallow American beech roots. Some trees show signs of old pileated woodpecker excavations where the crow-sized birds sought out carpenter ants. The path bears left over rolling terrain and intersects the Harrison Trail at an acute angle on the left. Stay straight on Deer Knoll Trail.

WOODLAND TO CHARCOAL

In the eighteenth and early nineteenth centuries, before the widespread use of coal, iron furnaces were fueled with locally produced charcoal. To make the huge quantities of charcoal required to keep the iron furnaces functioning, vast tracts of woodland were cleared. In addition to fuel to fire the furnaces, charcoal was also an important component used in the production of a wide variety of other products, including filters, drawing ink, gunpowder, medicines, and paint.

Charcoal making was a labor-intensive process carried out by men known as colliers. After cutting up to 30 cords (one cord is 8 feet by 4 feet by 4 feet) of wood (often American chestnut) to the proper length and seasoning it for a year to eliminate moisture, the collier used the logs to construct a mound in the form of a wigwam. Trees were cleared around the vicinity of the collier's hut in successively larger circles. The mound was then covered with ferns and sod to keep it from igniting completely. Air flow was controlled through vents in the bottom of the mound.

The collier spent about one month tending the slowly burning mound and lived in a hut of his construction nearby. Rock fireplaces are the only remainders today of such huts at Devil's Den. You can still find the rock-pile remains of a fireplace and bits of charcoal at the charcoal site along Laurel Trail. This is just one of 40 such sites identified on the Devil's Den property. Charcoal production, along with land clearing for agriculture, created a landscape that would be virtually unrecognizable to anyone living today. Whereas Connecticut today is fully 70 percent wooded, during the middle of the nineteenth century, 70 percent of the state was devoid of trees!

Descend gently and bear left on the rocky path. New York and then hay-scented ferns are common just before you reach another T at marker 5. Turn left onto Pent Trail, cross a seasonal stream, and head in the direction of the parking area. Pass marker 4 on the left where a small trail intersects. This also leads back to the parking area, but by a more circuitous route. A short distance farther, at marker 3, is the junction of the McDougal T. West Trail. Continue straight on the Pent Trail, marked with red-and-white blazes. Rock outcrops come into view on the left. The yellow concrete marker indicates the watershed land boundary. A marsh overlook on the right offers only a limited view. An observation area has been created just off the trail. Aquatic vegetation—buttonbush, lilies, and bur reed—is visible. Gaudy black-and-yellow tiger swallowtails sip nectar from the spherical flower heads of buttonbush in summer. A rock wall right of the roadway leads you back to the opposite end of the parking area from which you began your walk.

MORE INFORMATION

Open dawn to dusk. There are no restrooms. Pets, horses, bicycles, and picnicking are not allowed. Cross-country skiing is permitted on red-blazed trails. Register at the kiosk where you'll find trail maps and interpretive displays. A small donation is welcomed. Devil's Den Preserve, P.O. Box 1162, Weston, CT 06883; 203-226-4991 weekdays; http://www.nature.org/wherewework/northamerica/states/connecticut/preserves/art17963.html.

—R. L.

TRIP 17
THE WEIR PRESERVE

Location: Wilton
Rating: Easy
Distance: 1.1 miles
Elevation Gain: 50 feet
Estimated Time: 1.0 hour
Map: USGS Bethel, Weir Preserve map

This is a delightful ramble through 110 acres of lovely woodlands and old pastures, a great loop walk with young children, which features picturesque laurel thickets, sturdy stone walls, granite boulders and ledge outcrops, and pleasing meadows.

DIRECTIONS

From the traffic light in Wilton center at the intersection of Routes 7/33, turn onto Route 33 (Ridgefield Road). Travel north for 2.0 miles to Nod Hill Road. Turn right onto Nod Hill Road and follow it for 3.1 miles to the signed preserve entrance on the left. Park parallel to a stone wall on the left side of the road; there is room for about three vehicles (additional parking can be found at the Weir Farm Historic Site a half mile farther on Nod Hill Road, but trail directions commence at roadside trailhead parking).

TRAIL DESCRIPTION

Enter the Preserve, owned by the Weir Farm Art Center—the co-operating association with the Weir Farm National Historic Site, on a wide former woods road bordered on both sides by stone walls. The predominant tree is sugar maple; you also see white ash and black birch, and evergreen Christmas fern. Descend gradually to an intermittent brook with abundant spicebush shrubs. Aptly named shagbark hickory, contrasting smooth-barked ironwood (musclewood), and witch hazel, a fall bloomer, are also here. Winterberry, a deciduous holly, produces coral red berries, eaten by birds, in fall. On the left lies a seasonal wetland created by a 35-foot-long fieldstone dam across the brook, where moisture-loving sensitive and royal ferns thrive. The old roadway, blazed yellow, follows the length of the dam. Reach granite outcrops on both sides. Evergreen (marginal) wood fern caps the rocks.

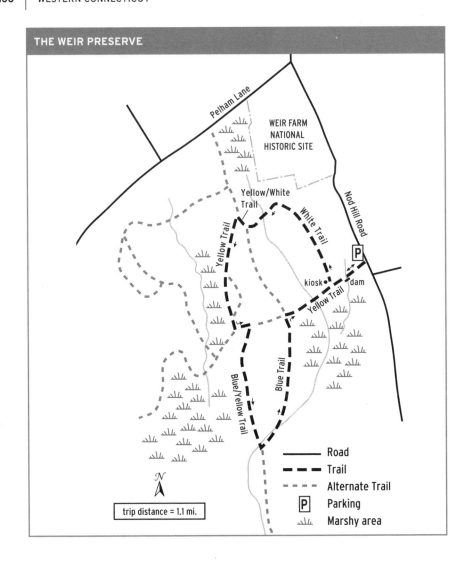

THE WEIR PRESERVE

WEIR FARM
NATIONAL
HISTORIC SITE

Pelham Lane

Nod Hill Road

Yellow/White
Trail

White Trail

Yellow Trail

kiosk • dam

Yellow Trail

Blue Trail

Blue/Yellow Trail

N

trip distance = 1.1 mi.

———— Road

- - - - Trail

· - · - Alternate Trail

P Parking

Marshy area

Red and white oaks appear just before a trail intersection on the right, 400 feet from the road. A kiosk complete with large trail map is located just beyond an opening in the stone wall. Turn right, toward the kiosk, onto the white-blazed trail. Here American chestnuts reach sapling height before the chestnut blight kills them. Black birches, from whose sap oil of wintergreen was once distilled, are common. A few American beech, red maple, big-tooth aspen, and red cedar (juniper) are also present. The cedar average 4 inches in diameter and took root when this still was pastureland. Pass through a substantial stone wall constructed of gneiss (pronounced *nice*) rocks. The gap is outfitted with a barway made of cedar posts and cleverly embedded horseshoes used to hold the cedar rails. Gray squirrels bound along the walls transporting hickory nuts and acorns to their winter larders. During the warm days of summer squirrels shelter in leaf nests high in the hickories.

At 0.2 mile, reach a Y fork and turn left onto a narrow path that soon enters woodland to continue on the Weir Preserve trail system (proceeding straight would lead you to the Weir Farm National Historic Site, former home of J. Alden Weir, a notable American impressionist painter; it's worth a visit). The trail continues as white-blazed. Pass through another stone wall fitted with cedar posts and horseshoe bar holders to enter a red oak and black birch forest with an understory of sassafras and striped maple—a small northern hardwood forest tree, unusual in this area, with green-and-white bark. Cross the East Branch of Comstock Brook, which flows seasonally through a culvert made of fieldstones. Strikingly plumaged and vocal red-bellied woodpeckers are common inhabitants of oak woods, their barred black-and-white backs unique in eastern woodlands.

Sweet pepperbush, witch hazel, and striped maple thrive in the moist soil below red maples. Curve left and climb slightly. Pass through a rock wall and turn right, ignoring the path going left. Thickets of laurel now appear along the yellow-and-white-blazed trail. At 0.3 mile, a yellow-blazed trail (somewhat difficult to see) turns to the left. Follow the yellow-blazed trail through dense laurel that towers to 9 feet. The week before Father's Day is reputed to provide the best floral show, while white, red, and chestnut oaks and red maples display brilliant foliage in fall; the red maples, when backlit, are flaming scarlet. Follow a gentle grade downhill on the yellow-blazed path and bear left at a rounded pink granite outcrop. Some of the chestnut oaks are fairly large, their leaves quite broad, with wavy margins. Turn left again and walk through heavy laurel growth and under a canopy of oak and red maple. Continue gradually downslope, then more steeply by granite bedrock outcrops and boulders.

Where the trail levels out, reach a large, handsome American beech with a 2-foot-diameter trunk; its smooth, light gray bark is characteristic. In fall, the bright yellow sunlit leaves of sassafras provide a pleasing contrast to the gray beech trunk, which serves as a backdrop. Continue straight, past the beech, and at 0.4 mile bear left at the T intersection where another fine beech specimen awaits. Follow the yellow trail left; note that the direction-of-travel arrows, however, are white. The path is crisscrossed by the surface root network of a stand of beeches, some quite sizable, while the stems of mountain laurel shrubs are picturesquely gnarled. The raucous cries of blue jays are a

FROM EDEN TO YOUR GARDEN

Snakes, quite frankly, have gotten a bum rap for millennia. Ever since evil was epitomized in the serpent that tempted Adam and Eve in the Garden of Eden, these scaled creatures have been the object of disdain by most of humanity. The fact that snakes are legless no doubt plays a major role in conjuring up the feeling of revulsion some feel toward them.

Although poisonous snakes do exist that pose some danger to people, in this part of the Northeast, poisonous serpents are rare indeed, and even those that are poisonous are highly overrated as far as their danger to humans is concerned. But the fear, or at least the distrust, goes deeper. Perhaps it hearkens all the way back to a primeval time on the African veldt, the cradle of humanity, where a misstep by our early ancestors might certainly have been their last.

Putting the irrational aside, snakes are truly interesting and attractive creatures when seen from a vantage point devoid of prejudice. Fourteen species of snakes are indigenous to Connecticut. Two, the northern red-belly snake and timber rattlesnake, are now found at very few sites. Seven species are irregularly distributed, and the remaining five are commonly found statewide. No doubt the most common of all is the eastern garter snake, named after the fashionable garters that once held up men's socks. Although highly variable of pattern, the garter snakes generally possess three dull-yellow longitudinal stripes, one of which runs down the center of the back. The background color is usually tan with darker blotches.

Garter snakes, which range farther north and have a wider distribution than any other snake, are born alive and are often found near water. In spring and fall they spend much of their time sunning themselves to maintain the correct body temperature. Garter snakes eat earthworms, insects, frogs, salamanders, birds, and small mammals. They have an amazing ability to locate earthworms by the scent trail the worms leave. Sometimes it is the attention-getting alarm cries of captured frogs that lead a person to one of these snakes. The larger females give birth in late summer, about 5 months after mating. In winter they den together in protected locations such as mammal burrows or rock outcrops, where these snakes appear to be able to withstand some freezing without consequent harm.

ubiquitous sound in these woods. Jays cache acorns for winter use. Yellow birch, a member of the northern hardwood forest community, now becomes common, and black birch increases as you reach a T intersection. The fall foliage spectacle can be eye-catching: witch hazel, both birches, tulip tree, and aspen all turn varying shades of yellow; red maple transforms from green into red and orange; and oaks take on a coppery hue. The yellow-blazed trail goes both straight and left; continue straight, slightly up and onto a low, rocky knoll covered with laurel and birches.

Walk straight along a gradual slope through laurel, oak, birch, maple, and tulip tree woodland. Come to a Y fork, blazed yellow in both directions. Follow the white arrow left and walk easily uphill. Reach another Y intersection at two American beeches (0.6 mile). Turn right onto the blue-and-yellow-blazed trail and follow it through the twisted stems of tall mountain laurel. Continue past a granite boulder split lengthwise and through sweet pepperbush, which blooms white in summer. The trail continues past more boulders and outcrops. Walk up and over an outcropping—a granite island in a sea of laurel—which offers a fine view of the laurel thicket to the right. Come upon an oddly shaped black birch that, after being bent over, rerooted and formed a photogenic arch—a monument to flexibility and tenacity. This species' scientific name, *lenta*, in fact refers to its pliable twigs. Chestnut oak, black birch, and maple are the major trees here, while witch hazel and beech dominate the understory.

Cross a bedrock outcrop, and walk across additional low ledges as the slope drops away to the right. You are now gazing at the midpoint of the big trees' trunks on the right. Now proceed gradually down. The trail turns left; but first, follow the 25-foot-long spur to the top of the ledge for a view of the woods. On the left is a wet area with robust cinnamon fern. For a nice view, follow the path to the left over the outcrop where it joins the blue-and-yellow-blazed trail again on the left. At 0.75 mile, the main trail turns sharply left and continues over rocks to a slanted T intersection. Both directions are blazed blue. Continue straight (east) here; the path curves left through more mountain laurel, Connecticut's state flower. The trail jogs through oak, maple, birch, and sassafras woodland and traverses another low outcropping along a minor slope. Houses are visible to the right. Cross more granite as you curve right and descend from the ledge, where large white oak and tulip trees reach up from this damper "lowland." The trail turns left ahead where a short stone wall section greets you. Ferns and shrubs fill the wet area on the right with greenery.

The path now climbs again to a modest ledge. On the right is a four-trunked red oak. During a mid-October visit, I gazed up to witness a migrating sharp-shinned hawk and its larger relative, a Cooper's hawk, spiraling upward. A bit farther along, at the base of a ledge, stands a huge double-trunked red oak on the right. The slope drops down to a red maple swamp 100 yards away to the right. Continue walking over low outcrops and then turn right. Fast against the trail is a granite boulder, one of the hardest rocks on earth. Granite from the property was quarried for the Brooklyn Bridge's foundations. After descending from the outcrop, swing left and pass through a stone wall and many (sweet) birches, then reach a T intersection, at 1.0 mile, immediately after a rock wall. Turn right to follow the yellow-blazed trail back in the direction of the trailhead and your vehicle. Watch for spicebush; it contains aromatic oils, and early land surveyors once regarded it as an indicator of fertile agricultural soils. In mid-October a hermit thrush was swallowing the high-fat-content berries in preparation for its flight south. Pass through a stone wall, noting the fine tulip tree on the right. Finally, gain the junction of the white and yellow trails; note the kiosk. Continue straight to reach your vehicle along Nod Hill Road.

MORE INFORMATION

The Weir Preserve is open dawn to dusk; the adjacent Weir Farm National Historic Site's hours are Wednesday through Sunday, 8:30 A.M. to 5:00 P.M. Neither charges a fee. Dogs, bicycles, and picnicking are not allowed on the Preserve. The Weir Preserve, P.O. Box 7033, Wilton, CT 06897-7033; 203-762-7479; http://www.nps.gov/wefa/index.htm.

—R. L.

TRIP 18
GREENWICH AUDUBON CENTER

Location: Greenwich
Rating: Easy
Distance: 3.0 miles
Elevation Gain: 180 feet
Estimated Time: 2.0 hours
Map: USGS Glenville, Greenwich Audubon Center map

This is a 295-acre National Audubon oasis with 7.0 miles of trails traversing rocky uplands and wildlife-rich wetlands. Special attributes of this loop hike include massive hardwoods—especially tulip trees—numerous rock outcrops, and fine birding.

DIRECTIONS
Take Exit 28 off Route 15 (Merritt Parkway); follow Round Hill Road north for 1.5 miles to John Street. Turn left and drive approximately 1.5 miles to the intersection of John Street and Riversville Road. Turn right immediately at the entrance sign into the drive leading to the center's parking lot.

TRAIL DESCRIPTION
After registering at the nature center, follow the asphalt path downhill to the trailhead on the left. Some fine birding can be had right in this area. Turn right onto the Discovery Trail and then walk left and cross a small wooden bridge along spring-fed Indian Spring Pond. In summer the small pond, which bullfrogs and the smaller green frogs call home, is coated with a layer of tiny floating duckweed plants. Follow the sign to the Discovery Trail to the left. Take the second trail junction for Discovery/Byram River/Mead Lake/Old Pasture Trails, heading past a small masonry structure that protects the spring flowing out from under it. Pass two huge tulip trees on the right; one is more than 4 feet in diameter! Tulip tree (also known as tulip poplar or yellow poplar) is the tallest species of the eastern deciduous forest, sometimes exceeding 100 feet. Native Americans constructed dugout canoes from their massive trunks. Stand next to this pair of forest giants and gaze up into their crowns to appreciate their majesty. The showy yellow-green, tulip-like flowers, appearing in early June, prove that they are related to

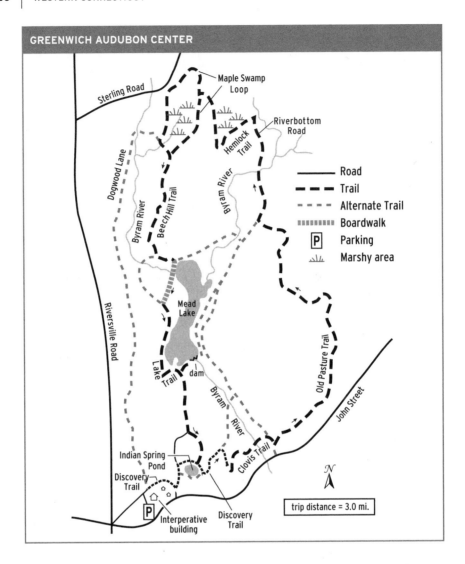

GREENWICH AUDUBON CENTER

Maple Swamp Loop

Sterling Road

Riverbottom Road

Hemlock Trail

Dogwood Lane

Byram River

Beech Hill Trail

Byram River

Road
Trail
Alternate Trail
Boardwalk
P Parking
Marshy area

Mead Lake

Riversville Road

Lake Trail

dam

Byram River

Old Pasture Trail

John Street

Indian Spring Pond

Discovery Trail

Clovis Trail

N

Interperative building

Discovery Trail

P

trip distance = 3.0 mi.

magnolias, not poplars. Sapling trees grow outsized leaves to help them in their competition with their giant parents—a leaf of one sapling here measured 14 inches across. Still, these woods are characterized mostly by American beech, sugar maple, black birch, and red oak—some also very large.

At 0.25 mile, reach a trail junction and follow the Clovis/Old Pasture Trails to the right. Schist rocks in the path sparkle with mica crystals. Christmas and spinulose wood ferns, the latter one lacy, are indicators of rich soil. A rock wall borders the path on the left, while a hillside drops away beyond it. Some of the taller trees here are black locusts—members of the nitrogen-fixing legume family. Recognize them by their deeply furrowed bark and compound leaves

You cannot help but admire the massive trunks of the Center's many towering tulip trees.

of numerous small leaflets. Sugar maple seedlings form a Lilliputian forest below their parent trees. The trail turns sharply left onto a downhill switchback, past a mowed grassy area with fruit trees on the right. The path swings right and crosses the brook on a section of boardwalk. Look for tracks of raccoon, eastern chipmunk, American crow, and other creatures in the fine silt. Garlic mustard, an alien, invasive plant with pungent foliage, grows here in profusion. Enter a small sunlit clearing colonized by thorny raspberry, rose, and hanging grapevines, and then reenter shaded forest. Skunk cabbage thrives along the brook. Cross a stone wall, descend a small hill, turn left, and then right to cross a wooden bridge over a flowing stream. This is the East Branch of the Byram River. Water striders skate on the stream's surface tension seeking insect prey. In summer, striking ebony jewelwing damselflies flutter along the stream. Males possess electric-blue abdomens and jet-black wings.

Regain higher ground and cross a stone wall at a T intersection with Riverbottom Road. Turn right toward Old Pasture Trail. Granitic gneiss (pronounced *nice*) boulders and outcrops are numerous. Cross a tiny intermittent streambed on a bog bridge; paved John Street is visible straight ahead. The path turns left to follow near the preserve boundary through young, open maple woods. The veery, a small, cinnamon-colored thrush, breeds here. Its descending flutelike song is one of the most enchanting sounds of the forest. Oriental bittersweet vines—some 3 inches thick—creep up the trees. This exotic invasive pest "strangles" its host in corkscrew fashion. The trail bears right and passes an open field where a nest box provides a breeding site for bluebirds. Stone walls are everywhere—at one time Connecticut had 25,000 miles of them! Enter a forest of beech and red oak, with bracken fern in sun-dappled glades, and pass a big glacial erratic on the right. Maple-leaf viburnum forms part of the shrub layer. Also present is another invasive exotic—Japanese barberry, a small prickly shrub indicating past soil disturbance.

A gray, rocky clifflike outcrop of gneiss rises to the right, below which scampering eastern chipmunks gather fallen acorns from the abundant white oaks. Bluish-green evergreen wood fern caps the outcrops, and New York fern softens the forest floor. To the left is a vernal pool where wood frogs and certain species of salamanders travel for annual courtship and breeding. In summer, the wiggling of tiny black tadpoles is obvious in the shallow water. Pass more outcrops on the right, one of which bears an uncanny resemblance to the arched back of a whale. Bisect another stone wall and curve left. Large black birches are common here, as well as tulip trees, red and white oaks, white ashes, shagbark hickories, and—in the understory—American beeches. Blue jay, eastern wood pewee, scarlet tanager, and northern cardinal are common breeding birds in this rocky woodland. Pass a large multi-trunked red oak on the right. Associated with the oak are tight-skinned and furrowed pignut hickory trees bearing five leaflets per leaf, while seedling sassafras trees have sprouted below them.

The path bears left and passes through a stone wall "boundary" into an open area with one nest box. Sassafras is colonizing this field. Now pass under the limb of a flowering dogwood, which opens exquisite four-petaled white blossoms in May. Yellow cinquefoil and blue-eyed grass bloom in early summer along the path. Walk through woodland briefly and then enter a second small field, also outfitted with a nest box. A few remnant red cedars are reminders that this was once all pasture. Bracken fern sprouts profusely in the sandy soil. Watch for butterflies such as little wood satyr in the clearing. Reenter woods briefly, passing through an old rock wall, and then glimpse a new field on the left as you approach a Y junction. Stay left and follow the Old Pasture Trail toward Riverbottom Road through a small field dotted with the yellow spikes of goldenrod in late summer. Bittersweet shows signs of invading this field, which also contains yarrow and black-eyed Susan, a well-known and attractive wildflower native to the Midwestern states. Reenter red maple–beech–oak woods and walk slightly downhill. Highbush blueberry, black birch, tulip tree, and maple-leaf viburnum are also present. Aromatic spicebush is very common; its leaves have a tangy citrus odor. The red fruits provide migrant thrushes and other birds with fat-rich fuel in late summer.

Pass through a small stone wall, swing left, and continue downhill. In late June, yellow-orange tulip tree petals litter the path. On the right stands another huge tulip tree—characteristically pillar straight with crosshatched bark much like that of an ash. Reach a T intersection at 1.2 miles. Turn right onto River-bottom Road in the direction of the Hemlock Trail and walk through an open woodland of red maple, beech, red and white oaks, and tulip tree, all with long, straight trunks. On the forest floor, Christmas and New York ferns add splashes of green. Each leaflet of Christmas fern is shaped like a tiny yuletide stocking. Unlike New York fern, it is evergreen. Pass through another stone wall and bear left, coming close to a very smooth, light-gray beech on the right. Reach a wooden bridge and cross the East Branch of the Byram River on a bridge of recycled plastic decking. Skunk cabbage plants poke up out of the floodplain. These fascinating plants generate their own internal heat, allowing them to melt through the snow cover of late winter. The impressive trunks of tulip trees stand like monuments in the woods. A rock outcrop emerges on the left as the stream parallels the path on the opposing side.

Follow the trail gradually uphill and at the top reach a dead end. From here, the Hemlock Trail turns left and follows alongside a hill through attractive oak-beech woodland. Many beeches are less than 3 inches in diameter and probably represent sprout growth from the roots of the larger trees. Hemlocks reappear as the trail bears right and then leads down into a bowl. An imposing ledge outcrop rises steeply on the left to a height of 40 feet. A little farther pass a wetland with skunk cabbage on the right. Raucous great crested flycatchers nest in tree cavities, while ovenbirds construct their domed-over nests on the ground. Listen for the ovenbird's ringing *teacher-teacher-teacher* in spring and summer. Walk by a huge beech on the right; it has a major branch broken off down low. Pass through yet another stone wall. While this was once a pasture, it now contains many specimen-sized beeches whose nuts are eagerly con-sumed by numerous birds and mammals.

Bear left and come to a T intersection at 1.7 miles; turn right (north) onto the Maple Swamp Loop. Then swing left, and left again; just below you to the right is gravel Sterling Road. Wood thrushes, with bright rust-colored heads and bold brown spotting on bright white underparts, summer in these oak and beech woods and winter in the Tropics. After passing through another stone wall, you are walking on the spine of a low ridge, with the land dropping off on both sides. After a couple of curves, a big rock outcrop appears on the left.

TULIPS IN THE SKY

As you walk the trails of the Greenwich Audubon Center, you can't help but be impressed by the sheer size and massive columnar form of the magnificent tulip trees, which are quite abundant in these woodlands. At the same time you may feel small and insignificant in their presence.

Tulip trees are fast-growing giants that reach their greatest dimensions in the cove forests of southern Appalachia. They are very shade intolerant but grow so quickly as to outstrip the growth of their competitors. They mature in 200 to 250 years. For sheer size alone, yellow poplars, as they are sometimes known, have virtually no rivals in our eastern forests. In the moist, rich, deep soils of the Appalachian forests, they sometimes attain heights of 150 feet and more. Some noteworthy specimens of *Liriodendron tulipifera* have grown to be 8 or 10 feet in diameter. It's no wonder, then, that the state of Tennessee selected this species as its state tree.

The flowers, which are pollinated by bees, are cup-shaped, 2 inches across, and gorgeous, the petals creamy greenish white with orange bases. In southern Connecticut they bloom in late May and early June. The trees produce many winged seeds, but most of these are infertile. Large crops of fertile seeds are produced at irregular intervals. Even the large leaves of these relatives of the magnolia are tulip-shaped.

The wood of these important timber trees is quite soft and easily worked to fabricate a variety of products. It is used to make plywood, crates, boxes, and other mundane items that are seemingly out of whack with its noble proportions. It is also used to make high-grade paper. Native Americans, and after them white settlers, used the long, straight trunks of tulip trees to fashion dugout canoes. Apparently it was such a canoe—fully 60 feet in length—that transported Daniel Boone, his family, and all their belongings westward to start a new life in the wilderness in 1799.

Turn right and come to an intersection with Dogwood Lane on the right. Go left and follow Dogwood Lane south to the Beech Hill Trail.

Although spring peepers are seldom seen, I was lucky enough to find one of these tiny tree frogs, with an X-like mark on its back, crawling up the wet, slanted surface of a nearby ledge after a shower. The friction disks at the tips of its toes enabled it to climb adeptly. In spring when the males of this, our smallest frog species, congregate in breeding choruses, their high-pitched calls resound like ringing sleigh bells. The Beech Trail leads to a junction with the other end of Dogwood Lane; turn left to follow the Beech Hill Trail a short distance to its intersection with the Lake Trail at 2.2 miles. Turn left at the Lake Trail. Soon reach a boardwalk that leads across a wooded swamp near the edge of Mead Lake on the left. The lake is covered with the floating leaves of fragrant water lilies. Clumps of tussock sedges and alder shrubs also thrive in the shallows. Reach a T intersection and turn left to continue on the Lake Trail toward the parking area. Here partially obscured views of Mead Lake on the left are possible. Watch for an isolated patch of low, creeping partridgeberry in the woods. Its tiny twin white trumpets bloom in late spring and early summer. The small, rounded leaves are paired and evergreen.

At the southern end of Mead Lake, the path turns sharply left and reaches a T intersection with the Lake Trail. Before turning right and heading back toward the interpretive building, you may want to turn left and walk out to the bridge over the spillway of the dam that created the millpond known as Mead Lake. The original stone core of the dam is more than 100 years old. After inspecting the dam, retrace your steps and continue south, past the intersection, on the Lake Trail. Walk uphill until you reach a vernal pond on your right. When the trail forks, you can go either way—both lead back in the direction of Indian Spring Pond. Watch for eastern cottontail rabbits emerging from sheltering shrubbery to nibble clover in the lawn near the pond, and listen for the sweet liquid warble of a rose-breasted grosbeak along the way. This black, white, and red bird is one of the most colorful of our summer residents. The left fork—Old Forest Trail—leads to another T junction at the pond; turn right and then left at the next intersection to retrace your steps to the interpretive building and your vehicle.

MORE INFORMATION

Greenwich Audubon Center—open daily, year-round, 9:00 A.M. to 5:00 P.M.—features regional natural history exhibits. Nonmember adults $3, children and seniors $1.50. Pets, bicycles, and collecting of specimens are not permitted. Picnicking is limited to the Hawkwatch lawn. Audubon Center in Greenwich, 613 Riversville Road, Greenwich, CT 06831; 203-869-5272; http://greenwich.center.audubon.org/.

—R. L.

2

CENTRAL CONNECTICUT

THE CENTRAL SECTION OF CONNECTICUT IS SANDWICHED BETWEEN the metamorphic mountains and highlands of the west and east. This area is home to the state's signature river, the Connecticut. The walks in this region explore the fascinating traprock mountains, from Sleeping Giant (Trip 29) and Bluff Head Ridge (Trip 33) in the south to Mount Higby (Trip 27), the Hanging Hills (Trip 25), and Talcott Mountain (Trip 24) to the north. Here Indian legends live on, and wildlife, from copperheads to bobcats, survives.

The central region also contains hikes that take you to caves to explore, from the overhang of Coginchaug (Trip 32) to the deep recesses of Indian Council Caves (Trip 21). In addition to these attractions are beautiful walks through the Sessions Woods (Trip 22) and Westwoods (Trips 34 and 35), where majestic rock formations mingle with the waterbirds and mysterious rock carvings of Lost Lake. You will be surprised that in this region of cities, suburbs, and thoroughfares so many lovely, private locations await your visit.

TRIP 19
MCLEAN GAME REFUGE

Location: Granby
Rating: Easy, with moderate section
Distance: 3.5 miles
Elevation Gain: 400 feet
Estimated Time: 2.0 hours
Maps: USGS Tariffville—CT, MA

At 4,446 acres, the McLean Game Refuge is one of the largest parcels of conservation land, state or privately owned, in Connecticut. Its many miles of well-maintained trails lead through extensive hardwood forests, along fast-flowing streams, past lush wetlands, and to the summit of a hill created by lava flows.

DIRECTIONS
From the junction of Routes 202/10, 20, and 189 in Granby, travel south for 1.0 mile on Routes 202/10 to a paved road on the right. There is currently no sign directing visitors to the refuge along the highway. Turn right onto the paved refuge entry road, past a yellow metal gate, and follow the road a short distance to its gated terminus at the parking area. A map of the trails and refuge regulations are posted here.

TRAIL DESCRIPTION
At the trailhead adjacent to the parking lot a map board illustrates the refuge's extensive holdings and trail system and lists its regulations. Walk past the wooden gate and enter a cool, shaded hardwood forest of red maple, red and black oaks, eastern hemlock, and black birch. A steep slope rises to your left, where brilliant scarlet tanagers nest high in the canopy, while on your right broad skunk cabbage leaves and fern fronds thrive in the waterlogged soil. Follow the broad roadway as it crosses Bissell Brook on a wide wooden plank bridge. The trail curves left and arrives at a trailhead on the right where a sign gives trail distances and blaze colors. The tall and eye-catching fertile fronds of cinnamon fern grace the brook banks to your left in spring.

Continue straight along the stream on the wide dirt path to the Trout Pond, as well as to the concrete dam that created it, on the left. A fence guards the shoreline, while Canada geese and their goslings approach visitors in hopes of

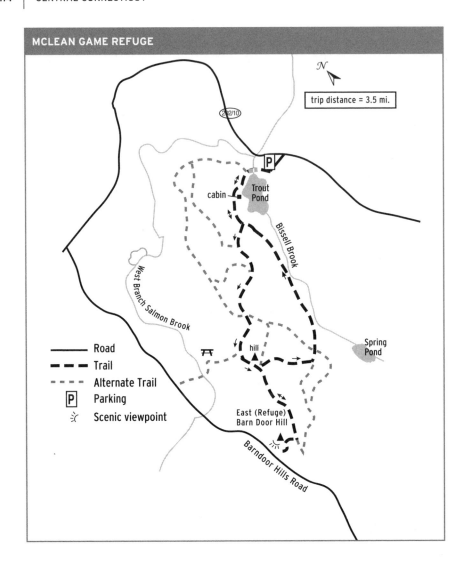

MCLEAN GAME REFUGE

trip distance = 3.5 mi.

202/10

cabin

Trout Pond

Bissell Brook

West Branch Salmon Brook

Spring Pond

hill

—— Road
━ ━ ━ Trail
- - - - Alternate Trail
P Parking
Scenic viewpoint

East (Refuge)
Barn Door Hill

Barndoor Hills Road

securing an easy meal. Restrain yourself and remember to "keep the wild in wildlife." Watch for painted turtles on logs basking in the sun. The trail climbs a low, sandy rise, and Senator George P. McLean's (1857–1932) log cabin overlooks the pond on the left. A pit toilet is located to the right of the path.

The trail now bears left and enters attractive pine, oak, and maple woods with some hemlock. Inconspicuous brown creepers hitch up the tree trunks using their forceps-like beaks deftly to pick insects and spiders from bark crevices. As you walk over this old woods road, watch for chunks of rusty-brown basalt, the first sign that lava once flowed and solidified below the surface of this land. At a Y junction, take the right fork.

Pink lady's slipper orchids bloom in June amid the accumulated needles of red and white pine. Another species that thrives in the sandy, acid soil of this pine-oak woodland is lowbush blueberry. The trail ascends gradually and curves left. Here the roadway has been cut over time several feet down into the sandy soil. Young white pine and hemlock line the path, and soft haircap moss forms a cushion atop the sterile soil. One of the loveliest spring wildflowers of these glacial soils is bird's-foot violet. Its delicate purplish violet blossoms and finely divided leaves make it easily recognizable. Seemingly always active are black-capped chickadees, which hang acrobatically from the ends of limbs in search of insects, spiders, and their eggs while continually whistling their territorial *fee-bee* songs. As you follow the old road to the left and slightly uphill, listen in late spring and early summer for the exquisite woodwind song of the wood thrush, one of the refuge's many birds that spend their winters in the Tropics.

Soon after reaching the junction of the blue-blazed trail (from Stony Hill) on the right, the trail curves left again. The rock outcrops are basalt, obvious by their dark brown, hexagonal fractures. Increasing eastern hemlock growth results in deepening shade and very little undergrowth in this section. Storms had toppled or snapped many shallow-rooted hemlocks just prior to my late-May visit. Proceed downhill, curving right, and then walk uphill, level off, and curve left. Soon reach a four-way intersection with a basalt slope on your left. This is one of the basaltic promontories known collectively as the Barn Door Hills. Turning right takes you to the picnic grove adjacent to the West Branch of Salmon Brook, where towering, mottle-trunked sycamores line the banks.

Turn diagonally left instead, toward the summit of East (Refuge) Barn Door Hill, where a fine view awaits you. This, too, is a wide old woods road leading past a 20-foot-high basalt outcrop on your left. Walk uphill through hemlock, black birch, and red oak woods, curve left, and arrive at a trail junction on the left. In spring, round green oak apple galls about the diameter of a quarter may litter the ground. These growths are caused by a tiny wasp that inserts an egg into the stem of an oak leaf; the plant reacts by producing the growth, thereby creating a protective home for the developing larva. Continue straight uphill on this blue-blazed trail toward the summit. Worm-eating warblers (named for the caterpillars they consume) build their nests in the leaf litter on the dry, oak-covered slopes. Listen for their sweet trills in spring and summer.

Tiny, white flower spikes and shiny green, heart-shaped leaves of abundant Canada mayflower dot the forest floor in May. The path levels off, climbs again, and soon reaches a narrow, blue-blazed path on the right that leads steeply up the hickory and oak slope past yellow-blooming star grass to the summit

The deep-cut leaves of the bird's foot violet give the species its common name.

of East (Refuge) Barn Door Hill. This path is short, and soon you level off and walk left to arrive on the basaltic summit ledges, 580 feet above sea level. Small-stature hemlock, birch, and oak grow in these scanty soils.

Here you are perched directly above a farmstead where cows graze in pastures separating this lava hill from another of the Barn Door Hills just to the southwest. The view of the other hill's cliff face, talus, and the surrounding rolling green countryside is excellent. This is a wonderful spot to bask in the sun and enjoy a snack before returning to the main trail. Follow the path back down the slope to the main trail and turn left, retracing your steps to the trail junction on the right. Turn right and walk on this wide old road, first on level ground, then gradually downhill. Light gaps created in the canopy by windthrown and damaged trees have allowed a host of white pine seedlings to thrive here. The trail curves left and joins with another wide pathway. Turn left and arrive almost immediately at another split in the trail. The blue-blazed trail turns right, but you should bear left, walking slightly downhill. The margins of the path are carpeted with Canada mayflower. These pine woods are also home to the lovely black-throated green warbler, one of some twenty species of small, active, and mostly colorful insectivorous birds that breed regularly in Connecticut woodlands and then undertake incredible annual migrations to and from Mexico and Central America.

FIRE AND ICE

The landscape so familiar to us today is actually just one snapshot in the vast library of photo albums known as geologic time. But graphic clues to the past lie all around us. The Barn Door Hills came into being some 190 million years ago, when what you now know as Connecticut and indeed North America were very different places. Connecticut had a tropical climate back then, with lush vegetation and dinosaurs constituting the dominant life forms.

As you walk the refuge trails, and especially as you make your way up the slope of the East (Refuge) Barn Door Hill, notice the dark, heavy stone that litters the woodland floor or juts out from it to create abrupt outcroppings. This basaltic traprock, as it is often called by geologists, is an igneous rock born of fire deep within the earth. As the molten material found its way to the surface through fissures and by way of volcanic flows, it solidified. In some cases, the molten rock did not reach the surface and cooled underground instead. As it cooled and shrank, it cracked into the vertical, often six-sided columns so characteristic of the dense, heavy rock you see today. The molten rock flowed to, or in some cases almost to, the surface through cracks in the earth's crust that formed as a result of the splitting apart of the supercontinent Pangea. One major result of all this was the creation of the Atlantic Ocean.

On the local scene, the half a dozen or so Barn Door Hills that jut up from the valley today are part of a generally north-south trending series of small traprock ridges that originally cooled below the earth's surface. Subsequent erosion of softer overlying rock layers have made these hills and others like them along the western edge of Connecticut's Central Valley visible. The ridges usually, but not always, have a steep slope on one side and a more gradual slope on the opposing side.

The steep, unvegetated slopes are prone to weathering through the cleaving actions of freezing and thawing. This creates a jumble of broken basalt at the cliff bases known as talus (Greek for *toe*) slopes. Thus, it is ice that in time reduces the erosion-resistant rock, born of fire, to rubble.

The earth is constantly recycling itself. Eventually the ridges will probably be covered in deep sediments again, no doubt to be overspread by lava flows and glaciers once again in their turn, ad infinitum.

Reach a major T intersection and turn left to return to the cabin at Trout Pond, near where you began the hike (turning right takes you to Spring Pond). The wide trail, which parallels Bissell Brook, is quite level as you walk under pine, oak, and birch trees. At this point the stream is screened by vegetation. Oak, hickory, and maple begin to predominate in the woodland as you continue. Here the songs and calls of red-eyed vireos, eastern wood pewees, and gray tree frogs fill the air. The tree frog has adhesive discs on its toe tips that enable it to climb and cling to branches high above the forest floor. Its grayish, lichen-colored skin makes it all but impossible to find. This 1-inch frog is quite vocal, however, and once you learn to distinguish its birdlike trill, you'll find that it is surprisingly numerous. The showiest trees in the May woods are flowering dogwood. The big, white, four-petaled blossoms of this small understory tree are unmistakable. The old road now parallels the brook more closely. Sizable hemlocks line the near brook banks, whereas red maple and skunk cabbage plants grow profusely in its rich flood plain. You may see a tiny blue-gray gnatcatcher as it flits about in the trees along the brook, its long tail acting as a counterbalance.

Soon come to the Y intersection near the Trout Pond. Continue straight through the pine-dominated forest. During the warm months the nasal voices of resident Canada geese will tell you that you've reached the pond, before you ever see it. The island in the pond hosts an abandoned bank beaver lodge, and old signs of the beaver's former presence still can be seen on tree trunks in the vicinity. Continue on the wide roadway back to the parking area. Notice bits of rusted barbed-wire fencing, left over from when this was pastureland, which you may have overlooked when you first entered the shaded forest.

MORE INFORMATION

Open daily 8 A.M.–8 P.M. in summer, 8 A.M. to sunset during rest of year. Free admission. Administered by the Trustees of the McLean Fund located in Simsbury. Bicycles are not allowed, and dogs must be leashed. Hunting, fishing, trapping, and camping are forbidden. Motorized vehicles as well as bicycles are not permitted. Horses are allowed only on yellow-blazed trails. No smoking or fire building is allowed outside the picnic area. McLean Game Refuge, 150 Barndoor Hills Road, Granby, CT 06035; 860-653-7869.

—R. L.

TRIP 20
PEOPLE'S STATE FOREST

Location: Barkhamsted
Rating: Difficult
Distance: 4.5 miles
Elevation Gain: 650 feet
Estimated Time: 3.5–4.5 hours
Maps: USGS Winsted, New Hartford

This loop hike combines history, nature, incredible mountain views, and features Manitou stones, glacial boulders, and a beaver meadow.

DIRECTIONS

From the junction of Routes 44/318, turn onto Route 318. Cross the Farmington River and turn left onto East River Road. Continue on East River Road for 2.5 miles to a parking area on the left (west) side of the road. Across the road from the parking area is a sign for the Jesse Gerard Trail.

TRAIL DESCRIPTION

Jesse Gerard Trail (yellow blazes) begins at the sign across the road from the parking area. From the edge of the woods where clumps of daylilies blossom in July, the trail enters a forest of white pine, hemlock, and maple. A few yards from the road, the trail forks left (north) and right (east). Turn left and begin a very steep climb up a bouldered ridge. This section of trail looks more like parts of the White Mountains of New Hampshire than it does Connecticut, which means it is beautiful but rugged and strenuous. As you hike through jumbles of boulders and groves of oak, maple, and ash, look for some of the wildflowers that grow in the sheltered crevices. False Solomon's seal is here, as is trillium, which displays its burgundy blooms in spring.

After a short but difficult climb, the path comes to a junction with the blue-blazed Robert Ross Trail, leaving right on a woods road, and the yellow-blazed Girard Trail turning left. Turn left (north) onto the Girard Trail, which leads through patches of laurel, chestnut oak, and maple. The glossy green leaves of wintergreen appear here and there along the trail, as does Indian cucumber-root. The grade is much more level here and becomes even

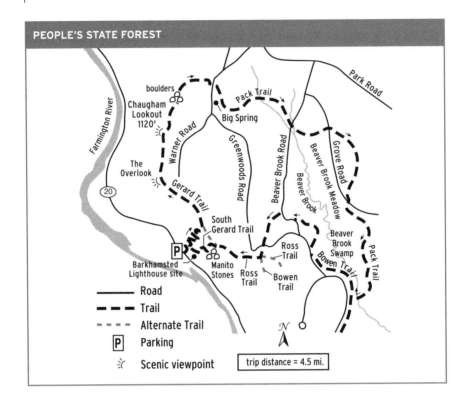

PEOPLE'S STATE FOREST

boulders
Park Road
Chaugham Lookout 1120'
Pack Trail
Big Spring
Farmington River
Warner Road
Greenwoods Road
Beaver Brook Road
Beaver Brook Meadow
Grove Road
The Overlook
Gerard Trail
Beaver Brook
20
South Gerard Trail
Beaver Brook Swamp
Ross Trail
Bowen Trail
Pack Trail
P
Barkhamsted Lighthouse site
Manito Stones
Ross Trail
Bowen Trail

——— Road

- - - Trail

- - - - Alternate Trail

P Parking

☼ Scenic viewpoint

N

trip distance = 4.5 mi.

more so at the crest of the ridge. A short side trail leaves left to a ledge with a limited view over the Farmington River below, while the main trail continues straight ahead. Continue through a hardwood forest of oak and hickory, accented with outcrops of ragged bedrock. Warner Road, a blue-blazed path, enters from the right (north).

After a short, steep climb, the path comes to a large rounded ledge called the Lookout, with spectacular views down the Farmington River Valley. The Lookout is nestled among red and chestnut oaks, red maple, white pine, and shrubby bear oak. Turkey vultures and hawks glide up and down the valley, while the songs of thrushes, juncos, and warblers float through the trees. On warm summer days, you can see people cooling off in the waters of the old quarry below and in the river to the south.

From the Lookout, the trail enters a beautiful, shady hemlock forest. Canada mayflower, with tiny spikes of lily-of-the-valley-scented flowers in spring, shares the forest floor with starflower and the tidy fronds of polypody fern. The cool hemlocks lead to the most spectacular viewpoint on the ridge: Chaugham Lookout. The view opens west down a steep cliff to the Farmington River below. To the north is the village of Riverton, with the Berkshire Hills beyond. Hemlock and white pine provide sheltered resting places all year long, and the mountain laurel that clings to the hillside adds a special loveliness when it blooms in late spring.

The trail continues through more hemlocks, passing through the narrow cleft between two immense glacial boulders. These truck-sized stones were transported to this spot by the glaciers that covered this area some 20,000 years ago. From the boulders it is a pleasant walk through tall, white pine above yellow birch and beech to the terminus of the Gerard Trail at Greenwoods Road. Turn right (south) onto the road and walk a few yards to Big Spring picnic area on the right. Here you can get a refreshing, very cold drink of water using the old red-handled water pump. Just south of the picnic area, turn left (east) onto the yellow-blazed Charles Pack Trail, a path that takes you into the heart of People's Forest.

This area of lowland forest is wet in spring and gets a little buggy at times in the warmer months. Familiar Indian cucumber-root and mountain laurel are joined by hobblebush, an open, thinly branched shrub with flat panicles of showy white flowers in spring. Partridgeberry, a creeping ground cover with lots of small, glossy green leaves, also grows here, as does blue-bead lily, with small, yellow springtime flowers and bright blue fruits in late summer.

After crossing a brook on a log bridge, the trail comes to Beaver Brook Road. Turn left and cross the bridge over Beaver Brook. Immediately after the brook, turn right into the Beaver Brook Recreation Area (sign). The path continues south, crossing the brook on stepping-stones beneath a stand of hemlock before climbing to a junction with Pack Grove Road. Cross the road and continue climbing, skirting a ledgy outcrop where the sharp calls of yellow-bellied sapsuckers can be heard in summer. The trail passes a huge, 150-year-old beech tree before heading downhill through a forest of beech, maple, and hemlock to meet Pack Grove Road once again.

Cross the road and continue downhill through hemlock and pine, passing a large boulder where trillium flowers in spring. Soon the remains of an old farmhouse appear on the left, its foundation composed of huge blocks of quarried stone. Tall ash trees loom overhead and shade trillium, doll's eyes, false Solomon's seal, and meadow rue. Near what once was the dooryard, daylilies still grow, a living legacy of flower gardens long abandoned.

From the foundation, the trail passes through a wet area and crosses Beaver Brook just before reaching the Agnes Bowen Trail (sign). Turn right (north) onto the orange-blazed Agnes Bowen Trail, which wanders along the edge of

The abundant thickets of mountain laurel along the trail make a late spring trip to People's Forest stunningly beautiful.

Beaver Brook Swamp. A short, unmarked path leads to a small open area near the beaver dam, where the wildlife of the swamp can be observed.

Life in the swamp is much different than that in the nearby forest, encouraging a host of different plants and animals. Elderberry mingles with swamp azalea, which bears small white, very fragrant blossoms in late spring. Summersweet forms thickets along the shore and bears spikes of small white flowers in summer. There are *Phragmites*, a grasslike invasive plant with mahogany-colored floral plumes in summer; yellow flag, a water iris with golden blossoms; arrowleaf; and bullhead water lily. Many species of ducks negotiate the waterway, and scores of songbirds, from red-winged blackbirds to wrens and warblers, either visit or live here. The booming croak of bullfrogs adds a peaceful tone to late-summer afternoons, and common water snakes and painted turtles sun themselves on rocks and driftwood all summer long. This is as spectacular a place as Chaugham Lookout, but in a completely different way. Each time you come here, it is possible to see something new—a delightful prospect indeed.

Return to the trail, which follows the shoreline past clusters of blue-bead lily and goldthread, to Greenwoods Road. Turn right onto the road and follow it about 100 yards to where the trail turns right into the woods. After a short walk, the path intersects Beaver Brook Road. Turn right and follow the road

MANITOU STONES

For thousands of years the Farmington River has flowed through the mountainous gap between American Legion Forest to the west and People's Forest to the east. In the 1700s, a narrow road was constructed along the bank of the river. Called the Farmington River Turnpike, it ultimately connected Hartford and Albany. Along the route were small, widely scattered English villages and a few Indian settlements. These villages served as a lifeline to travelers, providing accommodations, food, and shelter to those venturing out on the turnpike. One of these enclaves was in the gap along the Farmington River.

After a dispute with her father, Molly Barber, a woman from Wethersfield, ventured along the road, eventually reaching the Indian settlement in the People's Forest gap. She never left. She married Chaugham, a Native American, who lived in the hamlet, and the two made their home in a cabin near the roadside. The story goes that stagecoach drivers would look for the soft amber light that issued from their windows each evening as a sign they were drawing near to the cabin. Over time, the reliable light from Chaugham and Molly's cabin came to be called the Barkhamsted Lighthouse.

Today the Farmington River turnpike is gone, replaced by the winding highway called by the less romantic name of Route 20. Stagecoaches are gone, too, having been replaced with cars and trucks that speed down the highway. And of course, the settlement called Barkhamsted Lighthouse has been dark for generations. All that remains is the settlement's small graveyard on the hillside.

If you visit the cemetery, you will notice that each grave has a headstone and a smaller footstone. The stones are uninscribed, and each headstone has been notched at the corners so the marker resembles a rough image of a person's head and shoulders. These unique markers are called Manitou stones and were used by some Native Americans to mark the graves of their dead in the decades before the Revolution. It has been hundreds of years since the light in the window of the cabin by the turnpike last went dark and generations since Chaugham and Molly completed their life course. The cabin has returned to the earth, and all that remains as a reminder of Barkhamsted Lighthouse are some weathered stones on a hill. In a way it doesn't seem adequate; still, it is just enough to carry on the memory.

about 200 yards. The path then turns left, leaving the road and immediately climbing a short wooded stretch to intersect Greenwoods Road again. Turn right and follow the road about 50 feet. The trail turns left, reenters the woods, and quickly comes to the junction with the Ross Trail. Turn right (west) and follow the blue-blazed Ross Trail as it climbs past boulders and rocky outcrops. The path skirts a stony buttress to the right with impressive cliffs, and then descends along the hillside to the Gerard Trail. **Caution!** The junction is overlooked easily.

The Robert Ross Trail continues to slab the hillside, while the Gerard Trail, blazed yellow, leaves left (southwest) downslope. Follow the Gerard Trail down a steep, rough hillside. The path uses many switchbacks to ease the descent, but it is still tough on the knees, and the footing can be slippery. When the trail levels out, it passes through an ancient graveyard whose interment sites are marked with Manitou stones rather than traditional tombstones. This area is called Barkhamsted Lighthouse, a fascinating, though little-known, historic site (see essay in this chapter). From the graveyard, follow the trail the short distance to the parking area.

MORE INFORMATION

People's State Forest offers a campground, bathrooms, picnic shelter, and a nature museum. The museum is open weekends from Memorial Day to Columbus Day. Canoeing and fishing are possible in the adjacent Farmington River. Leashed dogs are permitted on the trails. Mountain bikes are permitted on forest roads only. Entrance fees of $7 per resident vehicle and $10 per nonresident vehicle are charged on weekends and holidays. People's State Forest, P.O. Box 1, Pleasant Valley, CT 06063; 860-379-2469; htpp://www.ct.gov/dep.

—C. S.

TRIP 21
INDIAN COUNCIL CAVES

Location: Barkhamsted
Rating: Moderate
Distance: 4.2 miles
Elevation Gain: 450 feet
Estimated Time: 2.0–3.0 hours
Maps: USGS New Hartford

This section of the Tunxis Trail is arguably the most attractive length of trail in the state. The boulders and outcrops, open hardwood forest, and mountain laurel thickets all combine to create a sense of benevolent wilderness found nowhere else. Here you have a most attractive out-and-back hike to an historic boulder cave, amid old foundations, ridge-top views, and beautiful forests.

DIRECTIONS
From the junction of Routes 219/318 near the Barkhamsted Reservoir dam, proceed east on Route 219 for 1.7 miles to a small parking area on the right, about 100 feet west of the intersection of Route 219 and Hillcrest Road.

TRAIL DESCRIPTION
From the parking lot, proceed north across Route 219 and enter woods of tulip tree, red oak, maple, hemlock, and ash, with clumps of mountain laurel and witch hazel beneath. Tulip tree's common name comes from its interesting tulip-like flowers of green and orange, which appear in the topmost branches in late spring. The blossoms are so well concealed that most people know them only by the occasional colorful petal that descends from the canopy and lands on the footpath. Beneath the ceiling of leaves lies an intricate matrix of cinnamon and Christmas fern, Canada mayflower, goldthread, and twisted-stalk, which have colonized the spaces between the boulders.

The path makes a loop right then another loop left before turning north into a dry woodland. At 0.1 mile, the path crosses an old woods road and enters a first-succession stand of sapling maple and black birch, evidence of fairly recent clear-cut logging in the area. From this disturbed woodland, the trail crosses a stone wall at about 0.3 mile and passes near a large white oak whose

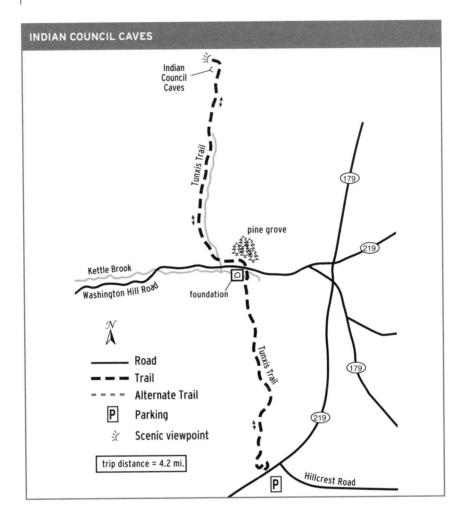

INDIAN COUNCIL CAVES

Indian Council Caves

Tunxis Trail

179

pine grove

219

Kettle Brook

Washington Hill Road

foundation

N

——————— Road

- - - - Trail

- - - - Alternate Trail

P Parking

Scenic viewpoint

trip distance = 4.2 mi.

Tunxis Trail

179

219

Hillcrest Road

P

boughs reach out toward the trail. It then enters a climax forest of hickory, beech, oak, and maple with scattered thickets of mountain laurel and witch hazel. The path continues north, climbing easily through picturesque woodlands where pileated woodpeckers live and wood thrushes sing in summer. Chipmunks are here, their sharp squeaks designed to remind you that you are only visiting the places where they live.

As the trail gains elevation, the soil turns rockier, passing over ledges of metamorphic rock called gneiss (pronounced *nice*). Chestnut oak begins to appear, and red-tailed hawks are frequent passersby. Many hawks, most notably the broadwing, migrate over these hills each autumn. Many of the redtails, easily identified by their rusty red tails, are true Yankees, staying throughout

**Large boulders make up the
Indian Council Caves.**

the year. They are often seen sitting atop a tall dead snag in winter or soaring high overhead in ever-widening circles in summer.

The path then crests a ridge and enters a beautiful woodland of rock ledges, wind-stunted oaks, blueberries, laurels, and pink lady's slippers. Coyotes love to come here, especially in the evening hours, to prowl the game trails in search of dinner. These woods are some of the nicest you can find anywhere in the state. Walk slowly and listen for the croaky laughter of ravens as they glide overhead. Passing over the top of a rocky, moss-covered outcrop at 0.5 mile, the path descends around the ledge by way of a hairpin turn. The treadway swings right (east) near a small wet area and proceeds along the base of the outcrop. Continuing through the woods, the path turns north (left), swings briefly northeast, and then resumes a northward course through thick stands of laurel.

A short distance farther on, the path turns southeast, descending along the edge of a wooded ledge before swinging east where abundant fern, starflower, and goldthread line the footway. As the path levels out, it merges with an abandoned woods road nearly overgrown with mountain laurel and fern. The walk through here is relaxing and pleasant, the hemlock, oak, and birch offering welcome shade on hot summer days.

The path then crosses a small brook and reaches Kettle Brook near a large boulder at 1.0 mile. The woods change to white pine, spruce, and hemlock before crossing Washington Hill Road at 1.1 miles. Nearby is the old clay pit used generations ago to make bricks. Just to the left, near a large sugar maple, are the remains of an old homestead. The house is long gone, but many of the perennials once planted in the garden still grow around the cellar hole. The glossy green leaves of vinca grow near the remains of the old foundation, and patches of ribbon grass grow in the sandy soil. You can recognize ribbon grass by the long white stripes that streak the leaves. These plants mingle with native goldenrod and milkweed. The yellow plumes of goldenrod attract bees in late summer, and the fragrant floral clusters of milkweed are a favorite of butterflies.

The trail crosses the road and enters a beautiful plantation of pine. The evergreen canopy far overhead provides welcome shade in summer, and on warm days this area is filled with a sweet, piney perfume. The path descends through the pines and again intersects with Washington Hill Road at 1.2 miles just above a brook. Turn right (north) and walk along the road about 100 feet to a junction. Here one fork leaves left (west) while another continues straight ahead (north). Continue straight ahead (north). A few feet past the junction, follow the footpath left (northwest) as it leaves the road.

The trail now makes an easy climb through increasingly attractive woods. Ground cedar, princess pine, and many types of ferns cover the ground beneath tall pine, cherry, and maple. To the right is a marsh where cattails, sedges, and the sculpted skeletons of dead trees can be found. Hawks frequently soar over the swamp, sometimes skimming just over the tops of cattails and other times making wide circles high overhead. Just past the marsh, the trail passes through a sea of ferns where deer often browse and birds sing from the trees. Soon the path merges with an old woods road at an exposed patch of bedrock. Continue north along the road, which soon narrows and fades back into a footpath as it passes through a grove of hemlock and laurel. After traversing a wet area, the trail makes a moderate climb to a rocky spot where the delicate blossoms of pale corydalis can be seen in summer.

After descending to and crossing a small brook, the path scrambles up a rocky cobble near a grove of dead red pine trees. Black-and-white warblers flit among the thick tangles of laurel as the path crosses an east–west Metropolitan District Commission (MDC) fire road at 1.9 miles. Continue north through a seemingly endless thicket of laurel in a woodland of red and chestnut oaks.

At 2.0 miles, the trail reaches the top of a rise, levels out, and swings right over a series of rocky hummocks. After a short, pleasant walk, you follow the trail east over metamorphic rock ledges studded with small crystals of ruby-red garnet. At 2.1 miles, a limited view opens from the ledge, while below, hidden by the forest, lie the boulder cave shelters called Indian Council Caves.

Blueberry grows in the shallow soil, and a small, gray-barked tree called shadblow, or serviceberry, blossoms here in spring beneath the oaks. From the ledges, the trail swings south and makes a steep descent past enormous cliffs and boulders to the caves. A fire road at the base of the cliffs runs east 0.8 mile to Route 179. The area is a jumble of house-sized stones resting against the steep cliff face. Centuries ago, Native Americans came to this place at the base of the cliff to hold councils. These events were important, ceremonial gatherings. There are many stony hideaways among the rocks. Some are large enough to explore, while others have become home to porcupines, raccoons, mice, and bats. Take some time to explore before heading back. To return to the parking area, retrace your steps.

MORE INFORMATION

Leashed dogs are permitted on the Tunxis Trail. Tunxis State Forest, c/o DEP Western District Office, 230 Plymouth Road, Harwinton, CT 06791; 860-485-0226. For more information about the Tunxis Trail, contact the Connecticut Forest and Park Association, 16 Meriden Road, Rockfall, CT 06791; 860-346-2372; www.ctwoodlands.org.

—C. S.

TRIP 22
SESSIONS WOODS WILDLIFE MANAGEMENT AREA

Location: Burlington
Rating: Easy, with moderate sections
Distance: 3.0 miles
Elevation Gain: 200 feet
Approximate Time: 2.0 hours
Maps: USGS Bristol, Sessions Woods trail map (available online)

This 766-acre state demonstration area for wildlife and resource management techniques features beaver ponds and wetlands, fine wildlife viewing, a great vista, and a waterfall. This is a wonderful loop walk with children.

DIRECTIONS
From the intersection of Routes 6/69 in Bristol, take Route 69 north for approximately 3.0 miles. Turn left onto the entrance road for Sessions Woods Wildlife Management Area. Parking is located 0.15 mile ahead on the right.

TRAIL DESCRIPTION
The trailhead is found at the wide graveled roadway immediately north (right) of the parking area. Visitors are asked to register. Follow the roadway by an iron gate, passing interpretive signs about the property's vegetation. Enter woodland of predominantly red maples, some quite large, as well as young black birches. Cross a culvert where spicebush shrubs shade the damp earth. In late summer, they produce bright red berries high in fat—just the energy source southbound birds are looking for. Spinulose wood fern clumps dot the forest floor. Begin walking upslope and, at the crest, note coppice growth of red maple on the right. Red maple is a prolific stump sprouter, and the thick new growth is indicative of recent cutting. Soon reach a selectively logged area. Note the blue blazes that demarcate the Tunxis Trail. This major footpath follows the Beaver Pond Trail for less than a mile before turning north. Lowbush blueberry thrives in the sunshine. Schist rocks sparkle with mica. Gneiss (pronounced *nice*), a banded rock, is also present.

Walk gradually downhill through a forest of white, red, and black oaks and reach a fenced deer exclosure about 150 feet left of the path. A solar-powered electric fence keeps the hoofed mammals out so wildlife biologists can study

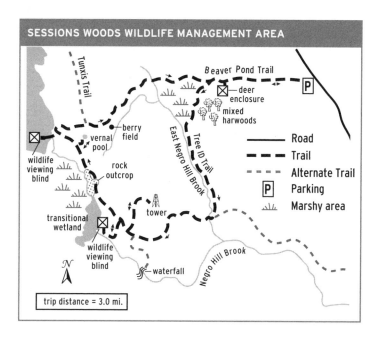

the effects of deer browsing on forest regeneration. Reach a small clearing on the right where bayberry has been planted as a wildlife food source. Diseased red pines were removed in 1985. At 0.25 mile, come to the beginning of the Tree Identification Trail on the left. A leaflet identifying the trees may be available at either end. No bicycles are allowed on this natural-surface woodland path. Follow it downhill through black, gray, and yellow birch woodland. Canada mayflower, princess pine, striped wintergreen, and hay-scented fern spice up the forest floor. Soft haircap moss borders the path. Level out amid numerous white oaks. Indian cucumber-root, which produces blue-black fruits in late summer, is named for its edible tuber. Some azaleas appear, as do American chestnut sprouts. The latter almost always die back due to the blight when they reach a height of 20 to 25 feet.

The slope drops off gradually to the right as you curve left. Reach a small stream on the right. In a good mast year, acorns, a critical wildlife food source, litter the path. Pass through a stand of New York fern—the small one—and chest-high cinnamon fern to the right. Hay-scented fern is the lacy species on the left. Arrive at bog bridges in a wet area leading up to East Negro Hill Brook. Sphagnum moss and New York and cinnamon ferns obscure the moist soil. Dusky salamanders hide by day under stones and logs here. This common stream salamander has no lungs, absorbing oxygen directly through its moist skin. Cross the brook on logs. To the right stands a 25-foot-high rock ledge with a boulder field below. Rock tripe, lichen that greens up after rains, forms a flaky covering over the granitic gneiss. Reflective mica crystals, some an inch across, are one of the boulder field's mineral components.

Continue walking through the little valley of birch and maple, with a slope rising up to the right. One yellow birch is 2 feet in diameter. There is also a stand of young and middle-age hemlock, mostly on the right side of the stream, indicative of a cooler ravine environment. Mosses and lichens pepper the moist outcrops and boulders, while the brook flows with a soothing trickle. Large white ashes, fond of damp soils, raise their crosshatched trunks high into the canopy. The wood of this tree, strong and durable, is favored for baseball bats. The path closely follows the waterway downstream. Where sunlight reaches the ground, patches of hay-scented fern create light green swatches. Yellow and black birches are numerous, while woodland asters bloom white in the late-summer woods. The summer quarters of a gray squirrel, a mass of leaves dubbed a leaf nest, will be forsaken for the warmth of a tree cavity in fall. Cross the brook after it makes a turn to the right. More spicebushes with red berries are established here. Red berries are designed to be attractive to birds since birds have excellent color vision, whereas fruits meant for dispersal by color-blind mammals are generally dark blue and sweet.

Pass a big white pine and walk through a sunny, fern-lined opening. An interpretive sign explains the virtues of a "3-log digger dam," which created the small pool brook trout utilize. Water striders skate on the surface tension, while 5- to 6-inch-long fish flee at the approach of a hiker. The trail is now wider and finely graveled again as you reach the junction with the main Beaver Pond Trail at 0.7 mile. Turn right, walk uphill, and cross the brook. If you look closely, you may see 3-inch-long brook trout in the pool at the right end of the culvert. The culvert has been partially buried to enable a natural streambed to form within it. Continue up the roadway, bearing right under birch and oak, where tufted titmice scold noisily. Mountain laurel, the Connecticut state flower, graces the steep slope to the left in mid-June. Rock sedimentation basins along the road prevent runoff silt from reaching the wetland.

Sweet fern, a fragrant fern look-alike, helps stabilize the sandy soil to the right of the road, which climbs and curves left. Small clearings have been cut to create edge habitat. Some plants have been fitted with wire or plastic mesh cages to prevent deer from nibbling them. While edge habitat encourages new growth sought by many species of wildlife, including deer, too much "edge" can be detrimental for some interior woodland-nesting birds, such as wood thrushes. Pass an informal woods path on the right. The forest canopy is composed of white, chestnut, and red oaks, red maple, and black birch, with some doomed American chestnut

Wetlands are dwindling resources that provide habitat for plants and animals, flood control, and contaminant filtration.

saplings. At 1.0 mile, reach a side trail on the left for the waterfall marked with a bench and sign as well as a large red pine with platy, pinkish bark. Follow the 200-yard trail into an attractive small ravine to the waterfall, which has a seasonal flow due to upstream beaver dams. Descend gradually, then more steeply, over wooden steps at the end to the flow. Negro Hill Brook tumbles through a jumble of large gneiss boulders, making a pleasing rumbling in the process. Tannins in the leaf litter color the pools a root beer brown. It is noticeably cooler in this small ravine. Watch your footing, as the rocks may be very slick.

Return to the main trail and turn left. The road passes through a shrubby clearing where eastern towhees whistle *drink-your-tea*. Almost immediately a short side trail on the right leads to an observation tower at 756 feet above sea level. Pass a very large twin-trunked black birch on the way to the 25-foot-high metal tower and bench at its base. From the tower, just above treetop level, you'll be treated to a wonderful 180-degree panoramic view toward the state's Central Valley, from Avon to Meriden. The Hanging Hills of Meriden and West Peak are visible to the right. This formation is part of the Metacomet Ridge, whose 190-million-year-old basalt rocks are actually the youngest in Connecticut. You'll see an early successional forest that has sprouted in the wake of a clear-cut. Interpretive signs give insight into the view, geology, vegetation, and management techniques.

Return to the main trail and turn right. In September, black-throated green warblers deftly pluck slender green caterpillars from the pine needles. Sheep laurel, a 2-foot-high relative of mountain laurel said to be poisonous to sheep, grows near the trail junction. Almost immediately reach another side trail on the left that leads to a wildlife-viewing blind. Turn left and walk on a wide chipped path through a 1985 clear-cut of diseased red pines, now regenerating mostly to oak and birch. Then enter a relatively shady oak forest. From the wooden blind, pickerelweed, bulrushes, and tree stumps are visible. Especially near dawn and dusk, you may be lucky enough to spy muskrats and other wildlife. Return again to the main trail and turn left. On a warm, sunny day, the evocative aroma of pine resin may waft to your nostrils.

Reenter woodland that holds low ledge outcrops. Reach a sizable boulder sloping up gradually from the road on the left; dark and light swirls in this gneiss rock make it look almost like a bundt cake. From its back, a better view of an old beaver flowage is possible; swamp maples here turn a brilliant scarlet in late summer. Walk left a short distance along the path lined with wintergreen shrubs bearing bright red fruits in fall to view a larger beaver dam. The big rodents were reintroduced into Connecticut in the early 1900s. Mountain laurel shrubs put on a dazzling pink-and-white June display in this sunlit clearing. Turn left after returning to the main trail. Pass over a small culvert and enter oak woodland with some red maple and abundant mountain laurel. At 2.1 miles, come to a graveled and signed side path on the right that leads to a wooden observation platform overlooking a 30-foot-long vernal pool. In late summer, the pool most certainly will be dry, for that is the nature of vernal pools. Velvety green moss encircles the depression, as do Juneberry and winterberry shrubs. Spotted salamanders make their way to this pool to breed during the rains of early spring, and the larvae must complete their development before the heat of summer dries this nursery.

Back at the main roadway turn right. Sheep laurel shrubs become common, and then you pass a water-control structure. On the opposite side is another side trail, which leads over boardwalks and bridges to excellent views of a red maple swamp. Azaleas, winterberry, and royal fern line the path, while bur reed, pickerelweed, and fragrant water lilies vegetate the standing water. A nesting platform for ospreys atop a dead snag has not been utilized. The vast majority of the population of this elegant fish hawk still nest coastally. Follow the path over more boardwalk to a wildlife blind that offers a nice, expansive view of the 50-acre, lily-covered pond. Breezes sometimes flip up the lilies' leaves, revealing the reddish undersides of the floating fragrant lily pads. An entire community of tiny organisms thrives on the leaves' gelatinous undersides.

To some, wetlands are the epitome of wasted and "unreclaimed" land, ugly places good only for hatching mosquitoes. In reality, wetlands are dwindling resources that afford countless benefits to humans and wildlife. In addition to providing habitat for plants and animals, wetlands are natural flood-control structures that absorb the abundant snowmelt and rainwater of early spring, preventing or greatly minimizing downstream flooding. Wetlands also act as ground-water recharge basins that slow stream flow and permit the water's percolation deep into the earth. And they function as natural filtration plants where contaminants can be transformed into less harmful or even benign compounds.

Each year wetlands are lost to the relentless tide of development, although wetlands-protection laws have stemmed the destruction to some extent. Pollution and acidification are also real threats. At last we have begun to appreciate the importance of what once were thought of only as wastelands. By acting to save and restore wetlands, we aid not only wildlife, but also ourselves.

Retrace your steps to the main trail and turn left. Reach another overlook of the swamp at a split-rail fence where the roadway takes a major bend to the right. Arrive at the junction of the Tunxis Trail on the left at 2.4 miles, which leads to East Chippens Hill Road and eventually to its Mile of Ledges section (see Trip 23). Remain on the wide graveled roadway. The road crosses a stream where a moisture-loving tupelo tree's foliage turns vivid shades of red and orange in autumn. Another short graveled path on the right soon leads to a "shrub release area," or berry field, where the removal of large trees has enabled the shrub layer to obtain more sunlight and moisture. Huckleberry grows along the edges, while pioneering gray birch has colonized the clearing. Note the 14-acre clear-cut in back of the Shrub Release Area, created in 2001 to benefit animals that require shrubby growth. Continue on the main road past a bench on the right. Yellow-flowered whorled loosestrife grows profusely along the road shoulders. Continue through oak-maple woodland where the land rises to the left.

Cross a small drainage where, even in late summer, spicebush, cinnamon fern, and small amounts of sphagnum moss testify to wetter times. On the left, wire mesh surrounds planted cranberry viburnum, or highbush cranberry, to keep deer at bay. At 2.75 miles, return to the start of the Tree Identification Trail on the right to close the loop. Continue for 0.25 mile on the Beaver Pond Trail back to your vehicle.

MORE INFORMATION

Open sunrise to sunset; there are no fees. Dogs must be leashed. The Beaver Pond Trail, boardwalks, and demonstration sites are wheelchair accessible. Cross-country skiing permitted. Bowhunting for deer and waterfowl hunting permitted in season; daily permit required. Portions of the property are also open for firearms turkey hunting by daily permit in season. Sessions Woods Wildlife Management Area, P.O. Box 1550, Burlington, CT 06013-1550; 860-675-8130; http://www.ct.gov/dep.

—R. L.

TRIP 23
MILE OF LEDGES AND TORY DEN

Location: Burlington
Difficulty: Moderate, but with challenging rocky sections
Distance: 4.25 miles
Elevation Gain: 300 feet
Estimated Time: 3.0 hours
Maps: USGS Bristol, Thomaston

One of the most rugged and interesting sections of the state's blue-blazed hiking trail system, this loop trail offers picturesque rock ledges, a few tight squeezes, and the historic Tory Den.

DIRECTIONS
In Terryville from the junction of Routes 6 (Terryville Avenue)/72, west of Bristol, travel north on Route 72 for 1.7 miles to Preston Road. Turn right onto Preston Road and drive east for 0.4 mile to its junction with East Plymouth Road. Turn left onto East Plymouth Road and travel 0.5 miles north to a wooden gate on the right. Park off the pavement; be sure not to block the gate. Parking is not allowed here sunset to sunrise.

TRAIL DESCRIPTION
The well-maintained Tunxis Trail begins on the east side of East Plymouth Road at a wooden gate. As part of the Bristol public water supply, it is posted against trespassing. Hikers, however, are welcome. Follow the level gravel tote road past a pine plantation on the right, lush with poison ivy. An arm of 1.3-mile-long Old Marsh Pond is soon visible on the right. Eastern towhee and gray catbird skulk in the thickets along the blue-blazed trail. Planted European larches border the pond, while sugar maple, white ash, red oak, and touch-me-not (jewelweed) flank the damp roadsides. Numerous grapevines drape the trees. When touch-me-nots' flowers mature into small pods, the slightest touch causes the pods to split explosively, hurling seeds a surprising distance.

After crossing two culverts, the roadway narrows amid black birch, maple, oak, and spicebush. Olive-and-white red-eyed vireos—6-inch-long neotropical migrants—are common nesting birds in these woodlands. Females weave lovely cup nests containing thin strips of birch bark at the ends of forked branches. Begin walking easily downhill along a slope to the left. Amid oak

MILE OF LEDGES AND TORY DEN

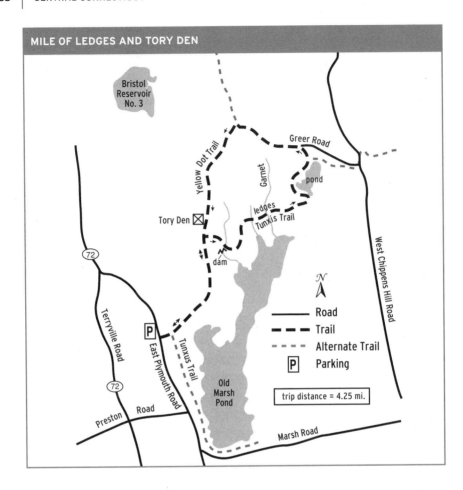

Bristol
Reservoir
No. 3

Greer Road

Yellow Dot Trail

Garnet

pond

ledges
Tunxis Trail

Tory Den ⊠

72

dam

West Chippens Hill Road

𝒩
⋀

	Road
	Trail
	Alternate Trail
P	Parking

Terryville Road

P

East Plymouth Road

Tunxis Trail

Old
Marsh
Pond

trip distance = 4.25 mi.

72

Preston

Road

Marsh Road

trunks festooned with climbing poison ivy vines, false Solomon's seal bears frothy white flowers at the end of its stems. Pass a big twin red oak on the left. In the low damp spots, meadow rue and smartweed bloom in summer. Cross a flowing stream bordered by spicebush and abundant skunk cabbage. You might find a green frog here.

Where the tote road forks, stay left. Cross another culvert where a few hemlocks have found suitable conditions, and begin a gentle climb. Stay left as the road splits again almost immediately and takes you through cutover red oak and hickory woods. Rock outcrops now protrude—the first of many to come. A few yellow birches, with fine peeling metallic bark, appear, while witch hazel and maple-leaf viburnum show up in the shrub-sapling layer. After more outcrops, the old logging road swings right. American chestnut sprouts, beaked hazelnut, and the flattened leaves of ground cedar club moss dot the forest floor. Mica crystals glisten in the rock at your feet. Hay-scented or boulder fern thrives in the sunlit openings, and lowbush blueberry and a few mountain laurel appear as the old road through this logged area levels off. Slash piles are still visible. The road bears left to avoid a seasonally damp spot marked by sedges, which have triangular stems, and smartweed. Evergreen wood fern, a rock specialist, caps the outcrops.

Red maples are vigorously resprouting in this selectively logged woodland as the trail narrows through a stand of hay-scented fern. Pass a large red oak and then walk through a gap in a stone wall. Notice the minerals quartz and mica in the boulders and outcrops to the right. A few white pines are present and below them, in the acidic soil, Canada mayflower. At the 0.75-mile mark, you'll reach a trail intersection. Turn right to continue on the blue-blazed Tunxis Trail. These oak woods have not been logged as recently. Joining the oaks are red maple, black birch, mountain laurel, American chestnut, and lowbush blueberry. A small plant, fairly common in dry soils and bearing light yellow trumpet-like flowers in summer, is cow-wheat. At the edge of a logged area on the right, the trail bears left into a dip and then up and over a ledge outcrop that forms a shallow bowl. The parallel-banded outcrop is gneiss (pronounced *nice*), a metamorphic rock altered under intense heat and pressure deep within the earth some 400 million years ago. Come to another shallow depression between ledges with laurel, witch hazel, sassafras, lowbush blueberry, and some chestnut oak.

While walking gradually up the next outcrop, note the layer-cake bedding of the dark gray rock upon which rock tripe lichen and common polypody fern have gained a foothold. Bear right and tread rather steeply over the outcrop. You are now standing on top of the ledges, with a sheer drop-off to the left. Light gray and green lichens decorate much of the darker-hued stone, and white cushion moss forms soft pillows on the rock. Wood thrushes sing their lovely *ee-o-lay* breeding songs from deep within this attractive oak woodland. Cross more exposed rock slabs and descend. The right-angle cleavage planes of the outcrop have created some convenient steps. Turn left and head down more steeply now over a jumble of flat boulders. Level out below the ledge and bear left. Walk over rocks along the left edge of another outcrop, and then turn right to climb up over this ledge. Pass boulders capped with polypody ferns. This is the top of another outcrop, with a sheer drop on the left. Come to an 8- to 9-foot-deep cleft in the ledge; swing right, then immediately left to descend through it. After emerging, turn left and walk steeply downslope. A few smooth-skinned, gray-trunked shad trees grow here. They bloom in April, when shad fish used to ascend rivers to spawn. In spring, hermit thrushes sing their ethereal songs, evoking a wilderness feeling as you travel this rugged terrain.

Follow the vertical cliff face decorated with mosses, ferns, and lichens. Note the quartz bands. Cross a jumble of rock slabs and blocks where horizontally bedded ledges rise up on the right, then descend to a wet area with fringed loosestrife, whose yellow, nodding flowers open in summer. Cross a stream via an old stone dam whose center stones have been removed. Both ends are intact, however, indicating its former height. Check the soft mud for tracks of raccoons and other mammals. Ascend the far end of the abutment and marvel at how the dam's builders transported these heavy blocks and maneuvered them into place. Eastern towhees, large and colorful members of the sparrow family, scratch vigorously in the leaf litter simultaneously with both feet and give a raspy *chewink* call from the safety of the shrubbery. Males are velvet black above with rusty brown flanks and white breasts, while females are warm brown above. Both possess fiery red irises. The trail swings left as you climb over a low outcrop. Walk between and over more outcrops to a small clearing created by bedrock; huckleberry, shad, mountain laurel, oak, black birch, and red maple predominate. Tiny wintergreen produces bell-shaped blossoms beneath the laurel in summer. Turn right and walk into a slight dip and then over ledge bedrock. Black-and-white warblers hitch along tree limbs seeking insects, looking like striped nuthatches.

Turn right along a 15-foot-high bedrock wall and then immediately left to make your way up through a shallow cleft; a rock on the right juts out toward hikers. Crest the lichen-covered ledge, with a dropoff to the right. Crawl up over the ledge and curve left. You can rest here, but beware the sheer dropoff to the right! I shared this perch with a white-tailed dragonfly, wasps, and ants as I ate lunch during a summer visit. You may wish to sample the ripe huckleberries if you're here in season. Then head downhill through low-stature oak, shad, and black birch, where white-breasted nuthatches are common year-round residents. Their nasal *ank-ank* calls are unmistakable. Bear right and descend at a sharp angle through a crevice colonized by black birch. Look back behind you for an impressive view of the ledge cliff. Walk down into a small hollow between ridges and pass through a small canyon about 100 feet in length. Bear right and cross more boulders. The rocky trail parallels a small outcrop on the left, curves left, and passes through another cleft, this one level. Within the cleft or fault, the air feels decidedly cooler. Climb out of this cleft, known as Bear's Den, on the right by employing natural steps in the 6-foot-high rock wall. Cross over the top of the 5-foot-wide "wall," turn right, and descend gradually.

Part of Old Marsh Pond is visible in the distance. The forest floor is studded with wild sarsaparilla, maple-leaf viburnum, Virginia creeper, and sessile-leafed

Climbing through bedrock fissures, including the one known as "Bears Den," adds excitement and variety to the walk.

bellwort beneath sugar maple and oak. Cross an intermittent stream through a boulder field and proceed easily uphill, past patches of New York fern. Bear around the left end of an outcrop and up to the right where a tulip tree stands tall and alone to the left. Cross the bedrock at a rather declivitous angle and swing left along more ledges where lowbush blueberry and Canada mayflower indicate acidic soil. Bear right and proceed over a low ledge where chestnut, red oak, hickory, shad, red maple, and lowbush blueberry fill the woodland. Descend over rocks, turn right, and then sharply left to level out. Patches of Christmas fern and princess pine club moss decorate the forest floor. Listen for the relaxing sound of running water ahead. Walk down and bear right to gurgling, rock-lined Garnet Brook. The sound emanates from a miniature waterfall 18 inches high. Even small irregularities like this help aerate the water. Cross the brook, which feeds the pond, on big flat stones. Green frogs often wait on streamside rocks for insects. Bear right, cross a stone wall in an area of small hemlock, climb a small slope over a low outcrop, and then level out again.

The Tunxis Trail undulates gently and passes a low outcrop and boulders on the left. Ghostly white Indian pipe, or corpse plant, pushes up through the decaying leaves, and striped wintergreen, with its variegated leaves and waxy flowers, blooms here in summer. Reach a trail intersection on the right just before a rock wall. Stay straight and pass the wall on the right and the junction of another trail almost immediately on the left. The blue-blazed trail turns left just before reaching a pond. Both fragrant and yellow bullhead lilies float on the surface, and at the far end, near Greer Road, sits the big, high mound of a beaver lodge. Return to the main trail and turn right. Climb over a low rock outcropping sparkling with mica. Pass a human-made mound of stone on the right, turn right, and ascend another ledge fairly steeply. The pond glistens through the trees below. You may also glimpse the Canada geese that nest here. Partial to beaver ponds, they often build their nests directly on the lodges.

Descend from the low outcrop and bear right under a low canopy of grape and witch hazel, the source of the astringent of the same name. Delicate maidenhair fern, as well as interrupted and Christmas ferns, thrive in the damp soil, as do moisture-loving basswood, ash, and spicebush. From this vantage point, there is an unobstructed view of the pond.

Now the path rises easily and moves briefly away from the water. Blue-headed vireo, eastern towhee, and chipmunk all began scolding as I passed through their domain on a late-July hike. Then return to the pond and follow its shore. Belted kingfishers use snags to scan for fish in the clear water, and male bullfrogs bellow from their territories. The imposing beaver lodge is now visible, and to the right of it are two others. Beavers have removed the trees on the far shore, and the increased sunshine reaching the dense mountain laurel there encourages considerable blossoming of the state flower in June and early July. Next, pass through a stone wall gap and descend to paved Greer Road.

Leave the Tunxis Trail and turn left onto the road. Follow it for about 0.5 mile and turn left onto the Yellow Dot Trail (yellow dot over blue) just before the pavement ends. Cross a seasonally wet streambed and climb the rather inclined hillside into oak and maple woods where red-eyed vireos are among the most common breeders. Vireos and warblers consume vast quantities of forest-canopy insects in spring and summer. Cross the boulder-covered slope, where mica and quartz crystals are prominent, and reach a T intersection. Turn left toward Tory Den, 0.75 mile south. Proceed through laurel and under maple and oak. Here olive-drab eastern wood pewees sally forth for flying insects. Red efts are quite common even here, a fair distance from the beaver ponds where they later live out their aquatic adult lives as red-spotted newts. Gain a cliff on the right, its face obscured partially by

TUNXIS TALES

If only the rocks could speak—oh, what tales they would tell! And so it is at Tory Den. Long after cataclysmic forces deformed the rock itself and much later exposed it at the earth's surface, long after earthquakes, tremors, and ice sheets jostled the slabs into their current positions, local inhabitants created a human history that is still being told today.

During the American Revolution, British loyalists—Tories—from the nearby Chippen Hill community used the den as a safe haven, taking refuge there when the patriots came calling. The den was owned during those days more than two centuries ago by one Stephen Graves. He was whipped by patriots for being a Tory, but his brother-in-law, Moses Dunbar, suffered a far worse fate for his lack of support for the fledgling nation. Dunbar was the only Connecticut resident who was hanged for treason during the Revolutionary War.

During the late 1800s Tory Den was also inhabited by a recluse known as "the Leatherman," who acquired that colorful moniker as a result of his habit of being attired entirely in animal skins.

leafy rock tripe lichen, which metamorphoses from brown to green after drinking in rainwater. A laurel thicket caps the outcrop. Both hermit and wood thrushes nest up here, hermits on the ground and wood thrushes usually about 10 feet up. Gray birch becomes more common along the undulating path, while chestnut oak is quite abundant.

Walk over bedrock where a small twin-trunked gray birch is anchored, then level out and bear left through a young forest of oak, birch, and maple. Walk down to a dip between ledges, swing left, and continue the gradual descent. Next, bear right and climb fairly steeply, level off, and then climb a low ledge. Witch hazel is the other prominent shrub in these woods. Handsome black-throated blue warblers are partial to mountain laurel thickets and often build their well concealed nests low to the ground in these shrubs. After leveling out again, the path traverses a big bedrock boulder and trends downhill. Bear left, descending with increasing steepness, and cross a small seasonal brook. Pass through a low damp spot adorned with tall, attractive cinnamon ferns; to the right stand ledge outcrops. Here we heard the enthusiastic song of a Canada warbler, a lovely 5-inch-long summer resident that breeds near wetland edges and damp woodland depressions.

Pass a noteworthy red oak on the left with seven trunks and walk over a quartz boulder covered partially with silvery green cushion moss; to the right is the damp bowl. The tongue-shaped leaves of pink lady's slipper crop up occasionally in these woods. Traverse a ledge with a short climb and bear left at the blocked connector trail on the right. A high cliff is visible on the right as you level out, and tulip trees grow in the depression below it. As the ledge continues, now 25 feet high, you'll see that slabs have broken off from the overhanging rock. Another damp area on the right contains cinnamon fern, wild iris, and sedge. Bear right, cross a low ledge outcrop, and swing left almost immediately. Brilliant scarlet tanagers, looking out of place in our northern forests, make the long flight each May from northern South America to return here.

Level off along the slope, bear right, and ascend a low outcrop. Continue walking to another ledge cliff ahead and bear left to arrive at the historic Tory Den on the right. A hideout for crown loyalists during the American Revolution, the 35- to 40-foot-long cavity consists of a stone slab resting against another rock, with a huge boulder forming the backdrop. Years later, the Den was the retreat of an animal-skin-clad iconoclast dubbed "the Leatherman." Continue south past the overhanging cliff and then gently downhill; soon you reach the intersection of the Tunxis Trail on the left. Continue straight for 0.75 mile back to your vehicle; watch for wild turkeys, especially in the logged areas.

MORE INFORMATION

Connecticut Forest and Park Association, 16 Meriden Road, Middlefield, Route 66, Rockfall, CT 06481-2961; 800-346-8733.

—R. L.

TRIP 24
TALCOTT MOUNTAIN

Location: Avon and Simsbury
Rating: Moderate
Distance: 3.1 miles
Elevation Gain: 500 feet
Estimated Time: 2.0–2.5 hours
Maps: USGS Avon

This is one of the most popular places to walk and enjoy nature in central Connecticut. On weekends and at other peak times, the Tower Trail gives plenty of opportunity to chat with fellow hikers— the old dirt road can become a little crowded. The Heublein Tower, featuring fantastic views, and King Philip's cave make this loop hike worthwhile anytime.

DIRECTIONS
From Route 44 in the center of Avon, turn onto Routes 10/202. Proceed about 2.9 miles to the junction with Route 185. Turn right onto Route 185 and travel 1.6 miles to the entrance to the access road on the right. Proceed up the hill and park off the road where designated. Parking is not permitted at the end of the road near the top of the hill, where a pad for the Lifestar helicopter is located.

TRAIL DESCRIPTION
The Tower Trail begins on the left side of the access road about 1,000 feet from the Route 185 entrance. A less crowded feeder path begins at the Lifestar helicopter landing pad, at the end of the access road.

From the helicopter landing pad, the trail enters the woods and proceeds south amid specimens of yellow birch, oak, maple, and hickory. Mountain laurel and clumps of witch hazel are the understory plants, along with tufts of Christmas fern. The path is wide and easy to follow as it begins gently to traverse the rocky hillside. The grade steepens as the woods change to waves of evergreen hemlock alternating with oak, maple, birch, and other hardwoods. At the junction of the feeder trail and the Tower Trail (0.3 mile), an unmarked path leads right, down the increasingly steep face of King Philip Mountain to a rocky enclave called King Philip's cave.

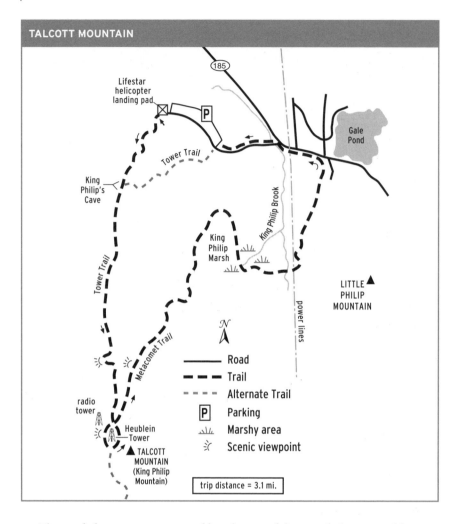

TALCOTT MOUNTAIN

185

Lifestar
helicopter
landing pad

P

Gale
Pond

Tower Trail

King
Philip's
Cave

King Philip Brook

King
Philip
Marsh

Tower Trail

LITTLE
PHILIP
MOUNTAIN

power lines

Metacomet Trail

N

— Road

- - - Trail

- - - Alternate Trail

P Parking

Marshy area

Scenic viewpoint

radio
tower

Heublein
Tower

TALCOTT
MOUNTAIN
(King Philip
Mountain)

trip distance = 3.1 mi.

The grade becomes steeper and breaks out of the woods into a scrubby area of red cedar, staghorn sumac, red oak, and hop hornbeam. In spring, round-lobed hepatica blooms near the edge of the ridge, its pale pink, blue, or white flowers providing a delicate touch to the stony landscape. Pink-eyed grass and a few black-eyed Susans flower in late summer, a month or so after the wild roses that also grow here have gone by. The plants of this area are representative of the type of community that thrives along all the basalt ridges throughout Connecticut. The plants and trees are a hardy group, accustomed to hot, dry summers and windswept, freezing winters.

The path continues along the edge of the ridge, with the Farmington River Valley sweeping away to the west. After a short stroll, a level area is reached where hang gliders launch their nimble craft into the sky. On summer days,

Heublein Tower crowns the traprock ridge atop Talcott Mountain.

turkey vultures often soar past the launch area, providing a feathered contrast to human-made wings. You can tell turkey vultures from hawks, even from far away, by the way they glide through the air. Turkey vultures rock back and forth as they soar, while hawks do not. From the launch area, follow the wide woods road south, away from the ridge, past a large chestnut oak. Striped maple, a small understory tree with green-and-white-striped bark, grows beneath the spreading boughs of beech, oak, hop hornbeam, and shagbark hickory. After passing a low escarpment on the left where rock climbers practice their sport, the trail joins the blue-blazed Metacomet Trail (1.1 miles) as it approaches the tower.

Follow the signs to the entrance of the 6-story-tall Heublein Tower (1.25 miles), perched in whitewashed splendor atop the highest point of Talcott Mountain (bathrooms are available at the tower). Gilbert Heublein constructed the tower in 1914 as a summer house where he entertained the likes of President Eisenhower. The 165-foot-high structure sits atop the already impressive 875-foot-high mountain. The tower's enclosed viewing area offers perhaps the finest views in the entire state, with a 360-degree sweep that encompasses most of Connecticut as well as bits of three other states. During foliage season, the viewing area can be standing room only. There are days, however, when bird song is still the predominant sound, and it is during these times that the uniqueness of the tower is most powerful. Designed to emulate the architectural style of Bavaria, the tower has been recognized as a National Historic Place since 1983.

From the tower, retrace your steps to the junction of the wide woods road called the Tower Trail with the Metacomet Trail. Head north on the Metacomet Trail, which almost immediately enters very attractive woods of white and red oak, hemlock, beech, and a few stump sprouts of American chestnut. Polypody fern hides in rocky recesses beneath the hemlocks, while chickadees and black-and-white juncos flit among the branches. The footway wanders through the forest, soon coming to a rounded ridge where colonies of evergreen bearberry grow in the rocky soil. The walk along the ridge is particularly enchanting, with beautiful views framed by a landscape of stone, tangles of mountain laurel, and stunted evergreen hemlock. After leaving the ridge, the path descends briefly and then passes a second ridge with winter views to the north and wintergreen underfoot. From the rocky outcrop, continue through a thick cover of mountain laurel that is stunning when it is in full bloom in late spring.

The trail then turns sharply right (south), descending through tall oaks and maples as it slabs the face of the ridge. It continues into the saddle between the basalt ridges of Talcott Mountain (also called King Philip Mountain) and those of the smaller Little Philip Mountain. This sheltered area is home to maple-leaf viburnum, mountain laurel, and wild azalea, which thrive beneath the tall trees. To the right is a small wetland called King Philip Marsh, which serves as the headwaters of the brook that also bears his name. The trail now heads generally east, passes beneath the power lines, then swings left (north) roughly tracing a course along the base of Little Philip Mountain, and crosses a feeder stream of King Philip Brook.

The path continues north until it meets Route 185 (2.6 miles) in a wet area of hardwoods and hemlock. Turn left (west) and walk along Route 185 the short distance to the parking area for Talcott Mountain State Park.

MORE INFORMATION

Talcott Mountain State Park offers bathrooms and a picnic shelter. Leashed dogs are permitted on the trails. Heublein Tower is open Thursday through Sunday 10 A.M. to 5 P.M., late May through the end of August; daily 10 A.M. to 5 P.M., Labor Day weekend through the end of October. No charge. Talcott Mountain State Park, c/o Penwood State Park, 57 Gun Mill Road, Bloomfield, CT 06002; 860-242-1158; http://www.ct.gov/dep.

—C. S.

TRIP 25
CASTLE CRAIG, CAT-HOLE PASS, AND EAST PEAK

Location: Meriden
Rating: Moderate, with challenging sections
Distance: 4.6 miles
Elevation Gain: 700 feet
Estimated Time: 3.0–3.5 hours
Maps: USGS Meriden

This is an out-and-back hike from Cat-Hole Pass through traprock ravines, past cliffs above the beautiful Merimere Reservoir to the views from Castle Craig atop the famous Hanging Hills.

DIRECTIONS

From Interstate 691 eastbound, take Exit 5 to the Chamberlain Highway (Route 71). Go north on Route 71 to a stoplight at the intersection with Kensington Avenue. Continue north on Route 71 for 0.4 mile to a pull-off on the right. A very small pull-off is sometimes available 0.2 mile farther north where the Metacomet Trail crosses the road. Westbound, take the Lewis Avenue exit, then turn left onto Lewis Avenue, and travel to its junction with Kensington Avenue. Turn left onto Kensington and continue to the Route 71 stoplight. Turn right (north) onto Route 71 and continue 0.4 mile to a pull-off on the right.

TRAIL DESCRIPTION

This walk is on the Metacomet Trail, which is marked with pale blue blazes. Turns are noted by two stacked blazes, with the topmost offset in the direction of the turn. From the pull-off on Route 71, walk north for 0.2 mile to where the Metacomet Trail crosses the highway, just south of the Berlin town line. This area is known as Cat-Hole Pass, because the narrow boulder slopes on either side of the road have provided shelter to bobcats for centuries. This area is certainly not wilderness, but I was fortunate enough to see a bobcat here in the 1970s, and they are probably still here.

From the road, the Metacomet Trail heads southwest into woods of black birch, maple, oak, and beech. The terrain is rough, with traprock boulders everywhere. A few yards from the road is a sign that reads "Warning Snake Area." If bobcats aren't enough of a thrill, Cat-Hole Pass is also famous for

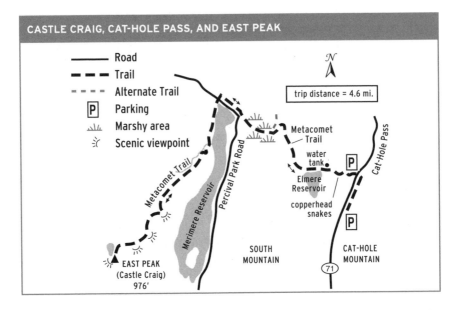

CASTLE CRAIG, CAT-HOLE PASS, AND EAST PEAK

———— Road
▬ ▬ ▬ Trail
▬ ▬ ▬ ▬ Alternate Trail
P Parking
⋎⋏ Marshy area
�▲ Scenic viewpoint

𝒩

trip distance = 4.6 mi.

Metacomet Trail

water tank

P

Elmere Reservoir

copperhead snakes

P

Cat-Hole Pass

Metacomet Trail

Percival Park Road

Merimere Reservoir

EAST PEAK
(Castle Craig)
976'

SOUTH MOUNTAIN

CAT-HOLE MOUNTAIN

71

its population of copperheads (see essay in this chapter). Most people who hike this section of trail consider the sign a joke. It isn't. It is there to protect the snakes from people who whack everything that slithers with a stick. Stay on the treadway, and most of the time all you encounter in Cat-Hole Pass are Christmas ferns, witch hazel, and a few songbirds.

After an easy, short climb, the path comes to an open area dominated by a large water-holding tank and the earthen dam of Elmere Reservoir. The trail leads across the dam (0.4 mile) at the north end of the reservoir. This is a beautiful pond with a wooded shore studded with boulders. In autumn, the colorful foliage reflects in the water, intensifying the color of the leaves. At the far end of the dam, an unmarked trail leaves left (south), and the Metacomet Trail continues straight (west). Follow the blue blazes along the stony bed of a usually dry wash through woods of red maple, oak, hemlock, hop hornbeam, and flowering dogwood above witch hazel, benzoin bush, arrowwood, and wild geranium. Just before beginning a gradual descent, a small, stone-lined spring is nearly hidden in the undergrowth on the left. Beyond the spring, the wide path enters a stand of hemlock sprinkled with large northern red oaks. An unmarked trail enters left as the main trail continues south.

To the right, a small brook trickles beside the path until the trail swings left (west), leaves the brook, and begins a moderately steep descent to the wetlands below at 1.0 mile. At the base of the hill, a dirt road enters right as the main trail continues straight. With wetlands on both sides, the tall forest gives way to lower tangles of benzoin bush and witch hazel. In early spring, benzoin bush

Castle Craig atop East Peak, from the Metacomet Trail.

lights up the still-leafless woods with tufts of fuzzy yellow flowers like tiny stars alight atop the dark gray branches. In late summer, the spicy aromatic leaves hide small green berries that ripen to a glossy red. Wood thrush and veerys particularly like the ripe berries, and people used them years ago as a substitute for allspice—perhaps giving this common wetland shrub its other name, spicebush. Marsh wrens dart about, as do vireos and warblers. In late fall, white-throated sparrows stop by on their southern migration, providing a few days when their cheery song can be heard.

The path continues along a level grade, passing a number of unmarked trails to the left before reaching Percival Park Road and Merimere Reservoir at 1.1 miles. Follow Percival Park Road across the dam at the north end of the reservoir. This long, narrow lake, embraced by red-brown, rocky cliffs on both sides, is one of the most beautiful bodies of water in the state. At the far end of the dam, turn left, leaving the road and scrambling up a short rocky ledge into the woods at 1.3 miles. The path climbs gently through a forest of oak and tulip tree, with lady's slipper and flowering raspberry beneath. The trail traverses the loose talus slope of the north shore, rising higher and higher above the water. The footing gets increasingly difficult in direct proportion to the view over the water becoming increasingly beautiful.

After crossing a deep cleft where a small stream runs, the path veers away from the shoreline and follows the brook up the ravine. A brief but steep climb up a rocky cobble is the first of a series of climbs through alternating

COPPERHEADS

When I was about 10 years old, I used to walk through the wooded wetlands at the base of the Metacomet Ridge. The columnar basalt cliffs rose hundreds of feet overhead, like a massive sculpture. Steep talus slopes composed of blocky boulders calved from the ridge. It was on that talus slope, bathed in the warmth of the south-facing mountain, that the copperheads lived. That much I had been told. But I was young and inexperienced and didn't know that, even though the den sites were in the rock slopes, during summer copperheads are not homebodies. In warm weather, the snakes wander from the den area on the hillside and explore the terrain below.

As I strode through the tangles of sweetshrub near a dried red maple swamp, I broke through the brush into an open area carpeted with tussocks of grass and shaded by red maples. I hadn't a care in the world at that moment, until I glanced casually down at where my next step would land. Copperheads are pit vipers, so called for the heat-sensitive organ, or pit, located between each eye and nostril. They are venomous snakes, with potentially lethal poison that they inject into the victim through a pair of long hollow fangs. That's the scary part. The reality is that the snakes are really pretty peaceful creatures that have a much more docile temperament than many nonvenomous snakes.

Copperheads have a pale, rusty-colored head leading to a thick, reddish-orange body marked with darker, saddle-shaped diamonds across the back. Many snakes, such as milk snakes, have coloration similar to copperheads, but only copperheads have a pink tongue, scales that have a central keel, a single row of scales under the tail, and the pit between the eye and nostril. Their earthy coloration makes them nearly invisible when viewed against a backdrop of fallen leaves and twigs.

The snakes pass the winter in rocky dens, usually on the south side of wooded mountains but sometimes on the edges of rocky talus slopes. In spring they disperse from the den site, wandering in a roughly circular loop a few miles long down to nearby low wetlands before returning, some 4 to 5 months later, to the den. They are not common snakes, and definitely prefer not to make your acquaintance. People who see them have a way of overreacting, often to the detriment of the snakes.

The coiled snake lay exactly where my next step would land. I froze in my tracks, balancing on one foot, while the other hung a foot or so over the copperhead. My mind raced through all the things I could do while half expecting the snake to suddenly rise and strike my leg. But the snake never moved—not even a twitch. After the initial excitement had subsided, I quietly backed away. When I had retreated a few feet, I stopped and admired the copper serpent for a few minutes.

Moses, as directed by Jehovah, crafted the copper serpent to heal his repentant people bitten by venomous snakes in the wilderness. If they gazed at the serpent after they were bitten, the people were healed. As I gazed upon the coppery snake in the woods, I was filled with a sense of awe at what an amazing creation this animal was. Despite all our knowledge, we cannot come close to duplicating it. Watching the snake left me with just a little more conviction that the world holds more beauty than anyone can ever appreciate completely.

hemlock woods and stretches of bare bedrock. Eventually the hemlocks yield to a grassy woodland of hop hornbeam, hickory, maple, and oak. The trail soon comes to the edge of the Merimere Cliffs (2.1 miles), where a spectacular sight awaits. Hundreds of feet below are the cool, blue waters of Merimere Reservoir, with a view of all of southern Connecticut stretching out beyond. This is a breathtaking stretch of trail with plenty of places to stop and marvel at the beauty of the creation around you. It is often much less crowded than the cliffs near the castle, and the combination of magnificence and solitude invites quiet introspection.

Continue along the cliffs, soaking up the seemingly endless views and passing bearberry, red cedar, common juniper, blueberry, oak, and hickory, all framed by the brown basalt cliffs. Soon Castle Craig appears through the trees, the stone turret looking like a misplaced medieval fortification. Follow the path to the castle, and carefully climb up the iron grate steps that spiral to the top of the watchtower, where the views are wonderful (2.3 miles). From the small viewing area, Sleeping Giant Mountain is to the south, with the skyline of New Haven just beyond. On very clear days, the pale blue reflection of Long Island Sound paints the far horizon with a pastel sweep of color. To the north, the tall buildings of Hartford fill the Connecticut Valley. The story of this unique building is nearly as fascinating as the view from its parapets.

At the turn of the twentieth century, a man named Walter Hubbard owned most of the land around East Peak. The generosity of Mr. Hubbard was responsible ultimately for the creation of Hubbard Park, the signature park of Meriden's famous city park system. Walter Hubbard had a dream of putting a castle on his mountain and hired a man named David Stuart Douglas to design a stone tower on the basalt crag of East Peak. Construction began on April 30, 1900. Park superintendent P. J. Quigly and his crew of expert Italian stonemasons worked all that spring, through the summer, and into the fall painstakingly creating Hubbard's dream. On October 29, 1900, the 32-foot-high tower was dedicated and has been a landmark of Connecticut ever since. The top of the tower is 1,002 feet above sea level (reportedly the highest point within 25 miles of the ocean between Cadillac Mountain, Maine and Georgia). To return to the parking area, just retrace your steps down the mountain on the Metacomet Trail.

MORE INFORMATION

Leashed dogs are permitted on the trail. Hubbard Park, City of Meriden, Department of Parks and Recreation, 460 Liberty Street, Meriden, CT 06450; 203-630-4259; http://www.cityofmeriden.org/CMS/default.asp?CMS_PageID=426.

—C. S.

TRIP 26
CHAUNCEY PEAK

Location: Meriden
Rating: Moderate, with challenging sections
Distance: 2.0 miles
Elevation Gain: 377 feet
Estimated Time: 2.0–3.0 hours
Maps: USGS Meriden, Middletown

For challenging climbs, memorable views, and benches by a lovely, quiet lake, you can't beat this short loop hike.

DIRECTIONS

From Interstate 691 in Meriden, take the Broad Street exit. Turn north onto Broad Street and travel 0.4 mile to Westfield Road. Turn right onto Westfield Road, pass over the railroad tracks, and proceed to the junction with Wall Street, which enters on the right. Continue on Westfield Road, passing beneath Route 15 and coming to the intersection with Bee Street, which enters on the right. A golf course is on the left. Turn left and follow Westfield Road for another 0.1 mile to the entrance to Giuffrida Park on the left.

TRAIL DESCRIPTION

From the parking area near the restrooms and caretaker's cabin, walk east through a grassy area in front of Crescent Lake dam. At the eastern end of the dam, a trail blazed with white markers heads left (north), and a blue-blazed trail continues straight ahead. Follow the blue blazes into a woodland of elm, maple, black birch, flowering dogwood, and arrowwood. The flowering dogwood is especially beautiful along the south flank of Chauncey Peak, where the blush-colored blossoms brighten spring afternoons.

After a moderate climb, the trail levels out ever-so-briefly before turning right (east) and proceeding through increasingly rocky terrain. Soon the path swings left (north) and begins the short, but memorably steep, ascent of the southern buttress of the mountain. The treadway is paved with small, loose traprock stones, which make the footing tricky. Near the crest of the ridge, large basalt ramparts appear that at first glance seem insurmountable. The trail negotiates the cliffs by threading through a narrow rock cleft. A brief scramble up the bare rock brings you to the top of this impressive ridge.

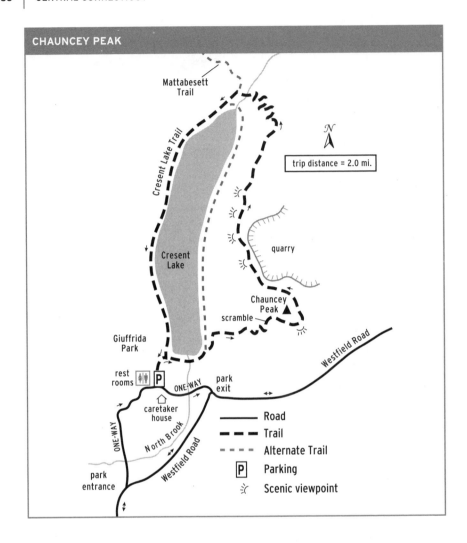

CHAUNCEY PEAK

Mattabesett
Trail

Cresent Lake Trail

trip distance = 2.0 mi.

N

quarry

Cresent
Lake

Chauncey
Peak ▲

scramble

Giuffrida
Park

rest
rooms 🚻 P   park
     ONE-WAY   exit

Westfield Road

caretaker
house

North Brook

ONE-WAY

park
entrance

Westfield Road

——— Road

– – – Trail

- - - Alternate Trail

P   Parking

🔆   Scenic viewpoint

On gaining the top of the cliff, turn right along the ridge and climb the
few paces to an impressive overlook. From the bedrock ledge, you gain beautiful views to the west, south, and east. To the west are the famous Hanging
Hills of Meriden with Cat-Hole Mountain and East Peak, decorated with
the stony silhouette of Castle Craig (see Trip 25). The Hanging Hills are also
called the Lion's Paw, for the shape of the four eroded basalt ridges that make
up the stately rock formation. To the south, far beyond the hayfields at the
base of the mountain, the skyline of New Haven is visible, with the sapphire-
blue hues of Long Island Sound discernible on clear days. To the southwest
is the Sleeping Giant, perhaps the most recognizable natural feature in Con-

necticut (see Trip 29). East of the overlook are the sheer traprock cliffs of Mount Higby (see Trip 27).

Follow the path along the ridge over traprock ledges dotted with staghorn sumac, red cedar, hickory, and oak. Staghorn sumac is a weedy little tree with soft, fuzzy stems and tropical-looking, pinnately compound leaves that turn bright shades of scarlet and orange in fall. Centuries ago, Native Americans used the berries to brew a tart beverage that looked and tasted like pink lemonade. Soon the trail leaves the ridge, swinging north into the woods and passing along the edge of a quarry. **Caution!** Use caution here, because the trail comes close to the edge of some very precipitous cliffs. As you walk through scrubby woods of hickory, red cedar, and linden, watch for a strange little plant called feverwort that grows in the dry soil of the mountain. If you see it, you won't forget it. Feverwort has pairs of large leaves decorated with wings near their base that clasp the stem. In early summer, small yellowish purple flowers appear in the axils of the leaves, followed in fall by hairy orange fruit.

The trail wanders to the western side of the ridge, where it leaves the woods in favor of a series of overlooks high above the sparkling waters of Prospect Lake. Some people refer to Prospect Lake as Crescent Lake, which is fine. And those who don't call it Prospect Lake or Crescent Lake refer to it by the less romantic epithet Bradley-Hubbard Reservoir—which is also fine. Regardless what name you tack onto it, it is a beautiful sight from high on the ridge. The trail continues northeast along the ridge, past lovely, open vistas that just seem to beg you to stop and admire the view. Rock climbers sometimes practice on the cliffs below, and on crisp fall days Canada geese can be heard honking as they paddle in the waters, while hawks soar overhead as they migrate to warmer winter climes.

The path then begins to descend the ridge through a picturesque forest of jutting boulders and bedrock mixed with evergreen hemlock. Brown creepers and kinglets mingle among the tree branches in fall and winter, providing welcome company. In the hemlock grove the path turns steeply downhill, swinging left and crossing a stone wall before leveling off near a drainage at the base of the mountain. From this T junction the blue-blazed Mattabesett Trail turns right and heads north. To the left is a well-worn path that goes south toward the lake, which can be seen through the trees. Follow the trail south as it soon begins to trace a scenic course along the lakeshore. A wooden bridge to the left escorts hikers onto a white-blazed trail that follows the rugged east shore back to the parking area. Continue straight ahead on the wide and easy path that follows the western shore.

The wind-swept trail atop Chauncey Peak.

The path stays close to the water, and thoughtful folks have placed many benches along the way. This gives ample chance to linger and watch the geese and ducks, or just stare out at the water. Chauncey Peak and Crescent Lake are only a few minutes from downtown Meriden, but sitting here on one of the benches or resting atop the mountain, you would never know a city is nearby. It is that peaceful. The shoreside path divides here and there into multiple trails. They all find their way eventually to the parking lot, but if you always choose the route closest to the water, the walk is much more rewarding.

MORE INFORMATION

Giuffrida Park provides bathrooms. Leashed dogs are permitted on the trails. Rock climbing, eating food outside the parking area, boating, swimming, and wading in the lake are prohibited. Giuffrida Park, City of Meriden, Division of Parks and Recreation, 460 Liberty Street, Meriden, CT 06450; 203-630-4259; http://www.ctparks.net/meriden/giuffrida.

—C. S.

TRIP 27
MATTABESETT TRAIL AND MOUNT HIGBY

Location: Middlefield and Middletown
Rating: Moderate, with challenging sections
Distance: 3.6 miles
Elevation Gain: 610 feet
Estimated Time: 2.0–3.5 hours
Maps: USGS Middletown

This out-and-back route takes hikers over some of the most exciting cliff walks in the state.

DIRECTIONS
From Meriden, take Interstate 691 toward Middletown. After the highway becomes Route 66, follow it east for about 0.4 mile to the traffic light and Route 147. Guida's Dairy Bar is on the left. Turn around at the traffic light and return west on Route 66 for about 0.5 mile to the beginning of I-691. There is a pull-off to the right. Park here and take the path the short distance to the Mattabesett Trail.

From Middletown, take Route 66 to its junction with Route 147. Travel about 0.5 mile west to the beginning of I-691. Immediately after the road becomes a limited-access highway, you find a pull-off to the right. Park here and take the path the short distance to the Mattabesett Trail.

TRAIL DESCRIPTION
The Mattabesett Trail along Mount Higby is marked with pale blue blazes. Turns are noted by two stacked blazes, with the topmost blaze offset in the direction of the turn.

From the pull-off where Route 66 becomes Interstate 691, a red-blazed trail enters the woods to the west. Follow the stone-covered path uphill about 100 yards to a flat area where the Mattabesett Trail, blazed in blue, meets an access trail from Guida's Dairy Bar, blazed in purple, on the right. Straight ahead is a largely unmarked trail used as a shortcut to the ridge. Though shorter, it is steeper with less reliable footing and more difficult to follow.

Turn left onto the Mattabesett Trail, which runs parallel to the highway on the left and the traprock talus slope of Mount Higby to the right. After a short walk, the path turns sharply right and attacks the steep slope, using occasional

MATTABESETT TRAIL AND MOUNT HIGBY

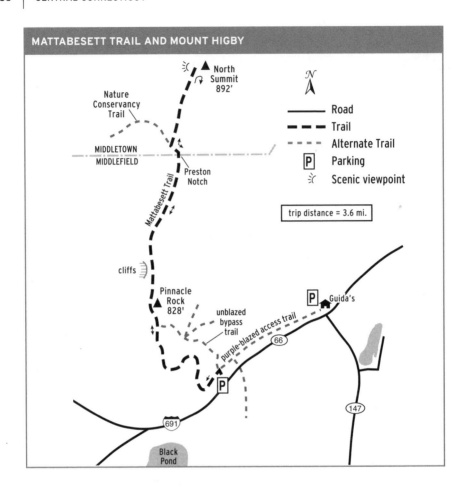

switchbacks to ease the ascent. This is a moderately steep climb that slows you down enough to enjoy the many types of plants that grow here. Oak and maple are the dominant trees, with a few glossy green Christmas ferns among wild sarsaparilla and creeping partridgeberry. The path climbs over a series of small traprock ledges, passing a large boulder where Black Pond is visible to the south. The forest of oak and maple now yields to an open, woodland savanna as the path enters an area of thin, dry soil on the ridge tops. This area is dominated by grasses and blueberries that grow among a rough landscape of rugged boulders beneath the trees. The open forest floor is shaded by widely spaced specimens of hickory, oak, ash, hop hornbeam, and red cedar.

As the trail crests a low rise, an unmarked trail continues straight while the Mattabesett Trail turns right and passes through a grove of stunted red cedar and hickory. It then descends into a small, steep-sided ravine carved by a vernal stream where hemlocks thrive in the cool, moist soil. The path crosses the stream and ascends the opposite bank to the crest of Mount Higby's famous traprock ridge. The trail proceeds north along the edge of the cliff, with peeka-boo views through the trees to the west of Meriden and the Hanging Hills. Aster and goldenrod line the path beneath staghorn sumac, linden, ash, and red cedar. The shortcut trail encountered at the base of the mountain now enters on the right at 0.5 mile.

Follow the blue blazes along the ridge a short way to the crest of Mount Higby. At 0.7 mile, a brief scramble to the top of a house-sized outcrop (the south summit of Mount Higby, called Pinnacle Rock) affords expansive views north, west, and south. To the south is the skyline of New Haven and the unique profile of Sleeping Giant Mountain in Hamden. Meriden and the four Hanging Hills (also called the Lion's Paw) are to the west, with Castle Craig visible atop East Peak. To the northwest is Lamentation Mountain, whose spine is studded with communications towers, and Chauncey Peak, with a large quarry devouring its eastern flank.

From the overlook, continue north along the open ridge crest, which offers nearly continuous, spectacular views. Colonies of bearberry can be found hugging the exposed traprock ledges and colonizing the shady spots beneath stands of bear oak. Bearberry is a creeping ground cover that grows along the exposed ridges of the Appalachians as far south as Virginia and is hardy enough to thrive as far north as the Arctic. It has small, dark green, very glossy evergreen leaves and cinnamon-red exfoliating bark. Clusters of pendant white-to-pale-pink flowers appear in spring and yield bright red fruits that look like tiny tomatoes in fall through winter. Wildlife, including birds and increasingly rare wood and box turtles, eat the fruit. Native Americans considered bearberry, or kinnikinick, a sacred herb and used it in religious ceremonies. Other plants growing on the ridge include bluestem grass, chokeberry, yarrow, wild mint, and butter-and-eggs, with snapdragon-shaped flowers in cream and orange.

As you walk along the bare basalt ledges, look closely at the stone's surface for long grooves etched into the rock. These scratches are called striations and were formed as the continental glacier advanced over the area during the last ice age. As glaciers move, they lift stones and boulders from the surface beneath and incorporate these into the ice. The larger stones scrape over the bedrock as the glacier moves, leaving behind telltale grooves to mark their passing. The striations not only convey the message that the glaciers were once here, but record the direction the glacier was moving when it passed by.

This section of the trail hugs the edge of the cliffs and is wonderful to walk. It is easily one of the most spectacular paths in the state. The footway wanders continually and teasingly close to the basalt cliffs, sometimes just inches from the edge of the vertical precipice. **Caution!** As beautiful as this area is, hikers need to be very careful here, especially children. There is no restraining fence, and from the edge of the basalt cliffs it is a 100-foot drop to the boulders below. The path continues north, entering thick woods before descending to a col called Preston Notch at 1.3 miles. Many years ago, a coach road ran through here connecting Meriden and Middletown. Traces of the old thoroughfare still can be seen on the upland section of the notch. To the left of the trail is a stone marker that delineates the boundary between Middlefield, which you are leaving, and Middletown. From the notch, a trail leaves left down the mountain. The path leads to Preston Avenue in Meriden, passing through land owned by The Nature Conservancy.

From this point, the Mattabesett Trail swings right and climbs the northern section of Mount Higby into more dry, woodland savanna. Along the path, the bright scarlet-and-yellow blossoms of wild columbine bloom in late spring and summer, along with blue-flowered flax. After a moderately steep climb, the terrain levels out, following the cliff edge to a series of lovely overlooks with views north, south, and west. The northern summit of Mount Higby (1.8 miles) is the last overlook before the trail begins to descend. It is grassy and largely private, as most people stay on the southern section of the ridge. The north summit is a perfect place to linger and have lunch before heading back to the parking area.

MORE INFORMATION

Leashed dogs are permitted on the trail. For more information on the Mattabesett Trail, contact the Connecticut Forest and Park Association, 16 Meriden Road, Rockfall, CT 06481-2961; 860-346-2372; www.ctwoodlands.org.

—C. S.

TRIP 28
WADSWORTH FALLS

Location: Middletown and Middlefield
Rating: Easy, with some steep sections
Distance: 3.3 miles
Elevation Gain: 100 feet
Estimated Time: 1.5–2.5 hours
Maps: USGS Middletown, Wadsworth Falls State Park map available online

This loop hike in Wadsworth Falls State Park offers waterfalls for every taste and the giant laurel.

DIRECTIONS

From Middletown, take Route 66 west to the junction of Route 157. Turn left onto Route 157; the park entrance is a few miles farther on the left. From Meriden, take I-691 to Route 66 and follow Route 66 to its junction with Route 147. Turn right onto Route 147 and proceed to the junction with Route 157. Turn left onto Route 157 and proceed through the little town of Rockfall. After leaving Rockfall center, the park entrance is a short way down the road on the right.

TRAIL DESCRIPTION

To get to the trailhead from the parking area, proceed through the picnic area to the bridge that spans Laurel Brook. The Main Trail, marked with orange, crosses the bridge shaded by hemlock trees and proceeds uphill into woods of birch, ash, apple, red cedar, and cherry, with an understory of burning bush scattered beneath. Round leafy squirrel nests are a common sight in the treetops. The footpath that leads to the swimming area and the parking lot enters on the right, opposite the Laurel Brook Trail.

The Main Trail proceeds south through the forest, passing three side trails on the left before coming to one of the treasures of Wadsworth Falls State Park, the giant laurel (0.6 mile). This exquisite specimen of mountain laurel is easily one of the largest of its kind anywhere. In colonial times, large mountain laurel were fairly common, and the extremely hard, durable wood was used to fashion a number of items, from tool handles to cooking spoons. But laurel grows slowly, very slowly, and once cut down, similar massive plants have never

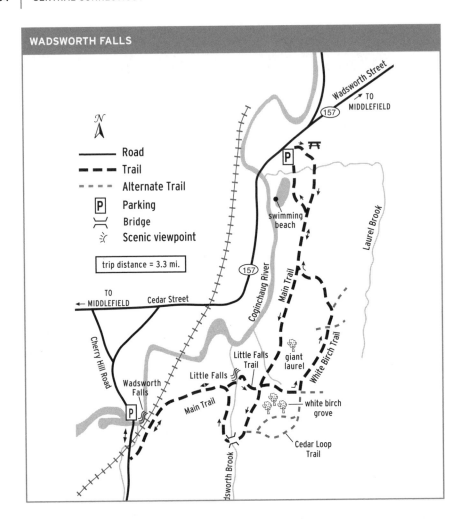

WADSWORTH FALLS

returned. The Wadsworth Falls giant laurel has stems nearly a foot in diameter and a leafy evergreen canopy 10 to 15 feet tall and more than 30 feet wide.

From the giant laurel, continue south along the woods road, crossing an intermittent stream spanned by a stone bridge. Hemlocks grow along the shallow banks of the stream, shading red trillium in spring. The hemlocks in this state park, as in so many other wooded areas of Connecticut, are suffering from an infestation of the hemlock woolly adelgid. An abundance of standing dead tree is the sad result. From the bridge, the woods become a blend of hardwoods including ash, oak, and beech interspersed with very large hemlock trees, some more than a hundred years old. The Main Trail then passes the white-blazed White Birch Trail on the left, followed by the blue-blazed Little Falls Trail on the right. The Main Trail crests a gentle rise and then descends

Graceful rivulets trip down Little Falls.

into a grove of red pine recently killed by red pine blight. Now only straight, gray-barked skeletons stand where once there was luxuriant greenery. Beyond the red pines, the forest again becomes dominated by hemlock, oak, and birch, with a few large, thick-trunked tulip trees. These beautiful trees grow very fast and straight, with some specimens reaching 100 feet tall. In spring, the upper branches bear upright greenish-orange flowers resembling tulips.

The trail heads downhill, crossing a small stream on a wooden bridge at 1.0 mile. The path then climbs away from the brook, passing the terminus of Little Falls Trail before heading downhill toward Wadsworth Falls. The Main Trail tracks through the woods, following alongside the railroad tracks before ending at the roadway (Cherry Hill Road).

To reach the falls, turn right onto Cherry Hill Road, cross the railroad tracks, and pass over the Coginchaug River, stocked with trout, on a bridge. Just over the bridge, reenter the park at a parking area. Cross the large grassy area to a series of stone and wooden steps that lead down to the riverbank at 1.6 miles. The fabled Wadsworth Falls pours from a fracture in the rock above. The volume of water that crashes over this escarpment is exhilarating to experience. On days when the flow is high, you can feel the thunderous pounding of water like the trembling concussion following a thunderbolt.

From Wadsworth Falls, retrace your steps to the terminus of the Little Falls Trail. Turn left onto the trail, which almost immediately comes to a sandstone promontory at the top of a steep ridge. Below, Wadsworth Brook traces a slender course over the edge of the ridge, cascading in a lacy tumult down the rocks. Follow the path as it swings left down the steep ridge to the base of the falls (2.2 miles), where the best views of the water can be enjoyed. Unlike the fairly uniform rock of Wadsworth Falls, the sandstone of Little Falls is layered. This layering, called stratification, causes the rock to erode and break away in fairly regular blocks. The result is a rock face that resembles a staircase and a waterfall that trips down these stony steps with unmatched grace and beauty.

The trail then crosses Wadsworth Brook, following the stream briefly as it flows down a run of bare bedrock. The path then turns uphill—away from the stream and its ravine—to pass through a hemlock and hardwood forest dotted with red trillium, bloodroot, and toothwort, which bloom in early spring. At the end of the trail, turn left (north) onto the Main Trail for a short way before turning right (east) onto the White Birch Trail. The White Birch Trail follows the course of an old abandoned road through waves of white birch trees into a wetland with many shrubs and vines, including benzoin bush, multiflora rose, greenbrier, maple-leaf viburnum, burning bush, barberry, and a little poison ivy. Jack-in-the-pulpit is a spring wildflower that grows here.

Continue through the woods to a multiple junction where the red-blazed Cedar Loop Trail leaves right (south), the yellow-blazed Laurel Brook Trail continues straight (east), and the White Birch Trail turns left (north). Immediately after turning left, the trail forks, with the White Birch Trail following the right fork. The woods here are a mix of many trees, including red cedar, maple, white birch, hemlock, and tulip tree. Wildflowers include red trillium and Canada mayflower, with its tiny spikes of white blossoms that smell like lily of the valley.

Many ski trails crisscross the White Birch Trail through here, and it is important to watch for the white blazes to be sure you remain on the correct trail. A green-blazed trail crosses, and the White Birch Trail continues northwest. At the next fork, turn left, following the white blazes west. After a short walk, the White Birch Trail ends at the Main Trail. From here, it is a short walk back to the parking area.

MORE INFORMATION

Wadsworth Falls State Park provides bathrooms, picnic sites, and a pond swimming area. Leashed dogs are permitted on park trails. Fishing is possible in the Coginchaug River. An entrance fee of $7 per resident vehicle and $10 per nonresident vehicle on weekends and holidays is charged. Wadsworth Falls State Park, c/o Chatfield Hollow State Park, 381 Route 80, Killingworth, CT 06419; 860-663-2030; http://www.ct.gov/dep.

—C. S.

TRIP 29
SLEEPING GIANT

Location: Hamden
Rating: Difficult
Distance: 3.2 miles
Elevation Gain: 620 feet
Estimated Time: 3.0–4.0 hours
Maps: USGS Wallingford, Mount Carmel, Sleeping Giant State Park map available online

Sleeping Giant State Park offers 32 miles of trails. This loop hike, where you live your own version of *Gulliver's Travels*, features rugged, rocky scrambles, views and more views, a four-story summit tower, wildflowers, and Indian Rock.

DIRECTIONS
From the junction of Mount Carmel Avenue and Route 10 (Whitney Avenue) in Hamden, turn onto Mount Carmel Avenue. The park entrance is on the left just past New Road.

TRAIL DESCRIPTION
From the parking lot, follow the narrow, paved road into the picnic area. As the road begins to swing from northwest to southwest, a blue-blazed trail leaves northwest. Follow the blue blazes around a moderately steep hill cloaked in evergreens to Axel Shop Pond. Turn right and immediately cross a wooden bridge over a small stream. In a few yards, the Blue Trail, now called the Quinnipiac Trail, swings left (northwest) and tackles the short but steep climb up the giant's elbow. One of the unique aspects of climbing on the Sleeping Giant is that you have to get used to climbing cliffs and ledges named for body parts. Hemlock groves cloak the rocky hillside, along with a few chestnut oaks. At the top of the hill the shallow soil yields to extensive patches of basalt, with fine views back over the pond below. From the giant's elbow, the trail follows the crest of the ridge through scattered clumps of red cedar, common juniper, oak, and hemlock. This already has been a challenging, though pleasant walk, but it is about to become spectacular.

At a cobble of boulders and bedrock, the path makes a very steep descent through ancient faults in the rock to a shallow pass that separates the giant's

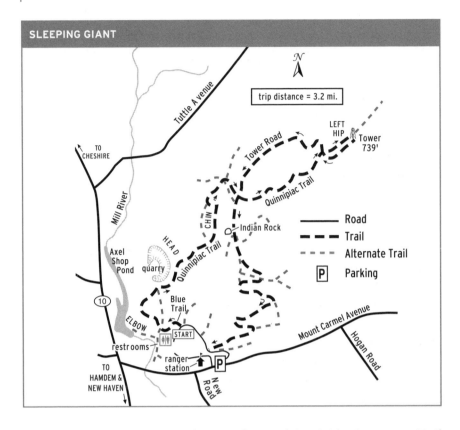

SLEEPING GIANT

trip distance = 3.2 mi.

N

LEFT HIP
Tower 739'

Tower Road

Quinnipiac Trail

TO CHESHIRE

Tuttle Avenue

Mill River

CHIN

HEAD

Indian Rock

Quinnipiac Trail

Road

Trail

Alternate Trail

P Parking

Axel Shop Pond

quarry

Blue Trail

10

ELBOW

restrooms

START

ranger station

P

TO HAMDEM & NEW HAVEN

New Road

Mount Carmel Avenue

Hogan Road

elbow from the dome of basalt forming the giant's head. The Quinnipiac Trail crosses the Red Trail in the saddle (0.4 mile), from which the massive buttress of Sleeping Giant is now in full view. Take a moment to soak up the scenery, for the trail ahead traverses some of the most difficult, and beautiful, hiking terrain in Connecticut. In fact, the next mile of trail more closely resembles New Hampshire's White Mountains, with a bare-rock trail bed and steep ascents, than it does a typical Connecticut state park.

From the saddle, the footway climbs smooth bare basalt up the giant's head, at times coming only a few feet from the cliff and a sheer drop of 300 feet to the abandoned quarry below. Bypass trails swing farther away from the cliff where a few cedars cling to the rock, then rejoin the main trail near the top of the hill. **Caution!** Use caution on this trail, as many people have died or been seriously injured here. The rocks are especially dangerous in winter or when they are wet.

The path climbs over several rock scrambles before it levels out at the top in an area covered with wild grapevine, red cedar, bluestem grass, and bayberry.

The rugged basalt landscape of Sleeping Giant is breathtaking.

Juncos hop frequently among the grasses looking for food, and in summer blue-headed vireos can be seen. The trail wanders across the giant's head, passing numerous craggy overlooks and secretive hideaways in the rock before reaching an area known as the Giant's Chin at 0.7 mile. The chin is another sheer cliff of basalt that drops away to a slope of boulders far below. The views from here are mesmerizing, and many hikers have idled away hours in this lovely spot.

From the chin, follow the blue blazes downhill through a hardwood forest sprinkled here and there with mountain laurel. At the base of the slope, the path crosses the Red Trail and then comes to a junction with the Tower Trail (1.1 miles) in the shadow of the cliffs of the Giant's Chin. Cross the Tower Trail and follow the blue blazes through rocky woods, passing over many forested cobbles. Follow the blazes carefully, for it is easy to lose the path among the boulders, trees, and laurel. After crossing the Tower Trail again, the footway wanders through deep thickets of laurel before emerging on the rocky scaffold called the Giant's Left Hip, where a four-story stone tower (more reminiscent of a castle than a tower) pokes into the sky at 1.6 miles.

The top of the tower offers a beautiful 360-degree view that includes the New Haven skyline and Long Island Sound to the south. On clear days, the north shore of Long Island can be seen. To the north are the Hanging Hills of

Meriden. From the tower take the Tower Path, a comfortable carriage road, back to the parking area. This is an enjoyable, easy walk through tall mixed hardwood forests and waves of laurel thickets. In spring, you can look for loads of wildflowers just off the path, especially near the wooded pass in the shadow of the cliffs of the Giant's Chin. Wild ginger, hepatica, and wild geranium are just a few of the flowers to be found here. A few yards farther on, as the path passes beneath the sheer cliffs of the Giant's Chin, you come to a large boulder (2.2 miles) at the edge of the talus slope. This upright boulder could be mistaken at first glance for one of the grand statues of Easter Island. The stone seems to hold the profile of a Native American, and its noble features are recognized easily. It was not carved or altered in any way. It is the result of the same natural processes that created the Sleeping Giant himself.

MORE INFORMATION

The Tower Road is maintained by the state of Connecticut, while the remaining trails are maintained by the Sleeping Giant Park Association, a volunteer, nonprofit group dedicated to preserving, maintaining, and expanding the park. Sleeping Giant State Park provides bathrooms and a picnic area. Leashed dogs are permitted on the trails. An entrance fee of $7 per resident vehicle and $10 per nonresident vehicle is charged on weekends and holidays. Weekdays are free of charge. Sleeping Giant State Park, 200 Mount Carmel Avenue, Hamden, CT 06518; 203-789-7498; www.ct.gov/dep. Detailed trail maps are available from Sleeping Giant Park Association, Box 185340, Hamden, CT 06518; www.sgpa.org.

—C. S.

TRIP 30
HEZEKIAH'S KNOB AND THE CHESTNUT GROVE

Location: Hamden
Rating: Moderate
Distance: 2.8 miles
Elevation Gain: 500 feet
Estimated Time: 2.0–3.0 hour
Maps: USGS Wallingford, Mount Carmel, Sleeping Giant State Park map available online

This is a unique loop walk in Sleeping Giant State Park with boulders, views from an overlook, and a stroll through a chestnut grove.

DIRECTIONS
From the junction of Mount Carmel Avenue and Route 10 (Whitney Avenue) in Hamden, turn onto Mount Carmel Avenue. Pass the entrance to Sleeping Giant State Park on the left and continue down Mount Carmel Avenue for another 1.9 miles to Chestnut Lane. Turn left onto Chestnut Lane and travel 0.8 mile to the trailhead and small pull-off on left.

TRAIL DESCRIPTION
This portion of Sleeping Giant Mountain is a wild web of trails that can seem confusing. Before hiking, it helps to reference the information kiosk and map near the parking area on Chestnut Lane, which displays the route and junctions of a number of trails. Also, detailed trail maps, courtesy of the Sleeping Giant Park Association, are usually available here. The Violet and Green Trails are marked with violet and green painted blazes. The Quinnipiac Trail that traverses the mountain is blazed in pale blue, and the equestrian trail is marked with horseshoe-shaped blazes.

From the kiosk, follow the Violet Trail northwest into a hardwood forest of beech, sassafras, maple, birch, red and white oaks, and hickory. Near a large red oak, the path crosses a stone wall where chipmunks live. Maple-leaf viburnum, a small, 3-to-5-foot-high shrub with maple-shaped leaves, thrives in the dark, loamy soil of the forest. In spring, maple-leaf viburnum's slender stems are topped with an open cluster of tiny white flowers. In fall, the deep green leaves turn a distinctive shade of reddish violet. Christmas fern and ground cedar also grow here. As the trail penetrates deeper into the woods, the forest

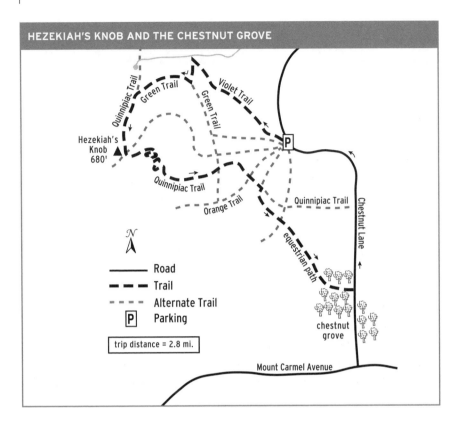

HEZEKIAH'S KNOB AND THE CHESTNUT GROVE

Quinnipiac Trail

Green Trail

Violet Trail

Green Trail

Hezekiah's
Knob
680'

P

Quinnipiac Trail

Quinnipiac Trail

Chestnut Lane

Orange Trail

equestrian path

chestnut
grove

N

——— Road

– – – Trail

- - - - Alternate Trail

P Parking

trip distance = 2.8 mi.

Mount Carmel Avenue

becomes a beautiful woodland dominated by large northern red oaks. Northern red oak is one of the fastest growing of all oaks, with dark gray-brown, richly furrowed bark. In early spring, the trees are decorated with 4-inch-long pendant tassels lined with tiny yellowish-green flowers. The acorns, which are about an inch long and egg-shaped, take 2 years to mature.

After crossing a second stone wall, the path swings uphill, passing patches of princess pine, partridgeberry, and more ground cedar. Just before the Violet Trail turns right and crosses a small stream, turn left (south) away from the Violet Trail onto a short unmarked connector trail. Follow the connector trail south a short distance to its end at the Green Trail. Turn right (west) onto the Green Trail, a wide woods road that proceeds gently uphill beside a stone wall before meeting the blue-blazed Quinnipiac Trail in a dense thicket of mountain laurel. This area in late May and early June is awash in pale blush blossoms that seem to float atop waves of emerald leaves. After seeing the springtime display, it is easy to understand why mountain laurel is the state flower.

Turn left (south) onto the Quinnipiac Trail and continue uphill through tall woods of oak, maple, and hickory with witch hazel, red cedar, and laurel

The trail wraps around Hezekiah's Knob, a cobble that provides a view to the southeast.

beneath. This section of the Quinnipiac Trail is an inspiring place, with huge, 10-foot-tall tangles of mountain laurel forming evergreen curtains on either side of the trail. The path ascends easily over alternating bands of exposed bedrock and soft earth, soon reaching a jumble of fractured bedrock outcrops. Like a prehistoric fortress dressed in shades of ghostly gray, this area is beautiful and vaguely unsettling at the same time. The fissured stones are home to small colonies of polypody fern, whose small, bright green fronds lend a bit of gaiety to the woods. The trail wraps around the rocky cobble, climbing at an easy grade to the crest of a feature called Hezekiah's Knob.

Hezekiah's Knob is what New Englanders call a "cobble," a cluster of boulders and outcrops that stands above the surrounding hillside. Its exposed position often makes it a bit breezier than the nearby woods. Ash, hickory, red cedar, chestnut oak, linden, and white pine all crowd atop the knob, but still leave room for a view to the southeast. Small colonies of staghorn sumac produce crops of red berries in fall, and in summer the pliant stems of columbine wave their tiny yellow-and-crimson flowers. Also, here is a shrubby tree called bear oak. This plant has leaves that look a bit like oak and a bit like holly. The acorns are small and gave the plant its name. According to tradition, the acorns were so bitter that the only animals that would eat them were black bears. Some people call bear oak, scrub oak, but there is no story in that.

The top of Hezekiah's Knob (680 feet elevation) offers fine views and is crossed by both the Quinnipiac Trail and the White Trail. Stay on the blue-blazed Quinnipiac Trail and descend past isolated specimens of wild rose, with pure pink flowers in summer, to a second overlook. From the second viewpoint, the path heads east through picturesque woods marked with stands of oak, pine, and hickory sprinkled here and there with grassy clearings. Soon the trail begins a serious descent of the knob, twisting down the steep hillside

SAVING AMERICAN CHESTNUTS

The American chestnut is one of the most majestic trees in the world. Its range stretches from the southern Appalachians to Maine and west through the prairies of Illinois. Before 1900, American chestnuts constituted up to a quarter of all the trees in the forest. They grew to stand 100 feet tall and up to 10 feet in diameter. The oldest of these giant trees were estimated to be more than 600 years in age. Their small, sweet nuts were produced in such quantity that everyone who wanted them could harvest all the nuts they needed for roasting, stuffing, and eating, and still leave plenty for wildlife. That was a century ago—it isn't the same now.

In the mid-1800s it became fashionable to purchase and grow Japanese chestnuts in many places of the country. This smaller species was grown in New York, New Jersey, California, and Connecticut. What no one knew at the time was that some of these trees were infected with a fungal disease later called chestnut blight. It was first recognized in 1904 in New York City, but was probably present, but unrecognized, in a number of other places along the East Coast at the same time. The blight, to which the Japanese chestnut was resistant, decimated the susceptible American chestnuts. Within 50 years, virtually all the groves and forests of American chestnut were dead.

Since the beginning of the epidemic, the Connecticut Agricultural Experiment Station at New Haven has been conducting research to solve the problem and restore the American chestnut to the forests. For many years these scientists, led by Sandra Anagnostakis, have made great strides against the disease. In 1972, a weaker form of the disease, disabled by a virus that ironically infected it, was found in Europe. This weakened disease has made it possible to keep American chestnut trees alive long enough to conduct more extensive breeding experiments—experiments aimed at instilling resistance in the American species. Today the Connecticut Agricultural Experiment Station has the finest collection of species and hybrid chestnut trees in the world. It is a tribute to the perseverance of the institution and its dedicated personnel.

The chestnut grove at Sleeping Giant State Park is an integral part of the effort to save the American chestnut. It is a very special place. As you stroll through the grove, be sure to savor the moment. It is one of the few places in the North America where you can still experience a walk beneath the spreading boughs of chestnut trees.

via switchbacks. At the bottom of the hill, the tall woods of oak, maple, and hickory return. Beneath the trees are small colonies of spotted wintergreen, with narrow evergreen leaves traced with white along the midvein. In spring, a slender flower stalk rises, bearing a pair of small, waxy white blossoms that look like miniature streetlights.

The Quinnipiac Trail crosses the Green Trail and then the Orange Trail. To return to the parking area, turn left onto the Orange Trail. To continue to the chestnut grove, proceed through the junction with the Orange Trail a few yards farther to the junction with the Equestrian Path. Turn right onto the horseback-riding trail, remembering that horses have the right of way. Follow the path downhill, generally southeast, and over a stone wall into a wide and grassy, easy-to-follow cart path that escorts you into the heart of the chestnut grove.

Few places are left in the country where a walk in the woods can lead you to a mature chestnut grove. This stand was grown by the Connecticut Agricultural Experiment Station (New Haven) over many decades for research into chestnut blight. The trees that grow here are a unique collection of species and hybrids derived from trees native to many different parts of the world. In early summer, they are decorated with long, pendant greenish-yellow flower clusters that have a sweet but mildly offensive odor. In fall, the green burs, which look like sea urchins, gradually turn brown. The first few frosts open the burs, exposing a cache of mahogany-brown nuts. Walk through the grove in fall and the prickly chestnut burs cover the ground beneath the trees; you can get a small sense of what the Connecticut's autumn woods were like a century ago. From the chestnut grove, it is a short walk to Chestnut Lane. Turn left onto Chestnut Lane and walk uphill to the parking area.

MORE INFORMATION

Sleeping Giant State Park provides bathrooms and a picnic area. Leashed dogs are permitted on the trails. An entrance fee of $7 per resident vehicle and $10 per nonresident vehicle is charged on weekends and holidays. There is no charge weekdays. Sleeping Giant State Park, 200 Mount Carmel Avenue, Hamden, CT 06518; 203-789-7498; www.dep.state.ct.us/stateparks/parks/sleepinggiant.htm. Detailed trail maps are available from The Sleeping Giant Park Association, 555 New Road, Box 14, Hamden, CT 06518; www.sgpa.org.

—C. S.

TRIP 31
BEAR ROCK

Location: Durham
Rating: Easy, with steep sections
Distance: 1.1 miles
Elevation Gain: 120 feet
Estimated Time: 0.5–1.0 hour
Maps: USGS Durham

Bear Rock is located within a section of the Conkaponset State Forest along the Mattabesett Trail. The rounded edifice of stone from which nature has carved the image of a bear's head has drawn me for many years. It is not overly high or difficult to climb, and the animals and vegetation can be found in many places. Yet it is unique in a most pleasing, completely undefinable way.

DIRECTIONS
From the junction of Routes 79/77/17 in Durham take Route 79 south and almost immediately turn left onto Higganum Road. Go 1.4 miles to a stop sign at the intersection with Bear Rock Road. Turn right onto Bear Rock Road, then almost immediately left onto Harvey Road. Continue down Harvey Road about 0.3 mile to the small pull-off. The pull-off is located near light blue blazes that mark where the trail crosses the road.

TRAIL DESCRIPTION
The path is blazed with pale blue marks. Turns are noted by two stacked blazes, with the uppermost blaze offset in the direction of the turn. From the pull-off on Harvey Road, near a small pond where spring peepers sing in April, head north uphill into a hardwood forest of oak, beech, and maple rising above an understory of witch hazel, mountain laurel, and isolated specimens of yellow star grass. Related to amaryllis, yellow star grass forms tufts of narrow, dark green leaves from which rise slender stems topped with beautiful golden yellow six-petaled flowers from spring to summer. If it is not in bloom, chances are you will never notice this little plant. But if you see it in flower, the lovely, delicate beauty of yellow star grass will stay in your memory for a long time.

At the crest of a low hill the trail levels out and passes through a grassy woodland shaded by oaks and sprinkled with tall thickets of mountain laurel

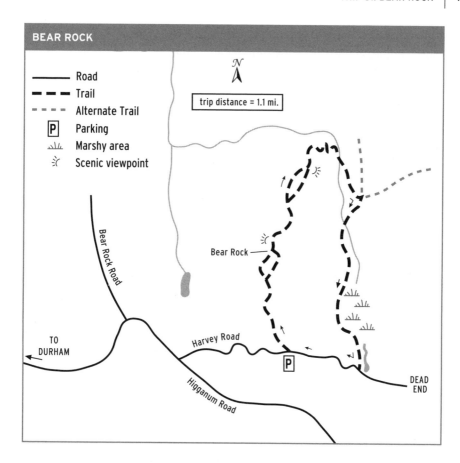

BEAR ROCK

——— Road
– – – Trail
- - - - Alternate Trail
P Parking
⫶⫶ Marshy area
⫶⧸ Scenic viewpoint

N

trip distance = 1.1 mi.

Bear Rock Road

Bear Rock

TO
DURHAM

Harvey Road

P

Higganum Road

DEAD
END

and a few wild azalea. In many parts of Connecticut mountain laurel is a shrubby plant that rarely grows above about 6 feet high. Along this section of the Mattabesett Trail, however, the laurel thrives, the twisted stems interweaving into tangles 10 feet high. The path repeatedly slips beneath their canopies of glossy evergreen leaves, forming verdant, magical tunnels.

The trail gradually descends past rocky cobbles where sweetly scented Canada mayflower mingles with wild sarsaparilla, starflower, princess pine, witch hazel, and ground cedar. Soon the tallest and most magical grove of mountain laurel appears. Standing over 15 feet high, the gnarled trunks look like a miniature medieval forest. In May and June, when the snow-white flowers decorate the tips of the stems, this place is enchantingly beautiful.

From the laurel thicket the trail sweeps through a moist woodland where summersweet grows and crosses a meandering stream. From the brook the path heads uphill through a well-drained woodland of white oak, chestnut oak, red maple, and beech. You find some rugged rock formations to the left and pink lady's slippers blossom here in late spring. Wild geranium and five-leafed cinquefoil flower in early summer along the trail beneath the spreading branches of flowering dogwood, which blossoms in spring. As the path continues uphill it comes to a ridge where the trail forks. The left (west) branch wanders up the rocky face of Bear Rock. The last section of the ascent is a rocky scramble that will be difficult for some people. The right (north) fork circles around the back of Bear Rock, gaining the top with no steep scrambles. Take either fork to the top of a large, rounded rock formation called Bear Rock. Unlike some overlooks that offer only a limited view for your effort, Bear Rock consists of a large area of open terrain and many places to sit and admire the view. Twisted pitch pine, serviceberry, and bear oak forest the thin, rocky soil, and mountain sandwort blossoms among the wiry woodland grasses.

To the west is the shallow pass called Reed's Gap. To the right are the easily identified grassy slopes of Powder Ridge Ski Area. Between Reed's Gap and Powder Ridge are the distinctive traprock cliffs known as the Hanging Hills. To the far right (north) the skyline of Hartford is visible, while in the valley below lie the picturesque villages of Durham and Middlefield. If you wonder why Bear Rock is named after an animal that had been absent from Connecticut for more than 100 years until the species reestablished itself in the 1980s, the answer is in the rock itself. A glance at the large outcrop and a liberal amount of imagination show that the cliff itself has been carved by nature to resemble the head of a bear.

Most people don't venture much beyond this overlook, but Bear Rock extends for a little way more. From the overlook the path rises to a rocky crest where mountain sandwort competes with pale corydalis in the infertile soil. The leaves of pale corydalis are similar to Dutchman's breeches, but the flower is something all its own. In spring to early summer pale corydalis bears slender, pale-scarlet tubular blossoms marked with a spot of yellow. They are hardy little things, surviving in bright sun or dark shade and thriving in the dry, gravelly soil.

The path continues through patches of huckleberry and blueberry, chokeberry, and wintergreen to an open rock ledge with an easterly view over the tops of a forest of maples and tulip trees. The trail then follows the ledge a short way to another lookout before beginning to descend through lady's slippers, wintergreen, and hemlock.

Follow the trail down the steep slope, weaving through boulders and past a stunning rock formation that juts out over the trail. In spring and after a rain, the rock drips a steady stream of drops on passersby. In winter the trickle of water is transformed into a pillar of ice.

The path leads to a small stream bordered by a narrow wetland. The trail wanders back and forth through the wetland, where trout lily and dwarf ginseng grow. Dwarf ginseng is a bit of a wallflower, no pun intended. It has three glossy green leaves and a small puff of white flowers in April. Its cousin American ginseng has been nearly exterminated from the wild, but, through all the exploitation, dwarf ginseng lives on. If you happen to recognize the plant on your walk, admire it and, please, leave it be.

From the stream the path proceeds past more rock outcrops to the junction with an unmarked snowmobile trail. The Mattabesett continues straight ahead. Turn right onto the snowmobile trail and walk through a beech forest studded with old trees. A stream appears on the right where wetland plants thrive, including skunk cabbage and summersweet. A little farther on, the stream enlarges into a small pond—the peeper pond—where all sorts of water-loving creatures live. Snapping and painted turtles are here, as are great blue herons and mallard ducks. And in spring, from April right into May, the peepers sing from every available spot. The pond borders Harvey Road. When you reach the road, turn right. The pull-off is only a few yards farther on.

MORE INFORMATION

Undeveloped sections of Cockaponset State Forest are open a half hour before sunrise to a half hour after sunset daily. Pets on a leash are permitted. Cross-country skiing, horseback riding, mountain biking, and snowmobiling are permitted. Cockaponset State Forest, 18 Ranger Road, Haddam, CT 06438; 860-345-8521.

—C. S.

TRIP 32
MATTABESETT TRAIL AND COGINCHAUG CAVE

Location: Durham
Rating: Easy, with steep sections
Distance: 1.5 miles
Elevation Gain: 100 feet
Estimated Time: 1.0 hour
Maps: USGS Durham, Haddam

This is a walk back in time to a rocky shelter used centuries ago by Native Americans, yielding a cliff-side cave, rocky forests, wildflowers, and blueberries.

DIRECTIONS
From the junction of Routes 79/77/17 in Durham, take Route 79 south for 0.9 mile to Old Blue Hill Road. Turn left onto Old Blue Hill Road and proceed 0.7 mile, where the Cockaponset State Forest lands begin on the right-hand side. Look for the blue blazes of the Mattabesett Trail entering the woods on right and park off the road.

TRAIL DESCRIPTION
The out-and-back walk to Coginchaug Cave is along the Mattabesett Trail, which is marked with pale blue blazes. Turns are noted with two stacked blazes, the uppermost offset in the direction of the turn.

From the trailhead near the top of the hill, the Mattabesett Trail on the right enters into a scenic woodland of yellow and black birch, beech, and sassafras rising above a shrubby understory of witch hazel and sweet pepperbush. Sweet pepperbush, also called Indian soap and summersweet, is recognized by its slender spike of dainty white summertime flowers. The plant prefers the moist, rich soils at the edges of wetlands. When the flowers are rubbed between wet palms, the petals produce a light, white lather.

As the trail wanders south, watch the edges of the path for ground pine and Virginia creeper, two vining plants that intertwine among the glacial boulders and bedrock outcrops. Other plants that live here include polypody fern, which forms colonies atop the rocks, wild azalea, and trailing arbutus. Deer are frequent visitors, but most of the hoof prints here are from passing horses.

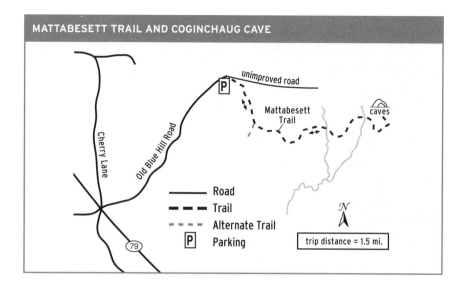

The horse and hiking trails coincide for a while, passing beneath the hardwood forest of hickory, northern red oak, and scattered clumps of mountain laurel. Soon the bridle path continues straight (south) while the trail turns left (east). Slender stump sprouts of American chestnut mingle with patches of Christmas fern and false Solomon's seal. After passing through beautiful tangles of mountain laurel that provide a striking floral display in late spring, reach a jumble of boulders on the right. The path now swings south, squeezing between the cobble of boulders on the right and a small stream on the left where sensitive fern, skunk cabbage, and sphagnum moss grow. The path crosses the stream near another large boulder whose west face is covered with a flat papery lichen called rock tripe.

From the stream, the path heads east, climbs up the hill between ragged rock outcrops, then turns north, scrambling up a stony trail bed to the ridge crest. The terrain levels out into hummocky, rocky plateau thick with blueberries, thorny vines of greenbrier, and groves of oak. From the hilltop the path drops off the ridge to a brook and enters a beautiful landscape of boulder piles shaded by stands of tall, straight hardwoods. The trail twists through this labyrinth of wood and stone, rising gently through groves of laurel and past stony ledges. The terrain now becomes steeper and the path passes through a gateway of bedrock just wide enough to squeeze through. It leads to the crest of another plateau. Wild azalea, blueberry, serviceberry, and mountain laurel form a thick understory beneath plentiful maples and oaks.

A narrow recess of bedrock creates the 20-foot-square, Cogincaug Cave.

A short unmarked path leaves left (northeast), terminating abruptly at the edge of a steep ledge. The Mattabesett Trail turns right (south) and descends immediately very steeply along the edge of the cliff. **Caution!** The descent is short but very slippery in bad weather. The path slabs the ridge and reaches the base of the cliff a few yards from the massive rock overhang known as Coginchaug Cave (0.75 mile).

Coginchaug Cave is a broad but shallow recess of bedrock. About 20 feet by 20 feet, it provides a dry, fairly comfortable spot to linger and relax. The mouth of the cave faces a small drainage forested with ash, oak, yellow birch, and beech. As you sit here surrounded by walls of cold, gray rock, it is interesting to imagine who, of the many that have used this place through the centuries, has been here before you. Native Americans came here centuries ago, their artifacts still discovered occasionally in the dry, compact soil.

While thinking about the past, take time to watch and hear the many types of songbirds in spring and summer, including warblers, thrushes (including veeries), and vireos. The birds are especially fond of the shrubby

MOUNTAIN LAUREL

Every elementary school student in Connecticut learns early on that mountain laurel is the state flower. All too often the lesson stops there, however, and the subtle wonders of this beautiful shrub remain unknown to many people.

Mountain laurel belongs to a genus of plants named *Kalmia* in honor of Peter Kalm, a Swedish botanist who came to North America for a brief time before the Revolutionary War. Although the plant is named for him, he didn't discover mountain laurel. The plant was known for centuries to Native Americans and was introduced into European horticulture in 1734, 14 years before Kalm ever got here.

Mountain laurel is a plant of open woods and thrives beneath the canopies of deciduous trees such as oak, birch, and beech. It needs a well-drained, acidic soil with lots of organic matter, such as leaf mold, to grow best. In the dappled forest shade, the emerald-colored evergreen leaves and irregular, twisted stems are welcome sights along any walk. But it is in spring when the bushes display their beautiful flowers that the majesty of mountain laurel is most apparent. In May or early June, clusters of rose-red buds atop the branches open to reveal snow-white, cup-shaped flowers. The inside of each blossom features ten tiny red dots. These dots mark small recessed areas that hold the anther, the pollen-bearing portion of the flower, in place as the blossom unfurls. As the flower opens, it puts tension on the filament, the thin, threadlike structure that connects the anther and the base of the flower. When a bee comes to the blossom, it bumps the filament, which then releases its stored energy like a taut bowstring. The anther pops out of its little pocket and dusts the visiting bee with pollen. The bee, completely oblivious to this ingenious display, gathers the nectar and flies off to another flower, where some of the pollen from the first flower is left behind and more pollen is gathered.

Mountain laurel is native to a broad region of the eastern United States, from New England west to the Mississippi Valley and south to the Gulf and Atlantic coasts. The leaves and flowers are toxic if eaten and should be kept away from children and overly curious adults. In Connecticut during colonial times, mountain laurel was called spoonwood because the very dense, hard wood made long-lasting cooking spoons.

Spoons and bees notwithstanding, the most loved aspect of mountain laurel is its stunning spring floral display. In spring, be sure to seek out walks that pass through especially thick stands of laurel. The masses of blossoms turn the evergreen thickets into ethereal, flowery clouds you don't soon forget.

tangles along the stream. To return to the trailhead, retrace your steps along the Mattabesett Trail.

MORE INFORMATION

Leashed dogs are permitted on the Mattabesett Trail. For more information on the Mattabesett Trail, contact the Connecticut Forest and Park Association, 16 Meriden Road, Rockfall, CT 06481-2961; 860-346-2372; www.ctwoodlands. org.

—C. S.

TRIP 33
BLUFF HEAD RIDGE

Location: North Guilford
Rating: Easy, with some steep sections
Distance: 2.1 miles
Elevation Gain: 430 feet
Estimated Time: 1.0–2.0 hours
Maps: USGS Durham; North Woods Trail System map and trail descriptions available online

Bluff Head is the name of a steep traprock ridge that makes up the eastern slope of Totoket Mountain. This is an especially nice loop ridge walk along basaltic cliffs with many wildflowers and great views.

DIRECTIONS

From Durham center, travel south on Route 17 to its junction with Route 79. Stay on Route 17 and proceed south the short distance to the junction of Route 77. Turn left onto Route 77 and travel south for 4.2 miles to the parking area on the right. From Guilford, take Route 77 north and pass under I-95 at Exit 58. From I-95, proceed north on Route 77 for 9.0 miles to the parking area on the left.

TRAIL DESCRIPTION

The walk over the Bluff Head section of Totoket Mountain is along the Mattabesett Trail, blazed in pale blue, and the Mattabesett Loop Trail, marked with pale blue blazes surrounding a central orange dot. It is part of the Northwoods Trail System

Just southwest of the parking area on Route 77, the blue-blazed Mattabesett Trail intersects with the orange dot blazes of the Mattabesett Loop Trail. Turn right (west), following the blue-blazed Mattabesett Trail as it immediately begins to scale the steep eastern slope of Totoket Mountain. The path is shaded with tall trees of ash, maple, and white pine, with an occasional understory of benzoin bush. Evergreen Christmas fern and spotted wintergreen mingle with wild geranium on the forest floor. The steep, heavy-duty walking doesn't last very long, and the grade soon begins to moderate. The woods change as you climb closer to the top of the ridge (0.2 mile), with beech, hop hornbeam,

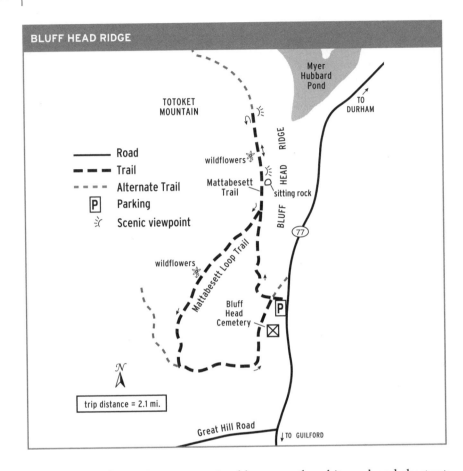

and hornbeam becoming more noticeable among the white, red, and chestnut oaks that predominate. Beneath the trees grow blueberry and a charming wildflower called pipsissewa. When not in bloom, pipsissewa can be recognized by its long, glossy evergreen leaves. Spotted wintergreen and pipsissewa are close relatives with similar-looking flowers, but spotted wintergreen has dark, reddish-green leaves marked in the center with a streak of white, while pipsissewa's leaves are solid green.

The trail hugs the edge of the cliffs as it continues uphill, with peekaboo views appearing through the trees. A small tree called serviceberry, or shadblow, thrives in the thin, rocky soil of the cliff edge. Serviceberry's delicate white flowers cover its slender branches in April. After a short, steep climb, the path reaches an overlook at the junction with the Mattabesett Loop Trail (0.5 mile), which enters left. Red cedar clings to the rocks, and turkey vultures often soar on the breezes over the valley.

Lyre-leafed rock cress clings to basalt cliffs at Bluff Head.

From the overlook, continue north along the Mattabesett Trail. The path is wide and easy to follow along the ridge. A little farther on, the woods become dominated by beech trees, which shelter thin clusters of mountain laurel. From the edge of the bluff, Myerhuber Pond comes into view to the northeast. After passing a boulder on the left, which is a nice sitting rock if you are tired, there is a stretch of cliff that is home to a vast number of interesting wildflowers. Clumps of lyre-leafed rock cress and early saxifrage grow directly from cracks and crevices in the cliff face. Lyre-leafed rock cress has dainty white, four-petaled, sweetly scented flowers. Early saxifrage has short, very stout stems above a rosette of fleshy green leaves. The fragrant flowers are small and white, with five petals. More wildflowers await the observant spring walker, including hepatica, with white or pink flowers, and Dutchman's breeches with dangling white, pantaloon-shaped blossoms. Adding to the beauty are isolated specimens of flowering dogwood, with white-petaled (correctly called bracts) flowers in late April or May.

The trail then climbs a short, steep section to a flat plateau and a lovely overlook (0.75 mile). From here, the waters of Myerhuber Pond are directly below. To the east is Mica ledge, while to the southeast are the bluffs called Broomstick Ledges. Far to the south, the waters of Long Island Sound are visible. Staghorn sumac, wild cherry, oak, and wild strawberry all grow around the traprock outcrops. Garter snakes also like it up here, preferring the grassy areas away from the cliffs.

From the overlook, turn back along the Mattabesett Trail and retrace your steps to the junction of the Mattabesett Loop Trail. Turn right onto the Mattabesett Loop Trail (blazed with orange dots). The trail heads west and then swings southwest through wide, open woods of hickory, oak, and maple. Many of the trees here are double or triple trunked. These trees arose from stumps left behind after the area was logged a few decades ago. As the path descends gently, you encounter occasional clumps of hepatica and trout lily flowers in spring. In fall, the squirrels are busy gathering nuts.

At a junction with an old road (1.5 miles) is a sign for the Loop Trail and mileages. Turn left along the dirt road, where the daisy-like flowers of bloodroot blossom in spring. Wild onion also grows here, with cylindrical green leaves and a potent small white bulb. Continue along the trail, passing wet areas where benzoin bush grows and coming to the Bluff Head cemetery on the right (2.0 miles). The parking area is 100 yards or so beyond the cemetery.

MORE INFORMATION

Bluff Head is protected and managed by volunteers from the Guilford Land Conservation Trust (GLTC). Leashed dogs and mountain bikes are permitted on the trails. For more information on the Mattabesett Trail, contact the Connecticut Forest and Park Association, 16 Meriden Road, Rockfall, CT 06481-2961; 860-346-2372; http://www.ctwoodlands.org. For more information on the Bluff Head area and Northwoods Trail System, contact the Guilford Land Conservation Trust, P.O. Box 200, Guilford, CT 06437-0200; http://www.guilfordlandtrust.org. Maps can also be purchased at stores in the area.

—C. S.

Location: Guilford
Rating: Moderate, with some steep sections
Distance: 3.3 miles
Elevation Gain: 120 feet
Estimated Time: 2.0–3.0 hours
Maps: USGS Guilford; interactive map on Westwoods website

The Westwoods Trails system is a wonderful surprise, in part for the array of natural wonders within its borders, and in part for its even being there. This sanctuary is found along the south-central shore, where tidy towns and homes have dominated the landscape for generations. Along the way to progress, however, people with foresight made room for Westwoods, which contains 39 miles of trails on 1,200 acres. This loop trail is great fun and features rocky granite outcrops and oak and hemlock forests.

DIRECTIONS

From Exit 58 off I-95, take Route 77 south (toward Guilford) about 0.5 mile to Route 1. Turn right (west) onto Route 1. Proceed 0.7 mile to Peddler's Lane. Bear left onto Peddler's Lane and drive 1.1 miles to the parking area on the left just past Dennison Road.

TRAIL DESCRIPTION

The system of trails at Westwoods is daunting to the uninitiated, but actually easy to figure out. All north-south trails are marked with circle-shaped blazes. Other hiking trails, marked with square or triangular blazes, weave back and forth intersecting the circle-blazed trails. A square-blazed trail and its connecting circle-blazed trail are marked with the same color. Crossover trails, which connect trails of different colors, are marked by Xs in the color of the circle trail they lead to.

From the parking area, follow the path through a small wooded area into a scrubby field where wild onion, daylily, wild rose, staghorn sumac, red cedar, and honeysuckle grow. At the far end of the field, the path reenters the woods and skirts a rocky cobble covered with bramble and greenbrier before heading

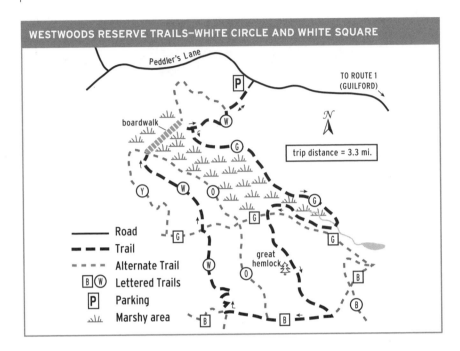

WESTWOODS RESERVE TRAILS—WHITE CIRCLE AND WHITE SQUARE

Peddler's Lane

TO ROUTE 1
(GUILFORD)

boardwalk

trip distance = 3.3 mi.

great
hemlock

Road
Trail
Alternate Trail
Lettered Trails
Parking
Marshy area

downhill to the junction of the White Circle Trail and the Green Rectangle Trail. Turn left onto the Green Rectangle Trail and continue easily downhill toward the marsh. The forest here is typical of the woods that grow atop the bedrock found in central and eastern Connecticut. Different species of oak dominate, with shagbark hickory, maple, ash, beech, and birch also mixed in. At the shore of the marsh, the trail swings to follow along its eastern perimeter, winding through heavily bouldered woods. In the marsh grows a collection of common wetland plants, including marsh marigold, skunk cabbage, and a woody shrub called summersweet.

The path leaves the edge of the swamp to wander briefly along a bedrock outcrop and then drops back down to the marsh. In early spring, the coarse but melodic song of red-winged blackbirds emanates from the wetland. The clear whistle of cardinals is also heard, as are chickadees and a variety of other songbirds. The trail passes through another very rocky stretch before crossing a small stream on stepping-stones. Leaving the marsh yet again, proceed uphill into plentiful clusters of mountain laurel sheltered by high trees before heading downhill to a stone wall just above the swamp. Turn left along the stone wall. This is a lovely stretch of trail, with the marsh to the right and large boulders and impressive ridges of gray bedrock to the left. At the eastern end of the wetland, the marsh has been transformed into a small stream with defined banks and cool water the color of English tea. The brown color of the water comes in part from tannic acid, a natural by-product of the trees, mosses, and other plants that grow in the swamp. After crossing the brook on a small log bridge, the path follows the brook upstream, weaving through a beautiful laurel thicket shaded by very large, hundred-year-old white pines.

The Green Circle Trail is crossed here and there by paths blazed with green triangles. Follow the green circles up a short but steep rise and cross another hiking trail. Continue straight ahead, climbing a short, steep rise and entering a cool hemlock grove studded with weathered bedrock outcrops and boulders. Some of the rock formations here are spectacular, and you could spend many minutes wandering off the trail to explore them. A short way farther on, the healthy hemlocks yield to a large area of dead hemlock trees. Near the center of this area are the remains of the great hemlock, a massive tree that was 200 years old before its death in the late 1990s. The dead trees, including the great hemlock, were killed by a small insect called the woolly adelgid.

This aphid-like bug is native to Asia and was accidentally introduced to North America many years ago. By 1985, it had spread to Long Island. When Hurricane Gloria swept up the East Coast that year, her winds carried the insects across Long Island Sound to Connecticut. Adelgids now infest nearly every town in the state. The devastation of Connecticut's hemlocks is a great concern, and for years it seemed little hope of effectively controlling the insect existed. Recent research by Dr. Mark McClure of the Connecticut Agricultural Experiment Station and others has identified a small black Japanese ladybug that is a voracious predator of adelgids. Thousands of the tiny solid black ladybugs have been released in Connecticut's forests, with promising results.

From the great hemlock, pass through a bouldered area, with some boulders as large as automobiles. Some of the stones here shelter small boulder caves. The trail climbs atop a bedrock ridge, passing more spectacular boulders and rock formations. Leaving the ridge, the path passes over a rise and comes to the junction with a Yellow Trail marked with triangles and the Blue Trail marked with rectangles. Turn right (west), following a wide woods road that winds gently downhill to a tea-colored stream. Cross the brook on a wooden bridge and pass the intersections of an orange-blazed trail marked with squares followed shortly by an orange-blazed trail marked with circles.

Continue along the woods road to a junction with the White Trail (marked with circles). Turn right onto the White Trail and almost immediately enter a labyrinth of granite bedrock and boulders, hemlock, and mountain laurel. The path continues uphill, weaving through the rocky landscape shaded by hemlock and mountain laurel. This is a beautiful, if a bit rugged, stretch and worth the effort. At the top of the ridge, the trail passes over a length of bare rock

Oak and laurel woods are one of the many environments hikers enjoy at Westwoods.

studded with the skeletons of dead hemlocks. It then swings downhill into a rock-lined canyon called the natural monument. This area is like an enormous sculpture, with some parts of the cliff weathered into soft, rounded forms and other sections fractured into angled blocks. From the natural monument, the White Trail proceeds through a mixed hardwood and hemlock forest, passing more rock formations along the way.

At the trail junction marked 22, where the path blazed with green squares crosses, continue straight, climbing to the crest of a hill marked by an extensive bald area composed of bare bedrock. This area is beautiful in every season of the year. Many people rest here, stretching out on the sunny rocks to idle away a few minutes. The bedrock continues gently uphill for about 200 yards. From the bald area, descend into thickets of laurel before quickly coming to another, smaller bald area with limited views over the woods to the west. From the vista, head downhill through laurel, passing a large rock outcrop on the right. The path crosses the Yellow Trail and comes to the beginning of a very long boardwalk, known locally as "The Plank Walk" that bridges a shallow, forested marsh.

The stroll over the narrow boardwalk is fun any time of year. Benzoin bush lights the wetlands with bright yellow-green flowers in very early spring, along with the shell-shaped blossoms of skunk cabbage. Later in the season, the vivid yellow blossoms of marsh marigold bloom, followed weeks later by wild iris. Highbush blueberry grows here, with small, sweet fruits in summer. Ruffed grouse can be found on the drier sections, their drumbeat mating call a familiar sound in April. In fall, yellow, red, and orange leaves float on the dark water as waterfowl fly overhead. From the boardwalk, it is a short walk along the White Circle Trail back to the parking area.

MORE INFORMATION

Leashed dogs and mountain bikes are permitted in the reserve. Volunteers from the Guilford Land Conservation Trust and its Westwoods Trail Committee manage and maintain all of the trails in Westwoods. The websites of the land trust and Westwoods include trail directions and maps. Maps can also be purchased at area stores. Guilford Land Conservation Trust, P.O. Box 200, Guilford, CT 06437-0200); http://www.guilfordlandtrust.org; Westwoods Reserve, http://www.westwoodstrails.org; Connecticut Forest and Park Association, 16 Meriden Road, Rockfall, CT 06481-2961; 860-346-2372; www.ctwoodlands.org.

—C. S.

TRIP 35
LOST LAKE

Location: Guilford
Rating: Easy
Distance: 1.5 miles
Elevation Gain: 40 feet
Estimated Time: 0.5–1.0 hour
Maps: USGS Guilford; Westwoods map and trail directions available online

Lost Lake, in the southern portion of the 1,200-acre reserve called Westwoods, is a large, brackish pond that was cut off years ago from Great Harbor just to the south by railroad and highway bankings. Since then, it can be called neither a part of Long Island Sound nor a freshwater lake. Rather it is something unique, and its special nature is a boon to those who visit it. Look forward to mysterious rock carvings and great birding

DIRECTIONS
From the center of Guilford, take Route 146 east. Proceed east, with the railroad tracks paralleling the road on the left for 1.3 miles. Just before Route 146 swings under the railroad tracks you find an intersection on the right where Sam Hill Road meets Route 146. Turn right; the small parking area is directly ahead and is so close to the intersection that it seems a part of it.

TRAIL DESCRIPTION
This natural area is webbed with a trail system that needs some explanation before people go off and explore. Here is a basic primer: All north-south trails are marked with circle-shaped blazes. Trails marked with square blazes weave back and forth across the circle-blazed trails. A square-blazed trail and its accompanying circle-blazed trail are marked always with the same color. Crossover trails, which connect trails of different colors, are marked by Xs in the color of the circle trail they lead to.

From the parking area, follow the White Circle Trail into woods lined with thorny greenbrier and seasonally fragrant honeysuckle. The path parallels the railroad tracks (on the left) and soon crosses a small wet area in a shallow swale. Climbing on a gradual grade with good footing, reach the junction of

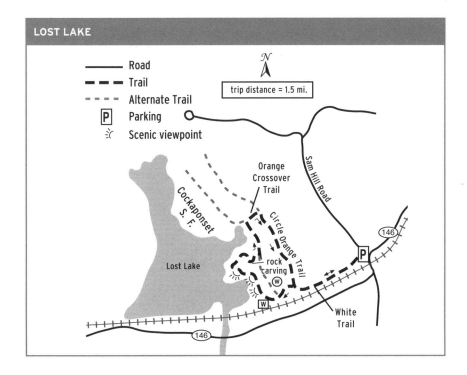

the White and Orange Circle Trails. Proceed straight on the White Circle Trail for a few yards to a second junction, where the White Circle Trail swings right and the White Square Trail goes left. Follow the white squares down a slight grade to a massive stone outcrop with numerous boulders gathered near its base. Clusters of mountain laurel bloom here in May and June beneath the spreading branches of black birch.

From the rock outcrop, the path heads downhill briefly before turning to follow a low ridge of bedrock. You have different ways to go from here, and old blazes mingling with newer ones make the treadway a bit difficult to follow. The path turns left, away from the bedrock ridge and toward a jumble of boulders near the shore of Lost Lake. The blazes lead you through a maze of large boulders and bedrock shaded by low-growing trees. Here rocky platforms reach like fingers out toward the shore (0.5 mile), offering private views of Lost Lake. For the next 200 yards, the trail skirts the shore with wide, beautiful views from a few selected rock outcrops. On quiet days, it is pleasant to sit on the rocks and observe the many different birds that come to feed in the shallows.

The railroad tracks form the very straight southern boundary of the lake. Along this shoreline grows a mix of grasses, sedges, and other wetland plants. Many waterfowl and wading birds come here to feed, including Canada geese, mute swans, a wide variety of ducks, great blue herons, and great and snowy egrets. Great blue herons are very large birds, standing nearly 4 feet tall with wingspans of 6 feet. They hunt frogs and fish along the edges of the lake by standing motionless for many minutes at a time, waiting for lunch to come closer. They stand so still that people often do not notice them until they fly off leisurely. Snowy egrets are smaller than great blue herons, reaching about 2.5 feet tall with a wingspan of 3 feet. Their plumage is pure white, which contrasts with their black bills. Snowy egrets often congregate in small groups in the shallows, where they run after schools of minnows through the water. You can sometimes observe these groups from this section of shoreline, but you must be quiet and still or they will fly off to a less noisy section of the lake. So many species of birds come to the shore and waters of the lake that each trip holds the potential for viewing the extraordinary.

Follow the white blazes as they guide you along the shoreline through blueberry, greenbrier, and serviceberry. The rocks along the shore often hold clusters of mussel shells, trash piles left behind by seabirds dining on the tender shellfish. Here and there along the way the path slips down to the bouldered shore, where wide, beautiful views of the lake await. The rocks here are covered with large, blackish-green lichens called rock tripe. These plants, part fungus and part algae, get most of their nutrients directly from the rock and do not need soil or much water to thrive.

The path climbs over bedrock and around boulders to a large outcrop of gray granite (0.6 mile). Chiseled into a protruding section of the rock are molding patterns of the type used to decorate marble columns and stone buildings. Nearby the bedrock is punctuated with numerous punch marks. It is like bumping into a stonemason's doodle pad. But the mysterious isn't over yet, for a few feet farther on is another stone, this one nearly at ground level, that has been carved into a drinking trough.

Follow the trail downhill to where it rejoins the White Circle Trail in a wet area thick with laurel and tall oaks overhead. The path continues north through a dense jungle of evergreen laurel that often not only lines the trail but arches over it, forming a leafy tunnel. Just to the right is another impressive granite cliff, which runs parallel to the trail.

In a wetland by a stream, the Orange Crossover Trail leaves right (0.7 mile). Turn onto the trail, which follows a lazy stream to the Orange Circle Trail. Turn right (southeast) onto the Orange Circle Trail. The woods comprise tall oaks, whose canopies amplify the sound of the wind as it blows in off the Long

TRAILS

"The surface of the earth is soft and impressible by the feet of men," wrote Henry David Thoreau, "and so with the paths which the mind travels. How worn and dusty, then, must be the highways of the world, how deep the ruts of tradition and conformity. It is remarkable how easily and insensibly we fall into a particular route, and make a beaten path for ourselves."

Thoreau saw trails, whether through the woods or in ourselves, as habits that could galvanize the mind and soul, turning them hard and thoughtless. It is easy to see paths that way, as a means of getting from one place to another while ignoring what is in between. Hiking or living in such a way may seem quick and even comfortable, yet is akin to choosing blindness over sight, or loneliness over love.

In the fall of 1847, Henry David Thoreau left the shores of Walden Pond. "I left the woods for as good a reason as I went there," he wrote. He left to continue his life's journey in other places, having harvested from Walden lessons he would carry with him wherever he went. The woods had taught him that when man "simplifies his life, the laws of the universe will appear less complex, and solitude will not be solitude, nor poverty poverty, nor weakness weakness. If you have built castles in the air," he wrote, "your work need not be lost; that is where they should be. Now put the foundations under them."

Everything that Thoreau discovered in the woods is still out there waiting to be found again. As you lace up your boots, walk in the woods for as good a reason as Thoreau left them behind—simplicity. It would be easy to gaze at the infinite complexities that are ubiquitous in creation and give up trying to understand it or appreciate it. Yet that is the reverse of Thoreau's message to us all. Instead of trying to approach natural beauty like an engineer, absorb it like a poet. Allow it to define itself to you by allowing yourself to be humble and open to its word. As Thoreau wrote at the close of Walden, "Only that day dawns to which we are awake."

Island Sound. In June, the pale white-and-pink flowers of mountain laurel are beautiful against the profiles of the many boulders and outcrops passed along the way. The path continues south through stands of chestnut and red oak and waves of laurel. At the junction with the White Circle Trail, turn left and follow the White Circle Trail the short distance back to the parking area.

MORE INFORMATION

Leashed dogs and mountain bikes are permitted in the reserve. Volunteers from the Guilford Land Conservation Trust and its Westwoods Trails Committee manage and maintain all the trails in Westwoods. Guilford Land Conservation Trust, P.O. Box 200, Guilford, CT 06437-0200; http://www.guilfordlandtrust. org; Westwoods: http://www.westwoodstrails.org. Maps can also be purchased at stores in the area. Connecticut Forest and Parks Association, 16 Meriden Road, Rockfall, CT 06481-2961; 860-346-2372; http://www.ctwoodlands.org.

—C. S.

3

EASTERN CONNECTICUT

THE EASTERN REGION IS FILLED WITH FISHING VILLAGES and rural towns. You'll find some of the most enchanting areas of shoreline in the state, from Hammonasset (Trip 46) to Bluff Point (Trip 48) and Barn Island (Trip 50). Along sandy beaches horseshoe crabs still congregate in spring, as do flocks of seabirds. In fall, scores of songbirds congregate in thickets of beach rose. North of the shore are hikes that take you through the haunting atmosphere of Chatfield Caves (Trip 45) and Devil's Hopyard (Trip 44). In spring the display of mountain laurel along Laurel Loop (Trip 41) and rosebay rhododendron in the Rhododendron Sanctuary (Trip 39) is spellbinding. But this region has even more in store, for in the northeast corner of the state are walks through Trail Wood Sanctuary (Trip 37) and, one of the most beautiful spots in the state, Rock Spring Preserve (Trip 38).

TRIP 36
BREAKNECK POND–BIGELOW HOLLOW STATE PARK AND NIPMUCK STATE FOREST

Location: Union
Rating: Moderate, with one challenging stretch
Distance: 6.1 miles
Elevation Gain: 100 feet
Estimated Time: 4.0–4.5 hours
Maps: USGS Eastford, Southbridge—MA; Nipmuck State Forest/ Bigelow Hollow State Park map available online

> **This trail presents you with a wild rocky country, straddling the Massachusetts border, which contains a scenic 1.6-mile-long pond with fascinating carnivorous plants, as well as luxuriant and eye-popping shoreline laurel blooms in early June.**

DIRECTIONS
From I-84, Exit 73, travel north on Route 190 for 2.3 miles to Route 171 in Union. Bear right onto Route 171 east and drive for 1.5 miles to Bigelow Hollow State Park. Turn left into the park, pass the entrance kiosk, and travel 0.65 mile to the Bigelow Pond Picnic Area; a parking lot is on the left. Hikers should not park at the boat-launch area.

TRAIL DESCRIPTION
Cross the paved park road and head up a gravel bank to the trailhead and map of the combined 9,000-acre properties. Trail options are well marked at a Y intersection where you should bear right, onto the white-blazed East Ridge Trail. The southern end of Breakneck Pond is 1.1 miles northeast. To begin this loop trail, walk under large white pine, eastern hemlock, black birch, and mountain laurel. Bracken fern proliferates in the sandy glacial soils. Soon enter a gravelly clearing regenerating to white pine. On an early summer visit, I found a handsome ringneck snake under a board in the clearing. These small serpents with orange bellies are harmless to humans and consume insects mostly. A tote road merges from the right. Enter shady hemlock, oak, and birch forest on a wide, pleasant roadway. Pass a small red maple swamp and cross a little stream. Male ebony jewelwing damselflies with electric blue abdomens flutter near the brook, where whorled loose-

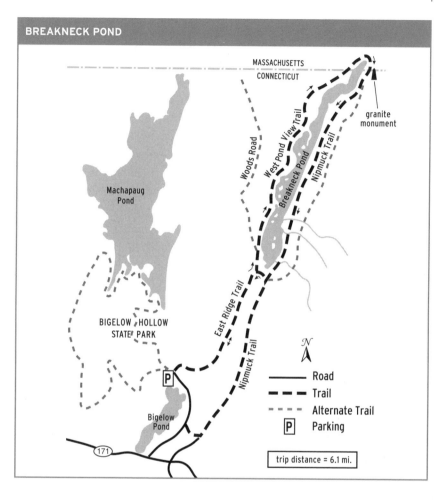

BREAKNECK POND

strife blooms yellow in summer. Reenter hemlocks (many young specimens line the roadway) and pass a borrow pit on the right.

At a Y intersection, follow the white rectangular blazes left. Note the near-total absence of vegetation in the deep shade as the wonderful aroma of needles permeates the air. Cross a railroad-tie bridge over a little brook. To the right, a small swamp lies thick with cinnamon fern, marsh marigold (actually a buttercup), and sphagnum moss. Green frogs call this home, and tiny brown winter wrens enliven the forest with their effervescent songs. The terrain rises gradually to the left—schist outcrops and boulders punctuate the slope. Reach a wetland about 200 feet left of the elevated old roadway and pass between former gateposts. Stay left at the Y trail split and come to a T intersection almost immediately at a shrub swamp. Shallow-rooted hemlocks have toppled into a swamp where royal and cinnamon ferns and sphagnum moss flourish. Turn left to follow the West Pond View Trail, blazed blue with a white dot in the center. It is 4.4 miles around Breakneck Pond from here.

Soon come to the narrow orange-blazed Pond View Trail on the right, which skirts the water's edge. Walk among fragrant white pine and blooming laurel in June and early July. Beavers have girdled some hemlock. Walk gently uphill, turn right, and swing left under exquisite laurel shrubs toward the shoreline. Reach a more open view of the pond's south end and more sign of beaver-cut and girdled hemlock. Hemlock is surely not among the rodent's preferred food plants, indicating perhaps that more desirable species have been depleted. Tiny, creeping partridgeberry display bright-white, four-petaled twin flowers in early summer that later produce red berries. Rejoin the blue-blazed trail at the T, turning right and walking over planks through a boggy area. Deep pink sheep laurel blossoms adorn both sides. A beaver dam is situated close by on the left, while the pond behind the dam is coated with floating duckweed. In summer, dragonflies patrol the pond shores and intercept insects in midair. Meanwhile, shiny black whirligig beetles gyrate en masse on the water's surface like bumper cars at an amusement park.

The white-on-blue-blazed trail swings right to continue along the shore. Follow this wide tote road for only a short distance before turning right, immediately past a big hemlock located on the right and onto a narrow trail that adheres tightly to the shore. This spot is easy to miss because of obscured blazes. Do not continue walking uphill on the roadway. This is the most demanding portion of the walk, requiring a climb over fallen trees and boulders. It makes you wonder whether this was what gave the pond its name! A steep, boulder-strewn slope rises on the left. You are now walking just below the parallel roadway from which this trail is virtually invisible. In early summer, the unassuming 6-inch-tall cow-wheat's pale yellow snapdragon-like flowers dot sunny patches along the trail. Climb easily for a short distance away from the pond through a laurel thicket. The forest, in addition to hemlock, includes red maple, red oak, and black birch. At three boulders, the trail turns right and heads down rather steeply toward the water. Pass by a few small striped maple, black and white oaks, and lowbush blueberry. Another islet of white cedar, where curious carnivorous pitcher plants send up their parasol-like, maroon-and-yellow flowers, appears. Near shore tiny least flycatchers spit out their unmusical, clicking *che-bek*.

Come to a vernal pool at the base of the rocky slope. Only the mounded trail ridge separates it from Breakneck Pond. The trail leads directly to the pond edge and swings left. Striking swamp white azaleas, wonderfully fragrant, grace the shore in late spring and early summer. Reach open oak woods with signs of camping. A few black spruce, which may be much older than their size would indicate, stand with the white cedar on the islets. Black spruce is a denizen of cold bogs, as are pitcher plants. This glacier-gouged hollow, a relict of the ice ages, acts as a cold-air sink within which such northern species can survive. In contrast, you'll also find a few bayberry or wax myrtle shrubs, more characteristic of the mild coastal region, growing on shore. Continue walking on the white-on-blue-blazed path through dry oak woods with bracken fern, sheep laurel, and a few highbush blueberry shrubs. The mountain laurel shrubs are 8 or 9 feet tall.

Back at the hemlock-lined shore, proceed along a small ridge from which you gain a nice view of the pond below. The trail bears left to a wooded swamp, where little common yellowthroats nest. The males sport black masks. Cross a wet spot easily on logs, rocks, and a short beaver dam. Turn right to follow the shore. Blue-headed vireos sing their measured, burry phrases from the hemlock. These 6-inch-long, bespectacled insect eaters build lovely cup nests, woven partially of white birch-bark strips, at the end of a forked branch. An impressive clump of mountain laurel, heavy with mounds of nickel-sized blossoms, may tempt a photo or two in season. Laurel flowers transfer pollen by smacking visiting bees with their spring-loaded, pollen-bearing anthers. The pond now is more open. White cedars have disappeared, replaced by larger islands bearing more substantial white pines. Skirt a damp spot along the pond edge and view oaks gnawed by beavers. While beavers generally cut softer species, they do also tackle dense and heavy oak. Proceed through a shaded hemlock stand and reach a narrow waterway between the mainland and an island; continue straight on the white-on-blue-blazed trail. From here, looking back south, you gain a splendid view of the pond. Climb gradually through stony oak, hemlock, and laurel woods to a point nearly 50 feet above the water.

Now pass big gneiss (pronounced *nice*) boulders to the left where polypody fern and leaflike rock tripe lichen obscure the gray rock surface. Rock tripe is brown when dry, becoming green when wet, as its component algae begin photosynthesizing again. This is a fairly young forest of black and gray birches, red oak, chestnut, mountain laurel, and a few white pine. On the left, pass more massive rock-tripe-encrusted boulders that form a tiny "cave" between them; you can explore this crevice. Both scarlet tanager, which prefers oaks, and black-throated blue warbler, partial to constructing its nest in laurel thickets, nest in these mixed woodlands. The trail skirts this glacially deposited boulder field, leading gently uphill through laurel. An outcrop on the left has a small black birch growing out of it. Drop down gradually past more lichen-covered boulders. Flashy 5.5-inch-long, orange, black, and white American redstarts fan their tails as they flit among the boughs searching for caterpillars to feed to their hungry brood. A bit farther along, a large boulder resembling the prow of a ship stands on the right. More angular, slanted chunks of rock come into view as you continue along the west side of Breakneck Pond. This line of glacial debris is known as a boulder train. Interspersed with mountain laurel, the boulders make for a lovely scene. On a tiny ledge of one rock I found an eastern phoebe's nest. Phoebes are among the earliest spring returnees, arriving back on breeding grounds by late March.

Descend along boulders. A small duckweed-covered pool is visible through hemlock below the steep slope on the right. Approach the pond and reach a tote road labeled Horse Trail. The gurgling of flowing water alerts you to a stream crossing. Turn right and cross the brook on stepping-stones. Continue on the tote road amid dense young hemlock. Walk through a wide, sandy area where the skeleton of an old truck decays. Pass a wooded swamp on the left, screened by trees, and arrive at a T intersection at 3.0 miles. Follow the old road right, along the shoreline. You are now at the northern tip of the pond in Massachusetts. A Louisiana waterthrush, a ground-dwelling warbler that builds its nest along the banks of clear streams, teetered along ahead of me before flying into the forest. A fence-like growth of young hemlocks lines the shore. Arrive at a granite monument marking the Massachusetts-Connecticut border on the left just beyond the hemlock, where the white-blazed East Ridge Trail splits off, climbing the ridge. Remain on the roadway, following the blue rectangles. Hemlock boughs overhanging the road make for a pleasing scene. In spring, blue flag irises decorate the shoreline.

After passing a big white pine, the trail deviates from the road by bearing right. The path can be difficult to locate near the shore. It becomes narrower, crosses a small flowing stream on stepping-stones, and wends gradually up the slope among hemlock and gray and black birches. Red squirrels have left middens of pinecone cores and scales, and the path is cushioned by the thick hemlock needle duff. Pass a small vernal pool to the left. The path undulates through attractive forest, made even more appealing by bountiful displays of laurel. Laurel produces more flowers in well-lit locations. This is now pine-oak-maple woodland where black-capped chickadees, ovenbirds, and red-eyed vireos reside. Pass a gneiss outcrop situated on the left, while on the right a 4-inch-diameter hemlock emerges from the top of another outcrop. Walk downhill through outcrops; on the left is a damp area with moss-covered rocks and cinnamon fern. Islands with tall pines lie offshore.

BOG CARNIVORES

The Venus flytrap, the one "meat-eating" plant known to almost everyone, is not native to and cannot survive the harsh climatic conditions of New England. But two other insect-consuming species—the pitcher plant and the round-leaved sundew—are reasonably common in the proper habitats: glacial relicts known as bogs. Bogs represent a nonrenewable natural resource in our landscape. The acidic conditions within bogs reduce decomposition of plant and animal matter to a very minimal level; the nitrogen plants require for survival is thus not readily available to them. This leaves bog plants with a major "vitamin deficiency." Insectivorous plants have overcome this dilemma by means of several ingenious strategies.

Pitcher plants are aptly named, as their basal leaves are fused into a tall urn lined with downward-projecting bristles. Rainwater accumulates in the pitchers, while sweet secretions from the plant lure insects to their doom. Flies and other six- and eight-legged creatures easily follow the downward-projecting hairs into the depth of the pitcher, but find it virtually impossible to climb out. Exhausted by their struggles to escape, they fall into the pool and drown. Digestive juices released by the plant soon reduce the insect's proteins to its constituent parts, including nitrogen, which the plant then absorbs.

Sundews have taken a different tack to reach the same end. Sweet droplets exuded from the tips of their reddish, tentacle-like leaf projections attract a wide variety of insects to the plant. Once the bugs alight, the extreme stickiness of the clear substance makes escape all but impossible. As the insects struggle they become ever more mired in the sweet embrace of the sundew's leaf. In time the leaf curls inward and then goes about digesting the soft portions of its prey. Upon closer inspection, I discovered that one of the sundews growing in a small colony along the eastern shore of Breakneck Pond had ensnared a small damselfly as well as several gnats and flies.

These highly specialized plants cope very successfully with the limiting conditions of bogs and sandy, acid soils by having evolved remarkable anatomical and behavioral adaptations. I always get a thrill out of seeing these carnivorous plants in the wild because they are such a wonderful example of the infinite variety and adaptability of nature.

You are now on a hemlock ridge above the pond; to the left a boggy area lies in the crease between ridges. The cheery notes of American robin, the Connecticut state bird, often ring through the woodland. Walk gradually downhill now, closer to the water, and cross feeder rills, the second larger and rockier. While following the shoreline closely here, I made an interesting discovery. A small antique glass bottle lying on the forest floor had been totally engulfed by mosses and fine hemlock roots so as to be all but invisible. So, given enough time, the work of human beings can be totally obliterated by the hand of nature. Pass an ancient rough-barked hemlock and then a hemlock snag riddled with deep pileated woodpecker excavations. Beautiful black, yellow, gray, and white magnolia warblers nest in these conifers, and tiny, mouse-like winter wrens utter their loud bubbly refrains from the shaded hollows. Descend the slope toward the pond and then curve left past an impressive straight-boled white pine. Arrive at a level spot along the shore where clumps of sticky-tentacled sundew plants passively trap unsuspecting insects. I noticed that one had ensnared a small damselfly as well as several gnats and flies. These bog specialists, like pitcher plants, supplement their nitrogen intake by absorbing nutrients from insects lured to their modified leaves. A nice view of the cedar islets situated along the far shore is possible here.

Pass through a small clearing where a leaning outcrop has been used as a fireplace. Farther on, one large red maple along the trail displays very shaggy bark. As you continue near the shoreline, note trees that beavers have chiseled the bark off. They consume the nutritious inner bark, or cambium layer, the tree's growth layer. If completely girdled, the flow of nutrients and water from roots to crown is cut, and the tree perishes. Arrive at an open grove of pine and hemlock showing more signs of unauthorized camping. The trail swings left and passes through a swampy hemlock-maple outflow on stones. Long beech fern, with its bottom pair of leaflets pointing downward, thrives in the moist rocky soil. Felled small hemlocks indicate that beavers are abroad. Another wetland denizen, a female wood duck, gave its characteristic squealing alarm call and fled at my approach. Come to another woodland clearing under white pine where the wonderful aroma of pine resin hangs thick in the warm air. Looking out toward the pond, notice that you are now opposite the tall pine islands. The trail bears left through laurel and brings you to another pond viewpoint clear of underbrush below white pine and hemlock. The pines must have colonized this once open ground first, since their winged seeds require full sun for germination.

Hemlock, in contrast, is extremely shade tolerant. From May through July, black-throated green warblers sing their buzzy *zee-zo-zo-zee* from the pine boughs. On the left, a hemlock-covered slope rises at a low angle. The waxy white blossoms of pyrola bloom under the evergreens. Cross a rock-strewn feeder brook and two sections of bog bridge where gulping green frogs live. A few witch hazel shrubs grow here as on the opposite side of the pond. Pass a small clearing. Later, spinulose wood and New York ferns add splashes of green to the forest floor. Walk through a boulder field vegetated by yellow birch and hemlock. Eastern chipmunks scamper over the woodland floor, seeking shelter from weasels and other predators among the rocks. An open view of the south end of the pond is possible here, and as you gaze in that direction, note the leatherleaf shrubs—another bog specialist. The largest frogs—bullfrogs—bellow from the shallows.

The trail swings left, passing the end of a stone wall on that side. Reach an orange-blazed trail on the right and turn onto it; this junction is difficult to see. Amble left along the swamp border, and in a short distance reach a T junction with the white-blazed East Ridge Trail, closing the pond loop. Walk straight ahead and retrace your steps 1.1 miles to your vehicle.

MORE INFORMATION

Bigelow Hollow State Park has accessible parking and picnic tables. Also pit toilets and a boat launch are available. Alcohol is not permitted; pets are allowed on leashes only. Open from 8:00 A.M. to sunset. Parking fees: Holidays/weekends $7 resident vehicle, $10 nonresident vehicle; weekdays free. Bigelow Hollow State Park, c/o Shenipsit State Forest, 166 Chestnut Hill Road, Stafford Springs, CT 06076; 860-684-3430; http://www.ct.gov/dep.

—R. L.

TRIP 37
CONNECTICUT AUDUBON CENTER AT TRAIL WOOD

Location: Hampton
Rating: Easy
Distance: 2.3 miles
Elevation Gain: 120 feet
Estimated Time: 1.5 hours
Maps: USGS Hampton; Trail Wood Sanctuary map

Trail Wood, the home of the late Pulitzer Prize winning nature writer Edwin Way Teale and his wife Nellie, offers stimulation, solitude, and inspiration. A wildlife-rich beaver pond, abundant fern variety, picturesque stone walls, and the author's writing cabin are some of the delights awaiting you along this idyllic loop trail— a fine hike with children.

DIRECTIONS
From Exit 91 off I-395, take Route 6 west for approximately 10.0 miles to Route 97. Turn right (north) onto Route 97 and drive 2.6 miles through Hampton to Kenyon Road. Turn left onto Kenyon Road and travel north for 0.35 mile to a farm lane on the left. A grassy parking area is located on the left after 0.1 mile.

TRAIL DESCRIPTION
These 168 acres, so beloved by Edwin Way Teale (1899–1980), now offer the same pleasures to visitors that first drew the Teales to its fields, woods, ponds, streams, and stone walls in 1959.

From the parking area, turn left onto the lane and walk toward the white farmhouse dating to 1806. Cross Hampton Brook, where fish, crayfish, and green frogs reside, on a stone bridge and continue up the gentle slope to the house. The old gravel lane is bordered by stone walls, the right one festooned with grapevines. Hay-scented fern is luxuriant along the lane and wall. A flower garden densely populated with showy blossoms in July attracts myriad butterflies, including elegant black swallowtails. Pass hickories on the left and curve right around the house. Trail maps and a visitor registry are housed inside the garage annex to the left. The effervescent song of the house wren celebrates the summer season as you follow the mowed path in spring and summer through what the Teales called the Starfield. Here they marveled at the depth and clarity

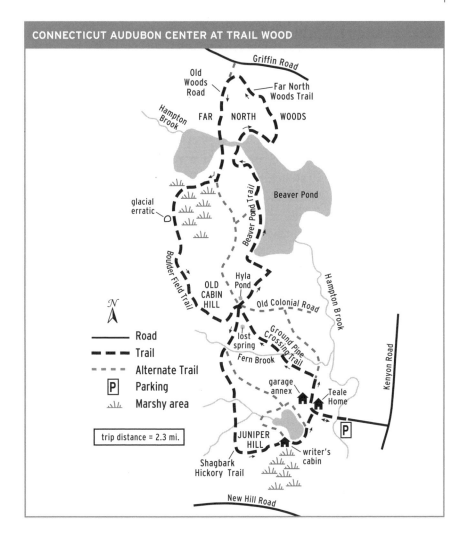

CONNECTICUT AUDUBON CENTER AT TRAIL WOOD

of the rural night sky. Uncut fields of wildflowers—Queen Anne's lace, black-eyed Susan, and spotted knapweed—provide sources of nectar for dainty and colorful American copper butterflies. Oriental bittersweet, an invasive exotic plant, is invading these fields.

Come to a trail intersection and turn left; you are now walking on Ground Pine Crossing Trail over Nighthawk Hill. Significant amounts of poison ivy edge the mowed path. The field to the left, Woodcock Pasture, is bordered by black oak, red maple, and quaking aspen. On summer days it is patrolled by dragonflies, while field crickets produce their soothing, if monotonous, chirping amid the rank grasses and wildflowers. The trail now curves right, entering moist deciduous woods of green ash, black oak, and red maple.

Cross the intermittent Fern Brook on stepping-stones. Skunk cabbage, interrupted fern, the club mosses ground cedar and princess pine (which give the trail its name), New York fern, royal fern, highbush blueberry, mountain azalea, and abundant spicebush shrubs thrive in the moist soils. Skunk cabbage, one of the earliest-blooming native plants, produces its own heat, enabling it to melt its way up through the snow cover! Woodland butterflies, such as northern pearly eye, with wings bordered by eyespots to fool predators, bask on leaves in patches of dappled sunlight. A sometimes damp depression on the right is usually dry in summer. Oak, ash, and hickory shade the path, while enchanter's nightshade blooms on the darkened forest floor. Its white flowers have only two petals.

Reach rock-lined Lost Spring on the left as the trail begins to rise slightly. The spring feeds a seepage area thick with skunk cabbage. At 0.35 mile, join the Old Colonial Road Trail on the right and two trails on the left, creating a wheel-spoke configuration. Proceed straight ahead to a sign for Hyla Rill/To Beaver Pond at a Y fork. Turn right toward a beaver pond and pass Hyla Pond—a vernal pool where salamanders and frogs play out their annual breeding rituals before the heat of summer dries their pool. An oak-covered slope rises gently on the right, where fall-blooming witch hazel and much shorter maple-leaf viburnum are common shrubs. Black birch, ash, black and red oaks, and chestnut saplings lead up to a stone wall cut by the trail, which now swings left. Ferns, of which there are 26 native species here, continue to be numerous. Christmas, hay-scented (thrives on rocky ground), interrupted, and New York (fronds tapered at both ends) ferns provide a feathery ground cover. Some components of a rock wall of flat Hebron schist flagstones built long ago glisten with mica.

The trail swings right, providing the first glimpse of the beaver pond through trees to the left. Red maple, Juneberry (shad), ironwood, white oak, black cherry, and highbush blueberry dot these open woodlands. Eastern wood pewees wait for flying insect meals to happen by. Arrive at the rather extensive pond created by North America's largest rodent in the early 1960s. Much of its surface is now covered with the floating pads and striking white blossoms of fragrant waterlilies. The stillness is broken by the amusing gulps of green frogs proclaiming their territorial rights. A portion of the beaver dam, across Hampton Brook, is visible to the right. The creation of this pond was a big surprise to the Teales, who chanced upon it one fall day. Stay alert for belted kingfishers as they rattle and fly with jerky wing beats, or a crow-sized green heron standing motionless and hunched over on a dead stump, completely absorbed in its quest for frogs.

Retrace your steps and take the trail on the right to cross a bridge over a tiny brook—the Teales' Hellebore Crossover. In summer, ferns steal the show—hay-scented, New York, royal, interrupted, and chest-high and taller cinnamon ferns are abundant, eye-catching holdovers from the Carboniferous era, long before the age of dinosaurs. Continue walking for intermittent views of the pond. I spotted an eastern phoebe, a 6.5-inch-long, olive-gray flycatcher, feeding insects to its two nearly full-grown fledglings on a red maple limb above us. Sections of stone wall dating from perhaps the eighteenth century, which once kept livestock out of planted fields, border what is now a beaver pond over whose placid surface dragonflies on gauzy wings capture insects. Cross a trail going left that leads up an oak-hickory slope to Old Woods Road. Turn right and take a quick left to drop down to the shoreline.

Large gray-green lichen rosettes, some likely older than the forest trees, decorate the stone wall on the right that you soon pass through. Note the huckleberry and maleberry shrubs. Colonists regarded maleberry as the male blueberry shrub, which of course it is not. Maleberry's "fruits" are small dry capsules. A glance at the pond in summer may reveal the small yellow pealike flowers of bladderwort protruding above the water's surface on slender stalks. Below the surface, the plant's bladders suck in passing minute life forms if the creatures are unlucky enough to touch a triggering bristle. Bear away from the pond and climb gradually into oak woods with a black birch and witch hazel understory. Wild sarsaparilla, sessile-leafed bellwort, and ground pine thrive in the rich soil beneath the woody growth. Now swing down and right, with walls on both sides and some sugar maples. Woodland wildflowers include rattlesnake plantain, whose attractive green leaves are graced by a network of fine white veins, starflower, and Canada mayflower.

Reach flowing Hampton Brook, the pond's source, and cross a bridge over it. Here jewel-like black damselflies flutter on ebony wings. A large yellow birch with four trunks stands on the left just before you come to a T junction. Turn right toward the Far North Woods and cross a dry (in summer) seep where the presence of skunk cabbage betrays the hidden moisture. Pass through a stone wall gap. Ghostly white Indian pipes push up through the rotting oak and maple leaves, taking their nourishment from decaying plants. Enter a small sunny clearing where some trees show beaver gnawing. A few bayberry bushes, more characteristic of the coast, grow here, as do the eye-catching, upturned, fiery orange flowers of wood lily. These gorgeous lilies bloom in midsummer.

Watch for the intersection of the Far North Woods Trail on the left where a red maple tree stands near a red cedar; this is easy to miss. Follow this trail left and through a gap in a stone wall. If you go straight by mistake, you soon come to the beaver pond. Here, Japanese barberry, an exotic invasive shrub, is a sure sign of prior disturbance. The trail now passes through maple-oak-hickory woods that also feature black birch trees and huckleberry shrubs. Striped (spotted) wintergreen, handsome for both its pendant white blossoms and its boldly patterned, dark-green and white foliage, blooms in summer. The two and three blossoms per plant may glow brightly in the dappled but intense sunlight like tiny lanterns. Climb very gradually through drier oak-hickory forest and follow the trail as it bears left and then goes lazily downhill. A vigorous growth of lacy New York fern may be spotlighted on the right when the sun is shining. Walk amid ferns and continue through another stone wall to a trail junction at 1.0 mile.

Turning right would take you to Griffin Road; instead, continue straight. Shortly come to a flowing brook giving life to sizable skunk cabbages and cross it on a bridge. Reach an alder shrub wetland on the right with red maples and horsetails, primitive green raspy stalks without leaves. Big leathery bracken fern stands thigh high along the sunny verge. Climb gradually now into dry oak woods where huckleberry bushes, hay-scented fern, Canada mayflower, and starflower are found. Reach a T junction at 1.3 miles. Turn right and walk down a very modest slope through oak, black birch, and chestnut sprouts. By late July, you can already find some ripe fruits on the highbush blueberries. As you walk over bog bridges through wetlands with skunk cabbage, spicebush, and jewelweed, listen for the lovely *ee-o-lay* song of the wood thrush. Spicebush has very aromatic egg-shaped leaves that exude a definite citrus odor. The foliage sustains the larvae of the exquisite blue-hued spicebush swallowtail butterfly. Bright red fruits appear in late summer.

From this low damp spot, walk slightly up and across a rock wall where tall white ash rise. Proceed uphill and pass a big black oak on the right; the slope drops away to the left. The songs of tufted titmouse, red-eyed vireo, and rose-breasted grosbeak floated to my ears in midsummer. These are just a few of the more than 144 species of birds recorded by the Teales during their years at Trail Wood. Large oak trees, widely spaced, are interspersed with smaller trees—hickory, ironwood, oak, and yellow birch. A glacial boulder (erratic) lies where it came to rest more than ten millennia ago. Look closely and you'll notice that it has been partially split. Drilled holes, 3- to 4-inch-long, bordering its edge indicate where iron rods were inserted. As you walk down the slight slope of the North Boulder Field, find more, smaller glacial boulders. Where the path levels off, remnants of barbed wire, indicating former pastureland,

A MAN FOR ALL SEASONS

Edwin Way Teale (1899–1980) was a meticulous and gifted observer and recorder of nature, a wonderfully insightful naturalist, and a gifted writer. I had admired Teale's writing for years, after reading such now classic works as *North with the Spring* and *Autumn across America*.

One excerpt from *A Naturalist Buys an Old Farm*; in which the author describes some of what he experienced while observing nature from a hollow brush pile of his own creation; reads as follows:

> There was the humming of bees among the mountain mint, the liquid monologue of the waterfall, the steely chorus of the meadow insects, the rushing of wind among the summer leaves. In the hot still days of August, the shrill cicada's song would soar above me among the treetops to end in a descending buzz and a dying sizzle.

Teale had a great gift in that he could explain in very understandable but at the same time evocative prose the extremely complex workings of the natural world. Usually his books dealt with the wilderness that lies just beyond our back doors. A world populated by creatures every bit as fascinating, albeit not as large and glamorous as, say, African elephants and lions.

Teale's philosophy of life on the land is summed up by these passages from the same book:

> We have experienced surprisingly little feeling of possession, of ownership. The deed is ours. But in our minds the trees own the land almost as much as we do. We are one with the robin among the wild cherries in the sunshine. We own Trail Wood together, we and every other wild creature that shares with us these country days.

> In our minds the sense of guardianship, of responsibility, surpasses that of ownership. Our title to the farm gives us the power to protect this small fragment of the earth, these woods, these streams, these fields, and all the inhabitants they contain.

Inside the desk of his writing cabin is this quote from a gravestone in Cumberland, England: "The wonder of the world. The beauty of the power. The shape of things. Their colors. Lights and shades: These I have seen. Look ye also while life lasts."

Edwin Teale certainly followed this admonition throughout his long and fruitful life. It was his credo, and it seems to me to be a fitting epitaph for him as well.

can be seen. The trail swings left. A stone wall runs to the right, and the privately owned land beyond it is partially cleared of trees.

Continue straight ahead past the informal trail junction on the left, and by an L-shaped former cabin foundation. Follow the path through oak-hickory-hazelnut woods as it bears left and downhill along Old Cabin Hill. At 1.6 miles, arrive again at the major six-way intersection. Take the first spoke to the right—the Shagbark Hickory Trail—and cross the dry (in summer) bed of Fern Brook. Come to an unmarked Y-junction almost immediately and take the right fork to Westwoods. This fork is easy to miss. Delicate maidenhair fern, regarded by many as the most beautiful of ferns, spreads airy fans above its ebony stalks. Plenty of Japanese barberry grows here, too, beneath the hickory and oak. Continue gradually down and cross a dry streambed. Red-bellied woodpeckers, which, like the wild turkey, wood duck, blue jay, and chipmunk, are fond of acorns, loudly call *churr-churr-churr* as they hitch up oak trunks. Arrive at a trail intersection on the left that leads downhill. Stay straight and walk through an area where sharp-hooked raspberry canes and prickly barberry shrubs predominate and Virginia creeper spreads its leafy runners over the ground.

Continue leisurely downhill under oak, hickory, and ash, by knee-high maple-leaf viburnum, and past jack-in-the-pulpit and Christmas fern, and then climb gradually into drier oak-hickory woods where pole-sized and smaller black cherries are common. The loud, insistent refrain of the ovenbird rings through the forest, where poison ivy is again common. Soon reach a T intersection. Turn left and walk downhill adjacent to a low stone fence that once bounded a pasture to the right. The modest shoulder of Juniper Hill rises to the left as you walk uphill. Few junipers are actually left now on Juniper Hill. Junipers, also known as red cedars, are sun-loving, pioneer trees that can't tolerate being shaded out by later arrivals. Step through a gap in yet another stone wall, bearing right. Edwin Teale once estimated that their property held nearly 5 miles of old stone walls! After 2.1 miles, arrive at Teale's hand-hewn log writing cabin overlooking a 1-acre pond built in 1963. This is where he did much of his reading and writing during the warmer months.

Turn right to head back toward the former Teale home. Above the far end of the pond stands a screened gazebo known as the Summerhouse. Cross the pond's outlet—Stepping Stone Brook—on a wooden bridge. Purple spikes of pickerelweed soften the shoreline in summer. Recent beaver activity in the form of a small dam immediately downstream of the pond is an interesting juxtaposition of human versus animal pond building. Alders grow thickly now along the pond shore to the left. After crossing the bridge, bear left on a mowed path up through Firefly Meadow. Reach a four-way intersection just below the house. Continue straight up to the lane. We watched a chimney swift fly down the redbrick chimney and back out again, probably just having fed a nest full of young. Turn right and walk 400 feet back to the parking area on the right.

MORE INFORMATION

The Connecticut Audubon Center at Trail Wood is open daily year-round, dawn to dusk. A pit toilet is located at the parking lot. Museum, writing cabin, and study open by appointment only. Admission is free. Connecticut Audubon Center at Trail Wood, 93 Kenyon Road, Hampton, CT 06247; 860-928-4948; http://www.ctaudubon.org/visit/trailwood.htm.

—R. L.

TRIP 38
ROCK SPRING PRESERVE

Location: Scotland
Rating: Moderate
Distance: 3.6 miles
Elevation Gain: 240 feet
Estimated Time: 2.0 hours
Maps: USGS Scotland

This trail is located on a fabulous 450-acre Nature Conservancy property with easy-to-follow trails and diverse natural habitats. This loop trail features wonderful vistas, the scenic Little River Valley, and striking fall foliage. This is one of my favorites!

DIRECTIONS
From the convergence of I-384/Route 6/Route 44 east of Manchester, take Route 6 east for 25.4 miles to its junction with Route 97. From the junction, turn south (left) onto Route 97 and drive 3.6 miles to the refuge entrance on the left. Parking for several vehicles is available off the pavement.

TRAIL DESCRIPTION
Enter maple-ash-oak woods and walk gradually downhill through an old stone wall to a kiosk on the left, where a trail map is posted. Beyond, another stone wall appears on the left as the trail curves right. Note the evergreen Christmas fern and attractive variegated foliage of rattlesnake plantain. In fall, woodland asters bloom white. Private property borders the wall to the left. At the point where both the wall and the path jog left, lowbush blueberry and shinleaf grow. Walk easily down through patches of hay-scented fern. Red maple, bitternut hickory, black oak, white oak, and black birch—some quite large—are the dominant trees. Most are young or of moderate age. The abundance of stone fences reveals that colonial farmers were very serious about keeping livestock out of their crops as well as those of their neighbors. Today they serve as handy lookouts and cover for scampering chipmunks. Pass through a stone wall of mica schist rocks. As the soil dampens, red-fruited spicebush appears, as does cinnamon fern. The latter reaches waist height in clumps of three to ten stems. Ruby-throated hummingbirds use the reddish fuzzy covering on the stems to line their walnut-sized nests. A Japanese barberry thicket on the

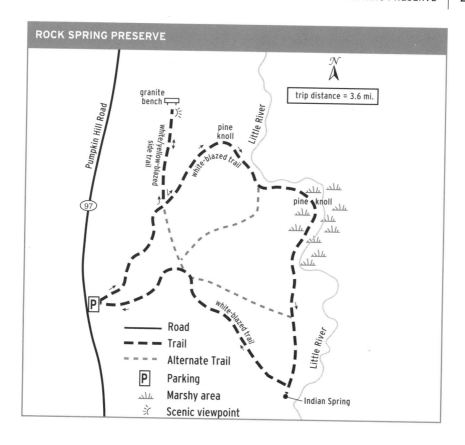

ROCK SPRING PRESERVE

Pumpkin Hill Road

granite bench

white/yellow-blazed side trail

97

pine knoll

white-blazed trail

Little River

trip distance = 3.6 mi.

N

pine knoll

P

white-blazed trail

Little River

Indian Spring

——— Road
- - - Trail
- - - Alternate Trail
P Parking
Marshy area
Scenic viewpoint

left indicates former soil disturbance; an effort to remove some of this invasive shrub is underway.

Cross a rocky intermittent brook bed. The rocks here are of another metamorphic type—gneiss (pronounced *nice*). Gneiss often shows gray and white banding. Christmas, cinnamon, and hay-scented species all flourish where a tiny drainage crosses the white-blazed path. The path turns right when you reach a stone wall. Aromatic spicebush shrubs now grace both sides of the trail. Another stone wall begins on the right and also crosses the path, which is littered with the golden leaves of black and yellow birches in autumn. The trees are mostly 8 to 12 inches in diameter. The wall veers away to the left, the slope becomes steeper, and the trail bears left. The abundant hay-scented ferns fade to light yellow after the first frosts. Ground cedar, one of the non-flowering club mosses, spreads by runners and forms rows of tiny evergreens. Even in fall, the ringing voices of spring peepers resonate through these open woodlands. Yet another rock wall begins on the right, with an abundance of sapling growth in the midst of the larger trees. Thick patches of dark-green Christmas fern thrive near the lower end of the slope, fertilized by nutrients washed down from above. Reach the end of the wall where it and the path meet an old woods road at 0.4 mile. Turn left and walk gradually uphill in the direction of the overlook.

The white-blazed trail picks up again on the other side of the road about 35 feet after you turn left. Continue straight on the road for now; you return to pick up the trail here later. The golden hue of frost-killed hay-scented fern is striking beneath the charcoal trunks of black birch during early October. The old roadway veers left, but the trail to the lookout continues straight. Be sure to follow the trail. In fall, the white-and-yellow-blazed path traverses dead bleached and brown skeletons of New York fern, which are tapered at both ends. Begin easy downhill walking, with stone walls on the right. Bear right, pass through a wall gap, and swing left. Descend to cross an intermittent brook where spicebush reaches 9 to 10 feet in height. The trail curves right after climbing out of the hollow. Cross a drainage, curve left, and climb gradually over gneiss outcrops. Tufted titmice noisily scold intruders as the distant ridge becomes visible through the burnished foliage. There is one last short climb to the viewpoint and an imposing gray granite bench. Black, white, and red oaks shade the overlook, while huckleberry (red foliage in fall) and lowbush blueberry soften the outcrop. Hickory (golden yellow), red maple (scarlet), ash (maroon), and black birch (bright yellow) also contribute brilliance to the autumnal spectacle. The view eastward at any time of year is wonderful.

After taking in this splendid scene, retrace your steps to the old road and continue about 100 yards to where the white-blazed trail turns left. Follow it and cross over a stone wall within rocky oak-hickory-birch woodland carpeted with ferns. Walk easily downhill, with the slope dropping away to the right. Cross an overgrown roadbed. Easily recognized shagbark hickory is present, and small black-and-white, spiny-abdomened spiders hang from silken threads. Feathery plumes of maidenhair fern are held aloft by the plant's slender ebony stems. Continue through thick Christmas fern growth and a fair amount of spicebush shrubbery. The white orbs of white baneberry, or doll's eyes, are indeed reminiscent of the porcelain eyes of Victorian era dolls. The trail bears right at a point where boulders squat on the left and continues gradually downhill. A stand of blue cohoshes straddles the path. In fall, they bear attractive but poisonous clusters of deep blue berries above their leaves.

Cross a drainage (a big ash rises on the left) and another intermittent brook. Walk over a stone wall amid oak, shagbark hickory, maple, and ash, and then reach white pines with 2-foot-plus-diameter furrowed trunks. Where the trail bears left, a mourning cloak butterfly flew rapidly and erratically by during an October walk. Climb easily up the knoll dominated by white pine. Tiny princess pine grows

Red (swamp) maples produce brilliant autumnal foliage along the banks of the scenic Little River.

thickly below its namesake and is joined by ground cedar, lowbush blueberry, and some poison ivy. Ghostly white Indian pipes poke from the pine duff. As they age, the pipe "bowls" turn upward. The trail then turns right and descends. Beaver-cut logs on the knoll seem absurdly out of place until you discover the wetland below. Husks of shagbark hickory nuts litter the path where red squirrels have opened them. Continue downslope and bear left under pine and oak, passing a very large multi-trunked white pine where the path levels out at Little River. Green frogs shriek and leap to safety at your approach until hard frosts send them into winter dormancy. Fish-eating belted kingfisher sometimes flash by, a sure sign that the river flows clear, and with a pleasing gurgle, over its gravelly bottom.

The shrub-lined path soon emerges from the trees and closely follows the streambank. Bank erosion has caused large trees to fall across the river. In October, a comma butterfly alighted upon the blue fruit cluster of a nannyberry shrub, while the shrill screams of a red-shouldered hawk resounded through the valley. The river makes a sharp turn to the left and then back around to the right to create a peninsula covered with broad-leafed deer-tongue grass. You can access the river at this location where the trail curves right. The foliage of autumnal red maple may be a brilliant red here, while the burnished gold of dead royal ferns enlivens the path. Cross a tiny feeder stream on a sturdy wooden bridge for a picturesque view of the colorful wetland to the right. In autumn, winterberry shrubs loaded with coral-red berries are visible on the opposite shore as the trail curves left. Old beaver cuttings are evident. Photo opportunities abound. At 1.5 miles, reach a trail junction on the right; this is a shortcut trail that leads back to the trailhead. Continue straight along the river, however. A tree-mounted sign reads "No Horses Beyond This Point." A giant oak has fallen across the river and serves as a convenient causeway for small mammals.

The trail now curves right, climbs away somewhat steeply from the river onto higher ground, and curves right to the top of a pine-oak knoll with an excellent view of the river. Continue gradually down the knoll's other side. The wooded river wetlands to the left are thick with dogwood and nannyberry shrubs. The ground drops off 8 to 10 feet just left of the trail, which skirts the wetland edge. More fine views of the river valley greet you as you follow the path within the floodplain. An old fallen oak tree serves as support for a beaver dam the big rodents have constructed partially against it. Emerge into a sunny clearing from which another, lower dam is visible. Here a green female katy-did came flying along and, to my surprise, alighted on a greenbrier stalk. Its brown, scimitar-shaped ovipositor was clearly visible. Continue walking past the end of the beaver dam and parallel with the river. New York and cinnamon ferns are common. Pass a big broken white pine, part of which has fallen into the river. You can examine the river from a pebbly bank here. Katydids utter their rhythmic *katy-did, katy-didn't* from the trees. Step over a fallen red maple from which two branches have grown upward to become surrogate trunks for the prostrate tree. The path is very close to the cutbank and no doubt will have to be moved as floodwaters continue to carve away this side of the channel.

More bright clusters of winterberry and many ironwood trees appear just before you reach a wooden bridge over a mostly dry feeder stream that enters the Little River from the left. The trail now bears right, away from the river and the floodplain, and enters a narrow red pine plantation. Virtually nothing survives in the constant shade cast by the pines, which are spaced 6 to 9 feet apart. After 100 yards of walking between pine rows, reenter natural woodland as the trail bears right, then left and uphill. A smaller trail splits off to the right. Continue straight up the gravelly knoll, another gift of the glaciers. Lowbush blueberry and a few pink lady's slippers exist in the acidic soil below the pine and oak. Emerge into a gravelly clearing with young white pine, quaking aspen, prickly dwarf juniper, and little bluestem grass. The trail turns left along the top of a gravel and sand ridge (actually a glacial esker) covered with oak, aspen, and pine. Reindeer lichen forms cushiony mats in a sunny clearing regenerating to white pine and oak. You also can see little bluestem, dwarf juniper, and shining sumac, with deep red fall leaves that glisten in the sunlight.

Reenter oak woods with ground cedar club moss as you continue along this glacial spine. Another small, sandy opening hosts sweet fern. Curve left over gravel and enter oak, black birch, and white pine woodland with abundant lowbush blueberry as well as dwarf juniper clumps. You can even see bayberry, usually found only in coastal areas, in the poor soil. Walk downward, curve left, and enter another cobbled clearing with little bluestem, a common Midwestern prairie grass, reindeer lichen, bayberry, and, in fall, violet-blooming stiff aster. Note the large ant mound in the clearing. Reenter forest, continuing downward and to the left, and reach a trail junction on the right. Turn here to head back to the trailhead, but first walk the 100 feet straight ahead to Indian Spring at 2.5 miles. A raised, round, stone springhead with a concrete lid contains an inscribed stone that reads, Old Bar One Indian Spring. A sign warns against disturbing the soils or stones around the spring. Note the water welling up in a depression and flowing away.

Return to the white-blazed trail and turn left. Ignore another small, unblazed side trail and walk steadily uphill into a young white pine grove, with lowbush blueberry and princess pine below the conifers. The trail curves gently right and leads to a stone wall on the left. Begin climbing to the top of the hill over a path of loose, glacially deposited pebbles and cobbles. Pass through a small grassy opening and soon reach the crest under oak and white pine. A few skeleton red cedars remain, shaded out by the broad-leafed trees. From this low ridge, the land falls away on both sides. Come to an informal trail on the left, but stay straight on the white-blazed trail. This is open oak woodland rejuvenated with the new growth of white pine. The path bears right at a small grassy clearing filled with lowbush blueberry, princess pine with spiky spore-emitting strobules in fall, and ground cedar club moss. Huckleberry shrubs are also common below the oak and red maple. Pass through a stone wall with a huge magnificent spreading and leaning white oak alongside it. It was spared the ax by a farmer who favored it for its shade and acorn bounty. Proceed right, over high ground under oak and birch, once again in the haunt of the vocal red-bellied woodpecker.

The trail undulates over a forest floor softened by grasses, Christmas and hay-scented fern, and wild sarsaparilla. It then curves right and takes you through an imposing stone wall that was originally 4 and even 6 feet wide in places. From here, the level path follows an old woods road to a four-way intersection at 3.2 miles. Turn left onto the white-blazed trail and walk steadily uphill under oak and black birch. Make a sharp turn to the left and pass through a rock wall where a big white ash stands on the left. Bits of rusty barbed wire embedded in the trunks represent what was once a major technological leap from stone walls for enclosing livestock. The path is mostly level now, but bears right and climbs a switchback, turning left. Pass through another stone wall, cross a damp swale,

FALL FINERY

In late summer, as the days gradually shorten, tree leaves halt their production of green chlorophyll as if on cue. The diminishing daylight brings about this change, and gradually, as the chlorophyll dissipates, the other pigments contained in the leaves assert themselves visually. In New England, the maples, both sugar and red, produce some of the most glorious autumnal foliage known anywhere on earth. Weather conditions leading up to this time can influence the quality of the show, but even during so-called poor foliage years, the pageant put on by Mother Nature has few rivals anywhere.

Only after the first frosts do the leaves reveal their most intense colors. Some leaves become a golden yellow, while others, usually the red, or swamp, maple, take on a scarlet-red hue as early as late August. Ashes are transformed into an odd but attractive maroon. The signature bright-yellow and fluorescent-orange foliage of the sugar maple is the most renowned among all the trees and the primary reason that the annual fall foliage spectacle in New England has spawned a multimillion-dollar tourist industry.

The trees, of course, are simply and elegantly preparing for the drought winter brings by hoarding most of their water and nutrients in extensive root systems below ground. When the hard frosts finally come, a layer of cells located at the attachment point of leaf stem and twig gives way, sending billions of spent leaves cascading to the ground and into waterways, where they are eventually broken down by bacteria, fungi, and a host of other microorganisms and soil invertebrates. The nutrients, far from being lost, are reduced to their basic building blocks and made available for incorporation into the tissues of other plants and animals, the ultimate recycling plant.

and continue climbing through lots of hay-scented, New York, and Christmas ferns, spicebush, red maple, ash, hickory, and oak. Bear right, paralleling a well-built chest-high rock wall on the left back to the kiosk straight ahead.

MORE INFORMATION

Rock Spring Wildlife Refuge is open dawn to dusk. Pets not allowed. The Nature Conservancy, Connecticut Chapter, 55 High Street, Middletown, CT 06457-3788; 860-344-0716; www.nature.org/wherewework/northamerica/states/connecticut/preserves/art5368.html.

—R. L.

TRIP 39
RHODODENDRON SANCTUARY

Location: Voluntown
Rating: Easy
Distance: 0.5 mile
Elevation Gain: 10 feet
Estimated Time: 0.5 hour
Maps: USGS Voluntown, Pachaug State Forest (Chapman Area) map available online

The Rhododendron Sanctuary in Pachaug State Forest is one of the most uniquely beautiful places in all of Connecticut. Savor the lovely native rhododendrons as you walk through a cedar swamp during this out-and-back ramble.

DIRECTIONS
From Voluntown center, take combined Routes 138/165/49 east for 0.4 mile to an intersection where Route 49 leaves left. Turn onto Route 49 north and follow it for 0.9 mile to the main entrance to Pachaug State Forest on the left. After entering the forest, proceed along the main road for 0.7 mile to an intersection. Bear left, pass over Misery Brook on a bridge, and enter the Chapman Recreation Area at 0.8 mile. Parking is straight ahead.

TRAIL DESCRIPTION
The trail is blazed with pale blue markers and was once part of the Pachaug Trail. Along the path, patches of shining club moss grow next to princess pine. Shining club moss, also called running pine, is a slender, glossy evergreen plant with hundreds of scruffy little leaves. The plant looks like a little green bottlebrush. Princess pine is also evergreen but looks like a small, 4-inch-tall pine tree growing on the forest floor. As different as these plants look, they are actually related closely, different species of the same group of plants called club moss. Mingling with the running pine and princess pine are clumps of wintergreen and colonies of Canada mayflower.

The path descends the short way to the cedar swamp and begins to traverse the wetland on a raised gravel walkway. To either side, wild iris, skunk cabbage, and sheets of sphagnum moss grow in the tea-colored water. Two types of trees predominate in the waterlogged soil: Canadian hemlock and Atlantic

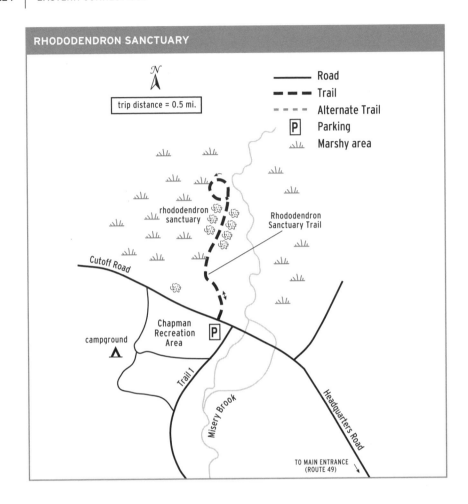

RHODODENDRON SANCTUARY

white lines beneath. It thrives in the cool climate of the wetland, but the standing water atop its roots does have an effect, inhibiting the passage of oxygen to the roots and slowing growth. The result is that even some fairly small trees in the swamp are actually very old. A 6-inch-diameter hemlock in well-drained soil is probably 20 to 30 years old, while a tree of equal size in the cedar swamp can be a hundred years old or more.

The other tree growing here is Atlantic white cedar, a beautiful tree with a strong, straight trunk and smooth, fibrous bark. The evergreen leaves are thin, scaly, and arranged like miniature fans. The wood of Atlantic white cedar is famous for being very resistant to rot. Untreated wood can survive for decades in swamps without rotting. As you proceed farther into the swamp, the first rhododendrons appear, mixed in with highbush blueberry and mountain laurel. As you continue to walk, these plants surround you. The gnarled trunks

Rosebay rhododendron growing in the Rhododendron Sanctuary.

reach up to 15 feet tall with deep, glossy evergreen leaves from 6 to 10 inches long. Crowning each branch is a large flower bud that opens in late June to early July, revealing a showy truss of white-to-light-pink flowers. Gorgeous.

About midway through the swamp, the gravel walkway yields to a boardwalk that guides you the remainder of the way. Near the looping turnaround at the end of the trail is a section where a patch of rhododendrons and the large hemlocks above them have died. The plants grow naturally in swamps yet were killed by too much water. For the last few years, beavers have been busy constructing a dam downstream from the swamp. As the water built up behind the dam, it raised the swamp's water level.

At first glance, it may seem that such a change would do no harm, but a swamp like this one is a very fragile thing. The swamp water damages soil structure, reducing the pore spaces that hold soil air vital to healthy plants. It also forces oxygen from the remaining pores in the soil. Some plants can survive by gleaning oxygen for the roots in different ways. One method relies on

ROSEBAYS

The rosebay is the largest rhododendron of eastern North America, with specimens reaching 35 feet tall. It is native from the coastal plain of Maine through southern New England, and from the Catskills through the Appalachians in northern Georgia. In the northern part of its range, the rosebay is uncommon, forming isolated and often widely separated colonies in swamps and marshes. Farther south, it thrives in the cool climates of the higher elevations of the Appalachian and Great Smoky Mountains, where it can form impenetrable stands in damp forests. It is a spectacular plant and lends a touch of the exotic to wetland forests.

Rosebays are one of two large rhododendrons of the eastern states, the other being the catawba, or mountain rosebay. Catawbas are smaller than rosebays, growing to 20 feet tall with 6-inch-long evergreen leaves as opposed to rosebays' 10-inch-long evergreen leaves. While rosebays sport blush-white blossoms, catawbas display trusses of deep rose to purple-lavender flowers. Catawba rhododendrons grow in a narrow belt in and around the Great Smoky Mountains.

As beautiful as these rhododendrons are in the wild, chances are you don't have to venture past your backyard to appreciate them. Many very popular rhododendron varieties are derived from these native plants. Catawba varieties include "Roseum Elegans," "Cunningham's White," "English Roseum," "President Lincoln," and "Charles Dickens." Rosebay varieties include "Album" and "Purpureum." Any and all of these plants can bring beauty as well as a touch of the wild to your garden.

the stable water level of the swamp. It is much more difficult for oxygen to pass from water into the roots than from soil into the roots. The oxygen content at the surface of the water is high enough so that it can pass relatively easily from the water to the roots. If the water level rises above the root zone, as happened when the beavers flooded the swamp, the plants suffocate. This is such an important and valuable habitat that when the beavers threaten the sanctuary, the dams are removed. Park personnel are monitoring the damaged area to see if the rhododendrons and hemlocks return.

The trail makes a short loop near the flooded area. Retrace your steps to return to the parking area.

MORE INFORMATION

Pachaug State Forest features two campgrounds and offers opportunities for mountain biking, swimming, fishing, boating, backpack camping, and a variety of other activities. Leashed pets are permitted on the trail. An entrance fee of $7 per resident vehicle and $10 per nonresident vehicle is charged on weekends and holidays. No charge on weekdays. Pachaug State Forest, c/o Bureau of Outdoor Recreation, Department of Environmental Protection, 79 Elm Street, Hartford, CT 06106-5127; 860-424-3200; http://www.ct.gov/dep/site/default.asp.

—C. S.

TRIP 40
MOUNT MISERY

Location: Voluntown
Rating: Moderate
Distance: 1.8 miles
Elevation Gain: 170 feet
Estimated Time: 1.0 hour
Maps: USGS Voluntown, Jewett City, Pachaug State Forest (Chapman Area) map is available online

Mount Misery is a pair of rocky promontories in Pachaug State Forest. Its low elevation (441 feet) allows many people who could not climb higher ridges access to the twin summits and their beautiful panoramic views. Also, enjoy plentiful wildflowers and songbirds along this out-and-back trail.

DIRECTIONS

From Voluntown center, take combined Routes 138/165/49 east for 0.4 mile to an intersection where Route 49 leaves left. Turn onto Route 49 north and follow it for 0.9 mile to the main entrance to Pachaug State Forest on the left. After entering the forest, proceed along the main road for 0.7 mile to an intersection. Bear left, pass over Misery Brook on a bridge, and enter the Chapman Recreation Area at 0.8 mile. Parking is straight ahead.

TRAIL DESCRIPTION

The walk to Mount Misery is along the Nehantic/Pachaug Trail, which is marked with pale blue blazes. Turns are noted by two stacked blazes, with the upper blaze offset in the direction of the turn.

From the Chapman Area parking lot, walk northwest down Cutoff Road past the trail to the Rhododendron Sanctuary (see Trip 39) on the right. Continue northwest down the forest road to the green gate. Pass through the gate and cross a small stream in a hemlock grove. Just beyond the stream, the combined Nehantic/Pachaug Trail enters the woods on the left (south). Follow the blue blazes into the grove of hemlock and white pine. The shady evergreens and the soft feel of needles underfoot make this section of trail especially inviting in summer. In winter, the grove is a refuge for such wintering birds as chickadees, titmice, downy woodpeckers, nuthatches, and brown creepers.

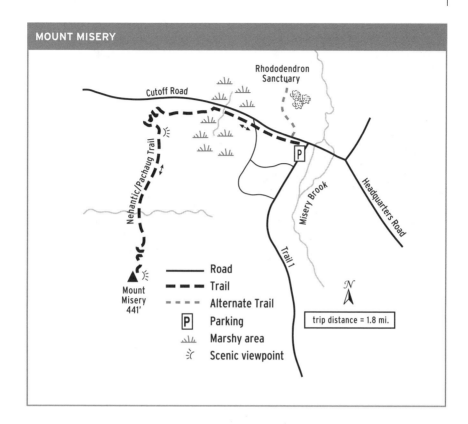

Sometimes small groups of kinglets also spend time in the shelter of the hemlock branches.

Beneath the trees are thickets of laurel and one or two Atlantic white cedars. As the path climbs the north slope of Mount Misery, the cool evergreens increasingly give way to oaks. The trail becomes rocky as the path weaves up the hill using a series of switchbacks. From May to late summer, warblers and thrushes sing in the woods. As the trail crests the hill, it turns sharply left (east) and proceeds through woods of white pine, hemlock, and oak to the first summit (0.5 mile), a bare rock shelf with a nice easterly view. This is a great spot (360 feet elevation) to stop and rest a bit. The frequent breeze here discourages bugs from bothering you too much in summer. In fall, the colorful foliage makes the view even better. An old windfall lies across the ledge, while wild cherry trees ring the bare bedrock.

From the first summit, the trail follows the contour of the ledge south, offering peekaboo views through the trees. In winter, this is a pleasant walk, with broad vistas available through the bare branches. The forest along the ridge is typical of rocky woodlands in southern Connecticut, with white pine, oak, and

The top of Mount Misery is a favorite place to take in the view and relax.

pitch pine. Colonies of lowbush blueberry blossom in late April and produce small but tasty berries in late July and early August. Wintergreen is another plant that grows along the path. This trailing woody plant has glossy evergreen leaves about an inch or two long. In spring, small white flowers appear, followed in late summer by bright red berries. Wintergreen is easy to identify because the leaves and berries always smell of wintergreen.

Soon the trail begins a gentle descent, passing isolated plants of spotted wintergreen and pipsissewa. Both these wildflowers have evergreen leaves and springtime waxy, whitish flowers with five petals. The path then comes to a small brook (0.7 mile) that marks the low point between the north summit and the peak of Mount Misery. Cross the stream on a plank bridge and begin the climb to the top of Mount Misery. The path becomes steeper as you pass through woods of beech, oak, and white pine. Isolated specimens of highbush blueberry offer tasty treats in late summer.

The grade steepens as the terrain becomes studded with boulders and rock outcrops. The last section of trail is steep and passes by a large rock from which there is a pleasing view before gaining the crest of the mountain at 0.9 mile. The summit area of Mount Misery is mostly bare rock ledge with scattered white pine, bear oak, and pitch pine. Thorny strands of greenbrier snake through the brush. The views from the bedrock ledges are more than worth the climb, with a panoramic vista to the south, east, and north that includes parts of Connecticut and Rhode Island.

One of the birds that frequents the ridge is the eastern towhee. The male has a black head and back and chestnut-colored sides, while the female has a gray head and back and chestnut sides. Towhees are frequent ground feeders and have a habit of searching for meals by quickly hopping forward and backward in dry leaves to uncover prey. These little birds make a great deal of noise while looking for food, which can frighten the heck out of people unfamiliar with the woods. A little investigation, however, reveals the innocent nature of the disturbance. To return to the parking area, simply retrace your steps.

MORE INFORMATION

Pachaug State Forest features two campgrounds and offers opportunities for mountain biking, swimming, fishing, boating, backpack camping, and a variety of other activities. Leashed pets are permitted on the trail. An entrance fee of $7 per resident vehicle and $10 per nonresident vehicle is charged on weekends and holidays. No charge on weekdays. Pachaug State Forest, c/o Bureau of Outdoor Recreation, Department of Environmental Protection, 79 Elm Street, Hartford, CT 06106-5127; 860-424-3200; http://www.ct.gov/dep/site/default.asp.

—C. S.

TRIP 41
LAUREL LOOP

Location: Voluntown
Rating: Moderate
Distance: 3.0 miles
Elevation Gain: 130 feet
Estimated Time: 2.0–3.0 hours
Maps: USGS Voluntown, Pachaug State Forest (Green Falls Area) map available online

This walk along Laurel Loop is in the Green Falls Area of Pachaug State Forest. You'll find old stone foundations, a forested marsh, and mountain laurel in abundance. This walk is a must for hikers with a love of laurel.

DIRECTIONS
From the center of Voluntown, proceed to the south junction of Routes 138/49. Turn south onto Route 49 and travel 2.0 miles to Fish Road on the left (a sign reads "Green Falls Entrance"). Turn left onto Fish Road and travel 0.8 mile to a pull-off parking area on the right. Park here and walk 0.2 mile farther down Fish Road to a junction where a tollbooth is placed in season. The trailhead enters the woods on the east side of the road near the tollbooth.

TRAIL DESCRIPTION
The Laurel Loop Trail is marked with a yellow dot in a pale blue rectangle. Mileages listed here are from the tollbooth.

Enter the woods on the eastern side of the tollbooth and pass through a forest of white pine, oak, and laurel. Get used to the view, because this oak and laurel forest, so typical of many parts of south and central Connecticut, seems to go on for miles. The trail proceeds gently uphill through a nonstop sea of evergreen laurel leaves. In June, this walk is spectacular, with frothy clouds of whitish-pink blossoms floating on glossy green leaves. These woods are home to many creatures as well as beautiful plants. Garter snakes are common in the dry woodlands and enjoy sunning themselves in the dappled light beneath the oaks. Deer come through from time to time, and even the odd coyote and fox are here.

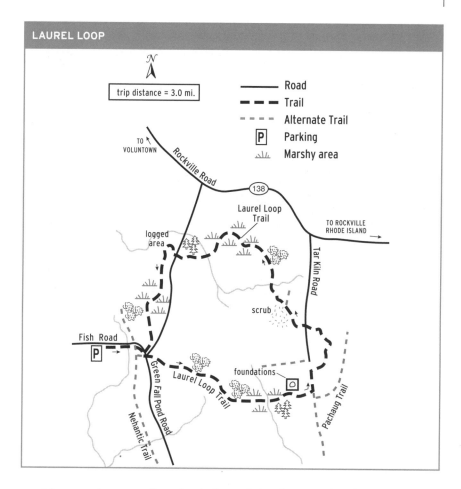

After crossing a small wetland, the path levels out. What follows is one of the nicest stretches of trail anywhere. For a long while, the laurel creeps up to the edges of the trail, touching your arms and shoulders as you pass by. The tall shade of the oaks is omnipresent, and together they afford a wonderfully relaxing serenity. Sometimes the laurel is only waist high, while at other times it towers over your head like an emerald-colored arch. In spring and summer, the migrant songbirds can be heard from the trees or within the evergreen thickets near the path.

The trail now takes an easy downhill course to a shallow swale with a small stream meandering through the bordering wetland. The laurel yields to bramble and greenbrier, an aggressive vining plant with grabby black thorns and clusters of blue-black fruits that persist from fall to spring. In addition to greenbrier and tall oak trees, ruffed grouse like this swampy area. They like to

Heaped stones create old fountains along the Laurel Loop Trail.

SPRING PEEPERS

Nearly 50 years ago, my mother and father built their home on the highlands above the Quinnipiac River in Cheshire. Long ago the rusty red soil had supported a farm, but the once cleared fields had quickly become the home of red cedar and northern red oak. Two immense shagbark hickories stood watch near the driveway, native trout swam in the pond behind the house, and spotted turtles lived in a small brook behind the horse barn. This was a place that had lots of things to keep an outdoorsy kid happy. One of the things I looked forward to most each year was the chorus of the peepers come spring.

Peepers are very small frogs, a little over an inch long, that spend most of their life hopping through the woods looking for spiders and ants to eat. They live around us all summer long, yet we rarely see them except during the week or so in early spring when they gather at the ponds to mate and sing. In winter, peepers spend the cold months under leaves and roots in the woods. As the temperatures drop, the frogs get so cold that their bodies freeze. But when the warmer weather comes, their bodies thaw out and they hop down to the nearest swamp to mate. This is when peepers congregate by the thousands in ponds and marshes. The song of a peeper is a high-pitched trill, pure and melodic when one or two are singing. When hundreds are singing at once, which often happens on a warm spring night, the crescendo can be so loud that it can hurt the ears.

As a boy, I could catch everything from frogs to dragonflies by hand. But peepers eluded me. Each spring I would hear them, but I could never find any. I would try to sneak up on singing frogs, only to have them fall silent and seemingly vanish. Every time I searched for them, all I got was wet. One spring evening, I convinced my father to don knee-high rubber boots and accompany me to the marsh. I figured there was strength in numbers. He carried the flashlight while I held on to the Mason jar with nail holes punched in the lid.

It took a long time for me to find any peepers careless enough to allow me to approach. Finally, however, I saw one clinging to a sedge stem that rose from the dark water. In a few seconds, I had him in my hands and put him in the jar. As the flashlight illuminated his tiny body, I remember being amazed that I was actually looking at the source of such joyous song. Then I allowed my selfishness to guide my actions and took the peeper home. I brought the jar upstairs to my room and placed it on my dresser.

I flicked off the light, climbed into bed, and waited what seemed like hours for the peeper to fill my room with the song of the outdoors. But the song never came. I realized a wonderfully important lesson: some things, no matter how beautiful, you just can't take home. I could capture the peeper, even take it home, but I couldn't capture its spirit, its *raison d'être*. The song of a peeper, like so many beautiful things, is an undeserved gift and as such cannot be purchased, stolen, or commanded. Instead it is a bounty for the humble and loving.

That morning I took the jar off the dresser and hiked back to the marsh. The songs of red-winged blackbirds singing from the cattails were the only sounds. The peepers, wherever they were, were silent. I unscrewed the top, lowered the jar to the water, and let him go.

That evening the peepers sang all night long. As I fell slowly into a peaceful sleep, the soprano chorus of hundreds of peepers slipped through my open bedroom window and filled the room with sound. On my dresser the empty Mason jar shone silent in the moonlight.

hide from predators (to a grouse, a hiker is perceived to be as much a predator as a coyote). They have a habit of waiting until you are almost on top of them and then burst out of the scrub with a thunderous flapping of wings to scare the life out of you. Folks who often walk the woods eventually get used to it, but I know some people who have been hikers for years and still jump every time a grouse flushes nearby.

From the stream (0.7 mile), it is a short walk through a dead red pine grove to a complex of stone foundations that are truly interesting sights. The stones are arranged in a Stonehenge-like pattern, producing a wall shot full of large spaces. From the foundations, the woods are open and lovely. The path is level at first and then begins a gradual climb to a scrubby clearing where a grassy woods road runs north to south (0.9 mile).

Turn left (north) and follow the grassy road through scrubby blueberry, laurel, and sheep laurel. Just before a rock barricade near private land on the left, the trail turns right, leaves the woods road, and enters the woods on the right. The trail wades through more waist-high scrub, passing a rock outcrop before coming back to the road, though this time it is paved and called Tar Kiln Road. Cross the road (1.1 miles) onto a wide grassy woods road that is easy to follow and comfortable to walk. Highbush blueberry affords a nice wild treat in late summer.

Laurel Loop Trail proceeds through a scrubby area and then abruptly leaves the woods road to the left while an unmarked path proceeds straight ahead. This turn can be missed easily. Look for a blaze on a tree to the left. The path then heads downhill into very thick tangles of laurel and crosses a small stream. The laurel is like a jungle through here, often growing well over your head. From the stream, continue through a patch of tall trees before again descending to a marshy area overgrown with greenbrier. A privately owned field is just to the right.

The trail then passes through a long section of mixed pine and hardwood, eventually coming to a stream spanned by a quaint wooden bridge at 1.9 miles. Cross the bridge and proceed through a cool pine grove that provides welcome relief on a hot summer's day.

From the pine grove, it is a short walk to the junction with a dirt forest road (2.0 miles). Cross the road and follow the path into a logged area. The trail continues downhill, crossing several wet, swampy areas beneath the shade of dark green hemlock trees. Laurel Loop then passes through waves of laurel, crossing more small streams before emerging from the woods near the tollbooth at 2.6 miles. From the tollbooth, it is a short walk back to the parking area.

MORE INFORMATION

Pachaug State Forest features two campgrounds and offers opportunities for mountain biking, swimming, fishing, boating, backpack camping, and a variety of other activities. Leashed pets are permitted on the trail. An entrance fee of $7 per resident vehicle, $10 per nonresident vehicle is charged on weekends and holidays. No charge weekdays. Pachaug State Forest, c/o Bureau of Outdoor Recreation, Department of Environmental Protection, 79 Elm Street, Hartford, CT 06106-5127; 860-424-3200; http://www.ct.gov/dep/site/default.asp.

—C. S.

TRIP 42
DAY POND STATE PARK/
SALMON RIVER STATE FOREST LOOP

Location: Colchester
Rating: Moderate
Distance: 2.6 miles
Elevation Gain: 170 feet
Estimated Time: 1.5 hours
Maps: USGS Moodus, Day Pond State Park map available online

Evidence of colonial era settlement and industry add to the enjoyment of a pleasant walk through rock-strewn woodland showing abundant signs of glacial action.

DIRECTIONS

From Route 2, take exit 16 (Route 149) in Colchester. Note the state park sign at Route 149 and follow it south for 3.0 miles. Take a hard right onto Peck Lane and drive 0.1 mile to Day Pond Road on the left (note the black-and-white sign). Follow it for 0.6 mile to the parking area on the right (second gate).

TRAIL DESCRIPTION

When the gravel road on the right is gated, park and follow it past a pit toilet on the left to the west end of Day Pond and the stone dam that was restored in 1935 by the Civilian Conservation Corps. The original dam, constructed by the colonial-era Day family, once powered a sawmill. The pond's root beer–colored water, stained by tannins, now tumbles unimpeded over the spillway. Cross the dam and immediately turn left onto the blue-blazed Salmon River Trail (North Loop).

An old wood road leads through forest dominated by smooth gray American beech, oaks, and yellow birch. The monarchs of the forest, however, are the towering tulip trees. Their columnar trunks are limb-free for the first 50 feet! At a small tributary of Day Pond Brook a blazed post indicates a left turn off the former road. Follow it to a buried cable right-of-way that becomes a shallow streambed during wet weather. Walk 50 feet left and re-enter the woods on the right. Flat mica crystals imbedded in the gneiss (pronounced *nice*) rocks

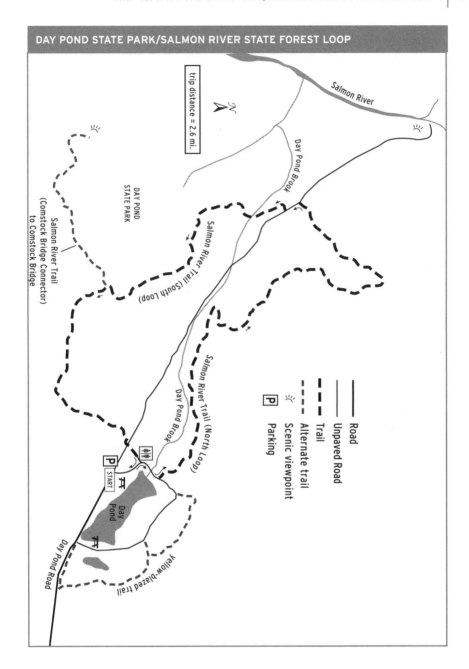

DAY POND STATE PARK/SALMON RIVER STATE FOREST LOOP

trip distance = 2.6 mi.

Salmon River

Day Pond Brook

DAY POND STATE PARK

Salmon River Trail (Comstock Bridge Connector) to Comstock Bridge

Salmon River Trail (South Loop)

Salmon River Trail (North Loop)

Day Pond Brook

Day Pond Brook

Day Pond

START

Day Pond Road

Yellow-blazed trail

Road
Unpaved Road
Trail
Alternate trail
Scenic viewpoint
P Parking

Scenic Day Pond Brook gushes year-round, fed by the impounded waters of Day Pond, just upstream.

sparkle like diamonds. You'll also pass rocks with large crystals of quartz, feldspar, and mica known as pegmatite as Day Pond Brook gurgles soothingly. After a few hundred feet, you'll leave the 180-acre state park and enter the nearly 6,000-acre Salmon River State Forest. Beware that the forest is open to deer hunting in the fall (except on Sundays).

A Lilliputian forest of princess pine club moss carpets the woodland floor and candle-like structures produce countless spores once used in primitive flash photography. You'll soon reach a trail junction; turn right and follow the blue-blazed path uphill. Turning left leads to the brook. This oak woodland has an evergreen understory of mountain laurel. Soon reach another break in the forest—a power-line clearing. Light-loving bracken fern and fragrant sweetfern (not really a fern) thrive here. Cross the right of way and re-enter oak woodland. Watch for an eye-catching glacial boulder the size of a cabin and topped by poison ivy. The path leads over ledges, through a gap in a fallen stone wall, and then downhill, within a shallow trough. After leaf fall, you'll spy a scenic ledge outcrop some 100 feet to the right.

More evidence of eighteenth century human activity is the rock wall that impounds a tiny brook, creating a shrub wetland filled with spicebush, winterberry, highbush blueberry, and ultra-absorbent sphagnum moss. You are again following an old roadway that leads eventually to a former farmstead. Once there, note what was probably a large rectangular stone pen on the left, now filled with evergreen Christmas fern. Another similar structure is located right of the trail. Tall non-native spruce trees are another clue to former settlement. Small foundations are situated adjacent to the pen, just before you reach abandoned Day Pond Road. Turn left to follow the road bordered by a substantial rock wall past a decaying automobile chassis (circa 1960) for approximately 200 feet. Note the remnants of barbed wire engulfed by a stalwart row of sugar maples along the former thoroughfare. It's difficult to imagine now that the wire once bordered pasture.

Turn right at the blue-blazed path (you've come 1.4 miles so far) to re-enter forest and then left when you reach a trail junction beneath white pines and shade-tolerant young hemlocks. You'll soon discover four more foundations adjacent to Day Pond Brook just before coming to a short wooden footbridge at what might once have been a mill raceway. After you walk gradually uphill through a stand of hemlocks, the path splits just before the powerline right-of-way. Turn right and cross the clearing bordered by raspberry canes. Such artificial clearings provide habitat for birds that require shrubby habitats for successful nesting. Shade-tolerant striped wintergreen plants are common

An eye-catching boulder the size of a small cabin was dropped here by a retreating glacial ice sheet.

in the forest beyond. On one autumnal outing I noticed tan, cushiony gypsy moth egg clusters adhering to tree trunks and boulders. Upon hatching, the caterpillars quickly defoliate oaks and other deciduous species, but generally the trees leaf out again creating a "second spring" in summer.

Proceeding gradually upslope takes you into dry, acidic woodland dominated by oaks, with a few red maples and hickories. Hop hornbeam and blue-beech or musclewood make up the understory, while huckleberry, maple-leaved viburnum, and blueberry compose the shrub layer. When you the reach the well-signed intersection with the Comstock Bridge Trail at a small clearing, continue straight on the Salmon River Trail South Loop. (The covered bridge is a 2.0-mile walk each way.) Almost immediately you cross the underground cable right-of-way and descend gradually to a tiny brook. Beyond, a massive house-sized boulder lies on the right where the retreating glacial ice dropped it. A mile-thick ice sheet burdened Connecticut for some 14,000 years! Old stumps of large trees attest to former logging. But the forest has since matured, creating favorable habitat for our largest woodpecker, the magnificent red-crested pileated. Listen for its somewhat maniacal call.

Finally, bear right at a stone wall and parallel it for a short stretch before turning left to pass through a break in it. This takes you across gravel Day

Pond Road (the paved section and yellow gate are visible to the right). Across the road, a gigantic sawn tulip tree log straddles the trail. Day Pond is visible ahead; turn right to return to your vehicle.

MORE INFORMATION

Day Pond State Park is open 8 A.M. to sunset. Leashed pets are permitted in picnic areas and on trails. Parking fee for resident vehicle weekends/holidays $7, $10 for nonresident vehicle. No fees on weekdays. Day Pond State Park, c/o Eastern District HQ, 209 Hebron Road, Marlborough, CT 06447; 860-295-9523; http://www.ct.gov/dep.

—R. L.

TRIP 43
BURNHAM BROOK PRESERVE

Location: East Haddam
Rating: Easy, with moderate sections
Distance: 1.7 miles
Elevation Gain: 170 feet
Estimated Time: 1.5 hours
Maps: USGS Hamburg, Burnham Brook Preserve map

Historic stone walls, a hemlock ravine and brook, ledge outcrops, and a huge glacial erratic imbue this 1,122-acre Nature Conservancy preserve with plenty of rural charm and atmosphere.

DIRECTIONS

From the north, follow Route 2 and then Route 11; take Exit 5 (Witch Meadow Road), turning right at the bottom of the ramp. Follow Witch Meadow Road for 0.5 mile and then turn left onto West Road and drive 2.5 miles to Dolbia Hill Road. Turn right and travel 0.55 mile up Dolbia Hill Road to the entrance on the right (second barway).

From the west, follow I-95 to Old Lyme, Exit 70, and turn left at the bottom of the ramp onto Route 156. Follow it for 9.0 miles to its terminus and turn right onto Route 82. Continue for 2.5 miles to Woodbridge Road, turn left, and drive 1.0 mile; then turn left onto Dolbia Hill Road. Follow it 0.55 mile.

From Exit 77 off I-395, turn north onto Route 85 and drive 10.0 miles to the traffic light at Route 82. Turn left onto Route 82 and drive 2.3 miles to Woodbridge Road. Travel for 1.0 mile on Woodbridge Road, turn left onto Dolbia Hill Road, and follow it for 0.55 mile.

TRAIL DESCRIPTION

This loop walk begins at a three-rail barway and proceeds into the woods on a wide lane demarked by sturdy stone walls. Oak, hickory, and sugar maple shade the entryway. Red cedars, now shaded out, border the lane on the right. To the left on the crest of Dolbia Hill are private hayfields. Wooden nest boxes in the large field host bluebird broods in spring and summer. Hay-scented ferns that take on a honey color in fall line the level path. The mosaic of forest canopy is composed of red maple, whose scarlet leaves are stunning in autumn against a cobalt-blue sky, black cherry, and black oak. Red cedar and

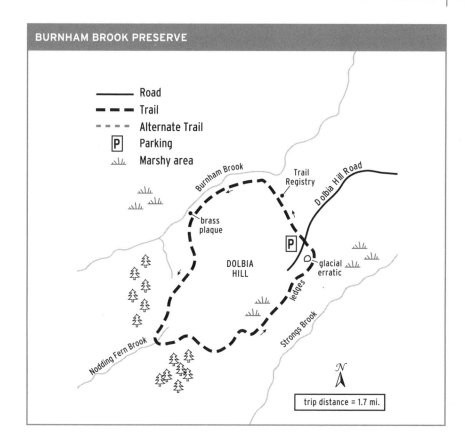

BURNHAM BROOK PRESERVE

——— Road
▬ ▬ ▬ Trail
▬ ▬ ▬ Alternate Trail
P Parking
⬤ Marshy area

Burnham Brook

Trail Registry

Dolbia Hill Road

brass plaque

P

DOLBIA HILL

glacial erratic

ledges

Nodding Fern Brook

Strongs Brook

N

trip distance = 1.7 mi.

sassafras form a second, lower tier, while highbush blueberry dominates the shrub layer.

Come to a trail junction on the right at an opening in a stone wall; continue straight and begin walking gradually downhill. Beyond the three wooden rails on the left, bucolic views of the field beckon. Periodic cutting keeps it from regenerating to forest. Pass a second stone wall gap; large, dark mica crystals are very apparent in the rocks at your feet. Pinkish feldspar crystals are also noticeable. Two oak species join the mix—white oak and chestnut oak—while black (or sweet) birch and sassafras are common.

Reach a sign and trail register (map available here) at the corner of a wall that was used as a convenient repository for additional rocks cleared in subsequent springs. Proceed straight downhill; the rock wall on the left continues. A stout grapevine with brown, shredding bark climbs high into a supporting white oak here. In fall, the foliage display is gorgeous. A low stone wall now begins on the right, bounded beyond by a sea of hay-scented fern. A few boulders repose on this gradual slope among the ferns, also known as boulder fern.

Common birds of the oak woods—bold and raucous blue jays and impudent tufted titmice—add their voices to the music made by fluttering leaves. As you continue, New York and hay-scented fern form a veritable carpet, while wild geranium blooms pink along the path in spring. At a yellow birch, the trail jogs right as the stone fence to the left bends away in that direction. Reach a brook that flows only during wet seasons. Spicebush shrubs indicate the moister soil. Cross the drainage and follow blue blazes, more numerous now, steadily but comfortably downhill. Both highbush and lowbush blueberries, ironwood, young American beech, and black cherry regenerate under the canopy of chestnut, red, and white oaks, red maple, black birch, and tulip tree. Chestnut oak seedlings, which do well on dry, well-drained sites, are numerous. Their wavy-edged leaves are not typically oak-like. Huckleberries, whose leaves are covered with minute resin dots, unlike those of the similar blueberry, appear.

Bear left at the base of the slope, walking on a terrace, with the slope dropping away to the right down to the brook that is as yet not visible. The trees—many of them beech—appear quite young, with few trunk diameters greater than 10 inches. The impression is one of rather open woods with little undergrowth. Hop hornbeam, an understory tree with thin, flaky brown bark, first appears here, along with many ironwoods with rippled, muscular gray trunks. Pass under a 14-inch-diameter hemlock, the largest so far, and then spot on the left one that is a full 2 feet across. The timber becomes larger as you pass around the end of an old fallen tree. Walk through an intermittent drainage; along its margins, a few Christmas fern as well as spicebush and New York fern find sufficient moisture. In autumn, the sugar maples' golden foliage is eye-popping. The dark green leaves of mountain laurel shrubs stand out as if polished, sunlight reflecting brightly off their leaf surfaces.

At a sugar maple, the trail turns right and proceeds downhill gently. A few small flowering dogwood trees, which blossom in May, stand on the right near two large ashes. Yellow birch becomes more numerous, and a thicket of gnarled mountain laurel, comes into view. Pass through a wall and bear left toward a large hemlock. Katydids, sounding far bigger than they are, call their names rhythmically from the foliage high above. Sometimes they shorten the verse simply to *did . . . did.* Enter laurels just above Burnham Brook and follow the path diagonally down. Hemlock and yellow birch are much more common in this cool ravine. Reach rocky, permanent Burnham Brook, a tributary of the Eight Mile River, which flows directly into Long Island Sound approximately 8 miles south. Outcrops of 450-million-year-old gneiss (pronounced *nice*) rock are visible on the far side. The trail, somewhat difficult to distinguish after leaf-fall, now turns left and parallels the brook. Interrupted fern and creeping partridgeberry line the path. Yellow birch is one of my favorite trees—the burnished-brass look of the curly metallic bark is unique; in winter, low-angle rays of sunlight reflecting off the yellowish trunks make them stand out in a most pleasing and easily recognizable way.

Cross a small feeder stream where leafy liverworts cling to the damp stones. Walk under a fallen but still living hemlock whose rootball is bedecked with moss and shining club moss. Hemlock is especially numerous on the north-facing left slope, while deciduous trees predominate on the sunnier, opposite side. In summer, resident hermit thrushes bathe in the brook. At a boulder on the left, the trail begins to climb above Burnham Brook. One old red maple trunk is blackened by fire. As you climb, the ravine grows deeper and more clothed in hemlock. A very large (2 feet in diameter), straight, and tall American beech stands at the point where the trail bears left, then right. At just under 0.5 mile, reach a brass plaque mounted on a boulder that commemorates the preserve's establishment in 1960. It is dedicated to John Ide, a donor and one of its founders. Horizontal ledge rock outcrops poke out just beyond the brook, exposed by water erosion. The trail now swings left and upslope, away from the brook, through open woods. A rotting piece of wood hid a 2.5-inch-long red-backed salamander on a late-October visit.

A rock wall comes into view above you on the left. The trail undulates as it continues along the shoulder of the modest slope. Skirt the end of a stone wall. A low wall, reduced to rubble, trails off at a sharp angle to the right. Pass a grapevine climbing up a hemlock just before you enter hardwoods—red maple, yellow birch, oak, and tulip tree—with patches of New York fern beneath. Walk by tulip trees that have 2-foot-plus diameters. From late summer, winterberry shrubs are adorned with bright red fruits. Grapevines with stringy bark hang down on the right from small trees, including hop hornbeam. Continue under a low overhang of winterberry. Another rock pile sits in the right angle of a stone wall on the left as you walk gently uphill. The stone fence to the left is formidable—chin high to an adult of average height. When first built, it took two strong individuals one long day to construct 10 feet of it. In 1871, the state contained 20,505 miles of them! Make a right turn at a young yellow birch displaying a double blue blaze. In fall, the ground is blanketed with spent leaves, except where turkey and deer have been foraging for acorns. Plenty of shade-tolerant hemlocks grow below the oak, maple, and birch.

Walk gradually downslope amid excited alarm cries of blue jays. Small rock piles are numerous on the forest floor. It is difficult to believe that what is now woodland once produced livestock rather than yellow birch and eastern hemlock. Where sunlight penetrates the canopy, ferns flourish. The path turns left at

False hellebore, with its attractive pleated leaves, is one of the first plants to emerge along brooks in early spring-well before its modest green blossoms.

a double-blazed black birch and continues through shady hemlock, oak, birch, and maple woods, with mountain laurel, the state flower, below. Gray squirrels gather acorns on the forest floor in preparation for the oncoming winter. Ledge outcrops are visible up the slope to the right, capped by dead hemlocks. Listen for the maniacal call of the pileated woodpecker, a crow-sized bird that requires extensive mature forest. Pass through a seasonally damp area. If you visit during dry periods, you may still hear water flowing beneath the rocks when you reach the brook bed. The trail, however, turns right just before you reach the brook's bank. This is easy to miss, as there are no blazes here.

Turn right and follow the bank. A double blue blaze now comes into view ahead as the land rises on both sides. Turn left at the double blaze, cross Nodding Fern Brook at nearly 1.0 mile, and bear right along the shoulder of a rocky talus slope. Gray gneiss ledges hem in the rocky brook channel downstream. Crusty greenish-gray lichens cling ever-so-tightly to the rocks of the slope, joined by green mosses. Evergreen wood fern also pokes up among the boulders. With a little imagination, the dark green mats of moss look like a forest seen from an airplane high above. Some of the moss has a furry quality—almost a green version of the forehead hair of a Hereford cow. Pass a four-trunked red oak on the left and continue uphill, soon reaching the top of the ledge outcrop. Virginia creeper vines cling to some boulders. From here, you'll be treated to nice views of the forest below, especially after leaf-fall.

Bear left and squeeze through a cleft in the rocks. A white quartz vein is evident at the top of one boulder on the left, immediately beyond the cleft. Follow along the top of the ledge as it bears left; you find many dead hemlocks here. Pincushion-like masses of silver mound moss line the rocks along the path. This scenic location is a fine place to relax and have a snack. The trail continues to climb and curve left, away from the cliff face, and then bears right under picturesque mountain laurel shrubs whose foliage is above your head. Pass an isolated boulder on the right and note that most hemlocks here are dead, killed by tiny sap-sucking insects known as woolly adelgids. Continue on rather level ground under white oak, red maple, and more laurel bushes. The slope drops away to the right. A surprising woodland singer is the familiar eastern chipmunk, whose clucks and chirps are uncannily birdlike to the uninitiated ear. Just below the ledge on the right runs an old cedar fence line, the wire long ago having disintegrated. Descend gradually as the trail parallels the outcrop.

Turn sharply right at a point marked by double blazes just before reaching the end of a rock wall on the right. Walk down to the old cedar-post fence line, bear right, and cross it diagonally. To the right are fine views of the ledge just crossed. Proceed toward a large windfall that was chain-sawed where it fell across the trail, but be sure to turn left just before it. The trail splits at the log; do not follow the right fork. Instead turn left and walk past the rootball of the fallen tree, up the slope under hemlock, black birch, and oak. This turn can be missed easily. When the path reaches the top of the cliff, bear left and follow along the outcrop. Oak and young beech trees predominate as the outcropping drops off sharply to the right. White-breasted nuthatches call *yank-yank* as they cling head down to the rough bark of white oaks, and huckleberry grows profusely here.

Continue walking near the cliff edge for a fine view of the forest below; a wooded ridge beyond is enhanced by leaf-fall. You are headed northeast now, over the top of these 40-foot-high ledges. The rocks are coated with the rosettes of gray-green leafy lichens.

Beyond a pair of trees (an oak on the right and a hickory on the left) 30 feet, the path turns right and heads with moderate steepness downhill off the ledge. To the right, rocks line the path. Before reaching a stone wall ahead, turn left at a blazed oak and walk easily downhill, adjacent to the ledges on the left above. You're progressing along the edge of a hemlock stand. On the

FENCES IN THE FOREST

Perhaps Connecticut should be known as the stone wall state. Given its very modest size, this state had an incredible 20,505 miles of stone fences in 1871, fully one-third of all fences in the state at that time. I've come to marvel at these byproducts of Yankee agriculture. Having grown up in the Midwest, I never actually took them for granted, but I never fully appreciated them either until reading about what went into their construction.

Stone walls—more accurately stone fences—served as real barriers that prevented grazing livestock from getting into one's neighbor's or, for that matter, one's own cornfields. And this was not taken lightly during the colonial era, when nearly everyone's livelihood depended upon subsistence agriculture. It was each farmer's solemn responsibility to keep his walls in good repair, lest he court the wrath of both his immediate neighbors and the community. To a far lesser extent, they also served as boundary markers.

It took two strong individuals one long day to build 10 feet of well-constructed stone wall. That included collecting the raw material the glaciers were so generous in providing and building a foundation that had to begin 2 feet below the surface to ensure that the wall would not be damaged by frost heave. A properly constructed wall was at least 4 feet high. The heavy stones—one cubic foot of granite weighs 150 pounds, for instance—were hauled by oxen (and later by plow horses) on wooden sledges known as "stone boats."

But why stone for fences? Stone was an abundant building material and wood was scarce, especially right after the Revolution. Every household burned 30 to 40 cords of firewood each year—a huge amount by today's standards. New England was, as a result, only 20 percent forested back then. Stone was a last choice, really, but these fences lasted forever if properly maintained.

Each spring the action of freezing and thawing ground water brought a new "crop" of tough gneiss or granite stones to the surface, which had to be cleared before planting could commence. Is it any wonder, then, that New England's rocky ground was abandoned for the thick, fertile, black prairie soils of the Midwest in the 1840s?

Today these walls, so seemingly out of place now, remain as picturesque reminders of a bygone era and as an important part of our shared agricultural heritage.

left side, Christmas ferns dot the forest floor under a cover of hardwoods. Notice the contrast between the sunny black birch, oak, and hickory forest and the shaded hemlock stand on the right. Pass through a small stand of flowering dogwood trees and curve right. At 1.6 miles, an enormous truck-sized glacial erratic rests off the trail to the left up ahead. Several other large boulders are also present where the ice sheet dropped them. Below the hemlock and witch hazel are mica-filled rocks that sparkle as you walk over them. More flowering dogwood and some ironwood make an appearance. A fallen beech has rotted off at the tip but survives as three tree-sized shoots that rise from its prostrate trunk.

Walk through a boulder field, with spicebush shrubs among the rocks, and reach a rock wall; pass "through" it. Tulip tree, birch, and abundant fragrant spicebush thrive in the damp area on the right. Walk beneath overarching witch hazel shrubs that produce straggly yellow but welcome fall blossoms and begin a steady uphill climb. White oak becomes common as you reach a stone wall halfway up the slope. A big chestnut oak stands on the right. Lifeless in the shade of the hardwoods are the remains of long-dead red cedars. The trail bends left and climbs gradually along the base of the hill, which you soon crest. Reach Dolbia Hill Road, turn left, and walk about 200 feet back to your vehicle.

MORE INFORMATION

Burnham Brook Preserve is open year-round, dawn to dusk. Pets are not allowed. The Nature Conservancy, Connecticut Chapter, 55 High Street, Middletown, CT 06457-3788; 860-344-0716; www.nature.org/wherewework/northamerica/states/connecticut/preserves/art18396.html.

—R. L.

TRIP 44
DEVIL'S HOPYARD STATE PARK

Location: East Haddam
Rating: Easy, with moderately challenging sections
Distance: 2.9 miles
Estimated Time: 2.0 hours
Elevation Gain: 300 feet
Maps: USGS Hamburg, Devil's Hopyard State Park trail map available online

With an extensive trail system on 940 acres of charming woodlands, featuring huge hemlocks and the swift-flowing Eight Mile River, this loop trail delights the hiker with a fine valley vista and picturesque Chapman Falls and the "devil's" potholes.

DIRECTIONS

From Exit 70 (Old Lyme) off I-95, follow Route 1 for 0.8 mile to its junction with Route 156. Turn right onto Route 156 west and drive north for 8.5 miles to the junction with Route 82. Turn right onto Route 82, travel 0.2 mile, and turn left onto Route 434 (Hopyard Road). Drive 3.2 miles to the park's main picnic area. The large gravel parking lot is located on the left, 0.35 mile after the right turn from Hopyard Road.

TRAIL DESCRIPTION

From the parking area, follow paved Foxtown Road left about 300 feet to the campground entrance on the left (you'll explore the falls at the end of this walk). Cross Foxtown Road to an unmarked, unnamed trailhead. Traverse exposed bedrock, go downhill, and reach the Vista Trail junction just before a wooden walkway over an unnamed brook. Orange blazes mark Vista Trail; turn left to follow the path upstream along the boulder-strewn brook on the right. Pass through tall mountain laurel shrubs with gnarled trunks and shiny green leaves only at their tops as you make your way up the gradual slope under the shade of red maple, yellow birch, and red oak. Here the clear stream is only 4 feet wide as it flows through sun-dappled woods. Caddis fly larvae drag their protective, inch-long stick cases about on the brook bottom, taking refuge under stones from alert brook trout. Hemlock covers the dark north-

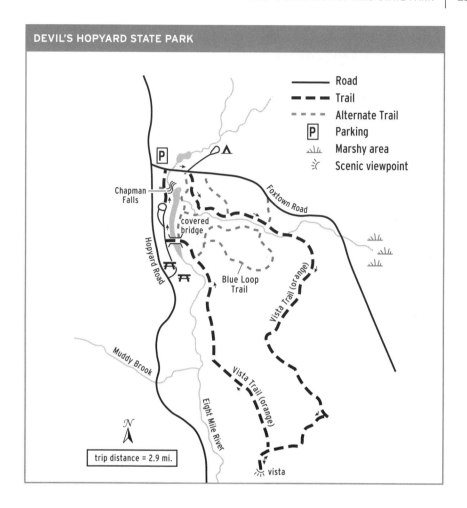

DEVIL'S HOPYARD STATE PARK

— Road
━ ━ ━ Trail
- - - - Alternate Trail
P Parking
Marshy area
Scenic viewpoint

Chapman Falls

Foxtown Road

covered bridge

Hopyard Road

Blue Loop Trail

Vista Trail (orange)

Muddy Brook

Vista Trail (orange)

Eight Mile River

N

trip distance = 2.9 mi.

vista

facing slope of a small ravine to the right. Pass a large boulder as you begin walking uphill, and listen for the emphatic sneeze-like song of the olive-green Acadian flycatcher as he gives his distinctive territorial vocalization from the shaded ravine.

Reach a big twin hemlock on the right and soon come to an unnamed fork—stay right (straight) on the main trail. The other branch goes downhill for a short distance to the brook. Here many mature American beeches are disfigured by blackish graffiti scars carved into their smooth gray trunks years ago. The path is well worn, with shallow beech roots exposed. Beech is a prolific root sprouter, as evidenced by the number of shoots—all clones of their parent trees. After 0.4 mile, cross the unnamed stream on rocks and begin a modest ascent. The brook now flows below you to the left as you turn right and

The swift-flowing Eight Mile River cascades over three tiers of erosion-resistant schist rock to form Chapman Falls.

walk under large white pines and then eastern hemlock and black birch, continuing uphill. A small yellow birch, the tree with peeling metallic bark, grows seemingly right out of a boulder just before the trail levels off.

Rock walls stand as mute testament that this was once open pastureland. Some of the large white pines have multiple, spreading trunks—a sure indication that they reached maturity in what was then an open, sunny environment. Notice that even a few red cedars, whose seeds germinate in sod, are still hanging on. But the woodland is now mostly white, red, and black oak, as well as black birch. Progress through a rocky, wet area under hemlocks where skunk cabbage, named for the fetid odor of its crushed foliage, grows. A massive white ash stands right of the trail. Recognize ashes by their tightly crosshatched bark. After entering the dense shade of a hemlock stand, come to a T intersection. Here an impressive frilly mass of fluorescent orange sulfur mushroom decorating the rotting hulk of a fallen oak caught my eye. It fairly glowed in the gloomy forest. Now turn right and pass a huge hemlock snag on the right, a portion of which is yet alive. Another trail enters from the left, but stay straight and follow the orange blazes gradually downhill. A slope rises to the left, and a stream trickles down on the right. Pass through a stand of dead, naked hemlock where sunlight striking the ground creates an anomalous dry spot. Some of the victims are 2.5 feet across. A tiny insect called hemlock woolly adelgid has killed many of the state's hemlock since the late 1980s.

Walk through another seep on stones, and then almost immediately cross the flowing trickle of a stream issuing from the left slope. As you cross it, note the tall cinnamon fern and skunk cabbage that find the soggy conditions ideal. The underside of one skunk cabbage leaf served as a projection screen for reflected sunlight as it bounced off the flowing water, creating a magical, dappled effect. Reach another T intersection, turn left, and follow the trail rather steeply uphill. Continue up through dead hemlock and living white oak and red maple. The rocks sparkle with mica, an abundant mineral in schist. This is the route's highest section. Come to another flowing (at least in late spring) stream with deciduous woods on the far side where red-eyed vireo, scarlet tanager, wood thrush, and ovenbird all nest in late spring and early summer. After passing a fallen tree, approach a ledge outcrop on the left. The trail turns right at a big hemlock snag. Black birch, or sweet birch, which contains a good amount of fragrant oil of wintergreen, is plentiful. Grassy-looking sedges carpet the forest floor on both sides of the trail. A prostrate, but still living, sugar maple lies on the left, and the evergreen fronds of Christmas fern decorate the woodland.

At 1.3 miles from the trailhead, come to another T intersection. Both directions are blazed orange. Turn left and walk downslope for 400 feet to the vista point.

Emerge onto a sunlit granite ledge with a fine southerly view of the Eight Mile River as it flows away toward the Connecticut between rugged hills clothed in a thick growth of hardwoods and hemlock. The clear, fast-flowing trout stream also forms a natural migration corridor for birds. The ledge's southern exposure gives rise to updrafts of warm air that enable turkey vultures to gain altitude. Three big black birds did just that as I stood on the warm bedrock gazing up at them. The abundant sunlight also stimulates mountain laurel to bud and put on a striking mid-June floral display. Sassafras, scrub oak (with woolly white leaf undersides), and black and white oaks also line the sunny clearing. Nearly 300 feet below and about 0.2 mile to the right, a nearly rectangular pond, backdropped by Hopyard Road, bucolic pastures, and tree-covered hills, lies placidly within the course of the river. While I ate lunch at the vista, a black-and-yellow tiger swallowtail butterfly alighted upon a mass of pink laurel blossoms to sip nectar. You, too, will probably want to linger here.

When ready to push on, return to the intersection and this time continue straight, uphill, then turn left and follow Vista Trail downhill. Pass by more rotting hulks of deceased hemlock. Sunlight, now able to penetrate to the forest floor, has induced a lush growth of ferns in the clearing. Listen for the melancholy whistle of the eastern wood pewee—*pee-a-wee*. On the right, above

HEMLOCK UNDER ASSAULT

The eastern, or Canadian, hemlock is an important and very beautiful member of Connecticut's upland forests, where it becomes especially common on cool, moist sites such as those found in the shaded ravines and Eight Mile River Valley of Devil's Hopyard State Park. Hemlock is exemplary in many ways. It is extremely tolerant of shade. Its tiny cones open only when dry, remaining closed when wet. The winged seeds they release thrive in deep shade, unlike those of white pine, which require plenty of sunlight to germinate.

With a life span that may stretch to six centuries or even longer, eastern hemlock is also one of our longest-lived trees. As the tree ages and matures, its bark cracks and furrows deeply, eventually revealing a characteristic cinnamon hue. Old-growth specimens of such girth are often 300 or more years of age.

But even towering hemlock have very shallow, albeit wide-spreading, root systems, which make them vulnerable to wind throw. The shallow roots snake across the park's trails in many places, and toppled trees are quite evident along the Vista Trail route.

This stately tree, one of our largest and most majestic species, is also unfortunately very susceptible to fire and insect pests. While fire has been largely eliminated as a major concern these days, insect pests continue to pose a grave threat to the welfare and perhaps even the continued existence of southern New England's hemlock.

The tree is now under serious attack from one of the tiniest insects, the hemlock woolly adelgid. This minute sap-sucking bug is related to the more familiar aphid. Its arrival in our region not only coincided with Hurricane Gloria in 1985, but seems literally to have been precipitated by that storm. Gloria, as you may recall, smashed into the Connecticut coast only 15.0 miles southeast of Devil's Hopyard. The adelgid had previously been unknown on this side of Long Island Sound.

This insect in its multitudes feeds on the sap of young hemlock branches, eventually killing the tree. A heavy infestation of the tiny creatures is capable of killing a massive hemlock in only one year. So far no effective means of combating the adelgid has been found.

the trail, sits a ledge nearly high enough for a person to stand up straight under. Now enter the deep shade of a hemlock grove and continue downhill. One old-growth hemlock on the right is fully 3.5 feet in diameter and perhaps several hundred years old! Cross over water flowing down from a rock outcrop on the right in this area of numerous old fallen trees. Reach Eight Mile River, its water stained root beer brown by tannin. Hemlock inner bark contains significant quantities of tannin, once used by the leather-tanning industry. The trail swings right and soon crosses a small feeder stream on a log bridge. Cliffs crown the rocky slope to the left.

Again reach the river, which has been stocked for anglers with trout and salmon, and turn right. An exquisite male black damselfly, with an electric blue abdomen, flitted over the bubbling stream and alighted on a royal fern growing on a little rock "island" when we were here. The gurgling water makes a soothing sound as it plays over the rocks. A jumble of boulders, topped with rock-loving polypody fern, juts from a talus slope on the right. Follow along the stream past a large uprooted hemlock that has fallen into the river. Here you can stand on bedrock at the water's edge and enjoy the cool air of the valley on a hot summer's day. Walk among sizable hemlocks, some dead, others living, just before beginning to climb a rocky slope. Tree roots lie exposed amid the jumble of stones. Follow along the ledge, where the rock has fractured in 90-degree planes, and reach its crest. A nice view of the river below presents itself as you peer through the hemlock boughs. Join a wider, orange-blazed trail on the right under the hemlock and bear left to enter deciduous woods of oak and red maple, with mountain laurel beneath. At 2.5 miles, meet the blue-blazed Loop Trail on the right, but continue straight on the orange-blazed Vista Trail. Listen for yellow-throated vireos that enunciate their burry phrases from above here.

Proceed through two cemented stone abutments with culverts but no water flowing through them and come to a covered bridge over the river. Nearly every bridge in the Northeast has its resident eastern phoebes. These olive-gray flycatchers, among the earliest spring arrivals, are partial to bridges over streams, where they construct their mud nests, covered with green mosses, on ledges of rock, metal, or wood. This bridge is no exception. Cross the bridge and enter the picnic area, which is especially busy on warm weekends. Turn right and follow the wide dirt path past a wooden log gate and then uphill.

Arrive at a wooden fence on the right where steps go downhill and then take the dirt path toward the left to obtain a fine view of Chapman Falls, which cascade over three tiers capped with erosion-resistant schist rock in a picturesque fall totaling 60 vertical feet. Potholes (once thought to be the devil's work) varying in diameter from a few inches to several feet pockmark the bedrock below the falls. These falls lie 15 miles north of Long Island Sound in a long-dormant fault zone that separates the Windham Hills region from the coastal slope to the south. The flow once powered a gristmill (until 1854) and a sawmill (until about 1895).

Return to the main path and follow a red cedar rail fence. Reach a trail intersection on the left, but stay straight. Cross a wooden bridge and come to a kiosk where a trail map and information is posted. The parking area is across Foxtown Road.

MORE INFORMATION

Devil's Hopyard State Park features a campground, a picnic shelter with grills, and pit toilets. Open from 8:00 A.M. to sunset, when the parking lot is gated. There are no fees to park or walk the trails, although a fee is charged for camping. Leashed pets permitted in picnic areas and on trails, but not in campground. Devil's Hopyard State Park, 366 Hopyard Road, East Haddam, CT 06423; 860-873-8566; http://www.ct.gov/dep.

—R. L.

TRIP 45
CHATFIELD TRAIL/COCKAPONSET STATE FOREST

Location: Killingworth
Rating: Moderate, with challenging stretches
Distance: 2.6 miles
Elevation Gain: 175 feet
Estimated Time: 3.0 hours
Maps: USGS Clinton

If you are a rock lover, this excursion along ledge faces, under rock overhangs, and over and through crevices is for you. Along the way, marvel at imposing ledge cliffs and outcrops, caves, and a perched glacial erratic.

DIRECTIONS

From the north, take Route 9 to Exit 9 at Route 81. Follow Route 81 south for 8.0 miles to Route 80 in Killingworth. From the rotary, turn right onto Route 80 west, and drive for 1.4 miles (0.3 mile beyond the entrance to Chatfield Hollow State Park) to the small gravel parking area on the left. Watch for a blue sign indicating Chatfield Trail. Do not park along the highway.

From I-95, take Exit 63 to Route 81 (north). Follow Route 81 for approximately 5.3 miles to Killingworth. From the rotary in Killingworth, turn onto Route 80 (west) and follow the above directions.

TRAIL DESCRIPTION

The blue-blazed Chatfield Trail leads over a rocky old forest road paralleling a stony brook bed. To the left a ledge outcrop appears—the first of many. The forest dominants are yellow birch, red oak, and sugar maple. Witch hazel and the evergreen mountain laurel are the common shrubs. The trail soon leaves the road and heads up toward the gneiss (pronounced *nice*) ledge. Pass the end of the outcrop and climb into a woodland of American beech and chestnut oak. Here the shrubs are sweet pepperbush and highbush blueberry; soon they are joined by huckleberry and maple-leaf viburnum. Solomon's seal, common polypody—a small fern—and mosses soften the rocks. In midsummer, the mechanical buzzing of cicadas fills the warm air. The high-pitched *pit-tee* call of the crow-sized broad-winged hawk, which nests in these woodlands, is often heard then.

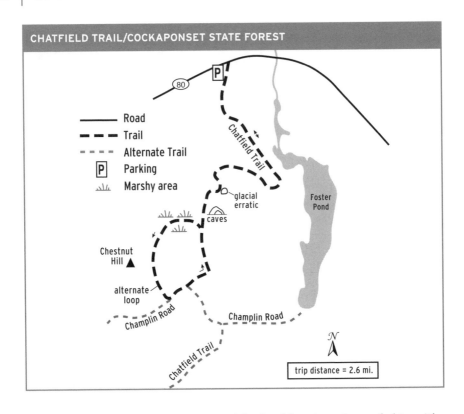

CHATFIELD TRAIL/COCKAPONSET STATE FOREST

——— Road
- - - Trail
- · - · Alternate Trail
P Parking
Marshy area

80

Chatfield Trail

glacial erratic

caves

Foster Pond

Chestnut Hill ▲

alternate loop

Champlin Road

Champlin Road

Chatfield Trail

𝒩
Λ

trip distance = 2.6 mi.

The trail climbs over an outcrop of flat boulders in staircase fashion. The rocks are dotted with greenish lichen doilies as white oaks appear. Cross the horizontally fissured bedrock mound where laurel and small red maples are common. Swing left at the top of the outcrop among stunted oak and birch. Huckleberry shrubs are numerous as you enter dry oak woodland. Walk easily downhill past lichen-spotted outcrops and then swing left around an outcrop past hickory and a few low sassafras trees. Come to a small sunny gap atop the gray rock ledge, where the trail makes a sharp left turn. Foster Pond is visible at a distance through trees. After crossing the ledge, follow a switchback in the trail to the right and descend. Cross a stone wall at the outcrop's terminus and then follow downhill along its face. The flat-faced cliff, its horizontal slabs seemingly placed one on top of another, rises above you, eventually towering 35 or 40 feet over your head near its end. Black birch saplings and false Solomon's seal have found footholds in the rock.

Hermit thrushes nest in the woodlands, raising and slowly lowering their rust-colored tails when agitated. Continue the gradual descent past the cliff face and through a boulder field where beech, sugar maple, and New York and Christmas ferns grow between the glacier-deposited stones. Rattlesnake plantain is present near the trail. The unmistakable bluish green leaves of this small orchid are marked with attractive white veins. Note the presence of hemlock snags. The pond again becomes visible as you pick your way through a boulder field. Climb up over an outcrop past live hemlocks. You can spy dead trees, too, and some that appear unhealthy. The hemlock woolly adelgid, a minute, non-native, sap-sucking insect, has killed them. The leaves of pink lady's slipper, the other orchid of these woods, protrude from the acidic soil, while princess pine, or tree club moss, adds its dark evergreen foliage to the scene.

Drop down momentarily from the raised, hemlock-topped outcropping and cross a rivulet, dry in summer, which feeds lily-covered Foster Pond, then climb back into hemlock woods with hay-scented fern in tree-fall gaps. Pileated woodpeckers have chiseled cavernous holes in the decaying trunks to reach the carpenter ants within. Indian tobacco blooms pale blue along the trail in summer. Native Americans smoked the dried leaves as a cure for lung ailments. Ironically, Indian tobacco contains a toxic substance used in gum and lozenges designed to appease smokers' craving for nicotine. This plant has been tied to human deaths and should never be used for self-medication. Bear left and descend gently. A thick growth of sapling black birch has colonized the openings where towering hemlocks once blotted out the sunlight on this rather steep slope. Begin descending, pass through another boulder field, and reach a low ledge cliff on the right. The rock wall is festooned with green moss, while small hemlocks protrude from the crevices. As the trees mature, their swelling roots and the actions of ice will eventually help to cleave apart the cliff. Walk down one long step and level out. The first "cavelet"—a diagonally vertical fissure—comes into view. You can walk in a short distance.

During an August visit, I noticed daddy long-legs with especially lengthy legs bounce along as they negotiated the moss and evergreen wood fern-covered rocks. Pass through a narrow slot created by an uprooted hemlock. Liverworts—tongue-shaped relatives of mosses—thrive on seepage at the base of the cliff. Small pickerel frogs likewise find the cool, damp conditions favorable. Continue along the cliff and pass a twin-trunked chestnut oak to the left and then a big hemlock to the right as the trail swings around it and over the outcrop. Proceed straight, not left, after the short climb to the level top. White pine makes its first appearance among the hemlock. The path bears left, past a few non-native Norway spruce, but these are predominantly pine-oak-maple woods, with mountain laurel and witch hazel in the shrub layer. As you walk downhill, a sunlit red maple stand—a sure sign of a swamp—comes into view. In contrast, the plantation white pines stand in rows. Their needles, five to a bundle, cushion the path. Sweet (coast) pepperbush forms a luxuriant growth

Chunks of gneiss rock, plied loose by the relentless forces of freezing and thawing, litter the floor of a 50-foot-long "cave."

in the moist soil. Beyond the pines to the right, the scene is one of nearly total domination by red (swamp) maple. The trail bears right, crosses a rivulet that may be dry in summer, and enters dry oak forest. After an undulation, the trail tops a low ledge outcrop studded with silver mound and haircap mosses as well as blueberries. Reindeer lichen, an important winter staple of caribou in the Arctic, forms a miniature forest on the rock.

Pass between boulders, then along the edge of a rather level boulder field, and turn right. A profusion of seedling chestnut oaks crowd and compete on the forest floor. More outcrops, then turn right and pass by angular rocks, some with obvious rusty pink feldspar crystals. Negotiating a short portion of the trail here requires a few easy tree holds. Reach the crest of the ledge vegetated with oak, black birch, red maple, and huckleberry. Note the shiny resin dots on the leaf surfaces of huckleberry. Climb up another low ledge where an oblong gray glacial erratic rests on two much smaller stones. The melting glacier left this souvenir of the ice age. Bear left and emerge into a sunny bedrock clearing where southwesterly views are possible after leaf-fall. A red cedar (juniper) has shouldered against the boulder, and clumps of little bluestem grass sprout in pockets of soil. This is a fine spot for a rest and a snack.

To continue, turn right and walk around the erratic to enter the low tree growth. Proceed downward over boulders and through a small boulder field—

another glacial reminder—and then over another low outcrop as the trail bears right. You find lowbush blueberry and huckleberry on top, their tasty blue-black fruits relished in late summer by mammals. Now swing left and descend along the outcrop's other side. Ledge stone, stacked like a layer cake, rises on the left. Bear right and walk along a 10-foot-high gray wall; then turn and go through a crevice between ledge and boulders. At one point you are forced to bend over to fit through. Slabs of fine-grained, black-and-white-banded granitic gneiss have broken off to form an overhang or cave high enough to stand up under.

Continue along the broken ledge face some 150 feet and make your way through a narrow cleft, this one requiring a short climb. Virginia creeper drapes the overhang, and Solomon's seal, with pendant pairs of deep-blue fruits in summer, adorns the rock. You are now looking down slightly into a larger cave roofed over by a 20-foot-wide ledge. This cave was created by the relentless actions of the elements as hunks of stone were pried loose from the overhang. Walk the overhang's 50-foot length. Sugar maple, beech, and oak rise in the adjacent forest. One beech, disfigured by a huge fungal canker, has fallen over and rests against the ledge. Quite a few beeches have sprouted right along the outcrop wall, and beech roots spread like varicose veins across the trail's surface. Clumps of shining club moss, reminiscent of bottlebrushes, dot the outcrop. The trail now diverges from the ledge and gradually bears left toward another; then it turns left at the end of that outcrop and bears left again. A fascinating spiny-abdomened spider known as a spined micrathena had strung silken threads across the trail one August day.

Come to a T intersection at a rocky old woods road. Use caution, as this can be a tricky intersection. Bear left onto the blue trail and walk among oak, with some beech, laurel, and witch hazel. At 0.9 mile, reach a junction with the Alternate Trail, marked by a sign on the right. Alternate Trail is blazed blue with an orange dot. Follow Alternate Trail down among rocks, under oak, blueberry, and huckleberry. Swing right along the spine of a low ledge and then down to its base within beech and oak woodland. Pass through a fern glade, cross a rivulet stream, walk over more rock, and then turn left at the end of the outcrop, following the path just below it. Posted signs indicate the edge of private property on the right; to the left runs the Cockaponset State Forest boundary. Sweet pepperbush sporting frothy white flower spikes in summer and the canopies of skunk cabbage signal swampy ground. Descend gradually through oak woods punctuated by ledges, bearing left at a low outcrop.

At the swamp edge, I inadvertently flushed a family of eight ruffed grouse. The young were nearly full grown. Their mother, all the while uttering odd

THE EGG AND US

As my wife Christyna and I passed back through the bedrock clearing marked by the glacial erratic, we watched another tiger swallowtail flying about in the sun. But this individual seemed to be moving with more purpose than usual. That purpose was soon apparent as the large, elegant insect fluttered above the leaves of a sapling black cherry in the clearing. We presumed it might be laying eggs as it gently touched the tip of its abdomen to the top of several leaves in turn.

Upon closer inspection we were delighted to find a tiny, round green egg adhering to the top of one leaf. No doubt the female butterfly had laid additional eggs on other leaves. We decided to try a little swallowtail husbandry by carefully removing the leaf and its attached egg and transporting it home. At home we placed the twig in a small jar of water to keep the leaf succulent and then put the jar in a small glass terrarium. We checked the egg more than once daily, and, to our delight, the egg hatched 8 days later. An 1/8-inch-long blackish caterpillar had emerged from the egg. It soon began to nibble on the cherry leaf.

From our butterfly field guides, we knew that black cherry was just one of the species' many preferred foods, and a number of young black cherry trees grew in our yard. The tiny larva grew and ate, grew and ate, and continued to do so. A molt reclothed the larva in a new green skin 22 days after hatching, and at its hind end it displayed a striking pair of "eyes." These feline orbs were actually just circles of orange and black pigment, but their role seems clearly to fool predators into thinking that this is the head of a more formidable creature. In reality, of course, the head is at the opposite end. Later, the caterpillar added to the illusory effect by holding up the rear end in such a way that its appearance as a head was enhanced further.

A week after its color change, it began visibly to react to sound. If we made a sudden sound, it responded with a quick movement, leading us to believe that it was capable of hearing. Over the course of the rest of the summer and into the fall, we continued to pick fresh fodder for the caterpillar while it continued to increase in size. On some days we could actually hear it chewing. From our reading we also realized that it would not form a chrysalis and emerge as a fully formed butterfly this year, as a monarch butterfly would have. Instead, as fall advanced, we knew it would simply crawl down and pupate among the leaf litter that had accumulated at the bottom of the terrarium. Only next spring would it finally emerge as a gorgeous adult tiger swallowtail.

One day in late October, when the caterpillar had reached 1 inch in length, it disappeared as expected into the bottom of the terrarium, and under the dry leaves molted into a brown chrysalis. As I write these words, we await the spring and the miraculous ultimate transformation of the tiny green egg laid so many months before.

mewing sounds, herded them away, out of harm's way. Bear left, drop down over rocks, turn right between outcrops, and cross a seasonal brook. Find maple-leaf viburnum shrubs under their namesake tree. The viburnums join sugar maple seedlings and Christmas fern. Both flourish in rich limy, or neutral, soils. Each leaflet of Christmas fern resembles a tiny Christmas stocking. Continue your measured descent through another boulder field and cross a brook on stones. Spicebush, with incredibly fragrant foliage, characterizes such moist soils. Now bear right and left, through lacy New York fern, and climb gradually to a ledge capped with polypody fern. The name (Latin for "many feet") refers to its matted, spreading roots. Walk left along the ledge face, turning right to climb over it. Here I found a very vigorous jack-in-the-pulpit perched on a rock pedestal. In August, its cluster of berries was still emerald green.

After you gain the top, turn right and then immediately left and climb gradually to another formation, whose 25-foot-high horizontally bedded mass is apparent. The crevices had provided a female eastern phoebe with a perfect nesting shelf 6 feet up. Feldspar and a quartz vein are visible in the rock on the lower part of the cliff. The trail bears left, rounds a huge boulder, passes a stone wall, and fords a brook that even in a dry season usually has pools with resident green frogs. Gravel Champlin Road is 40 feet beyond at 1.3 miles. Turn left onto the road and follow the blue and orange blazes; to the right is posted, private land. The road and trail cross a brook. Here Alternate Trail ends and rejoins the blue-blazed Chatfield Trail. Turn left and follow it to the north into the forest (do not take the main trail branch, which follows the road south). The path turns right twice to follow along a cliff face. A switchback on the left leads you up through a low crevice. Turn right at the top. You're walking in open woods of chestnut and white oaks, and then through greenbrier and huckleberry with a rock wall on the right. Hickory and oak long ago overtopped the red cedar that colonized a former pasture.

Cross a stone wall and pass to the right of a 30- to 40-foot cliff. On the left, note the false Solomon's seal, which has starry white flowers in a cluster at the stalk's tip. Turn left and follow the blue blazes, ascending steeply under a jumble of elephant-gray gneiss bedrock. Follow the blue blazes along the crest. A screened view through cedar, hickory, and oak is possible in summer. I was charmed by an eastern chipmunk that retreated to a rock crevice—a protective cave of its own—and then turned to watch my approach with some apprehension. Leave the oak knoll, reenter taller oak woodland, and come to an intersection with a woods road. Follow blue blazes to the right and walk uphill on the old roadway. Soon pass the junction with Alternate Trail on the left. Follow the blue blazes that leave the woods road to the right and return the mile back to the parking area.

MORE INFORMATION

No fee for parking at the trailhead, but admission to the state park is $7 per resident vehicle on weekends/holidays, $6 on weekdays; $10 per nonresident vehicle on weekends/holidays, $7 on weekdays. Chatfield Hollow State Park features accessible restrooms, a picnic shelter, and a swimming beach. Open from 8:00 A.M. to sunset. Chatfield Hollow State Park, 381 Route 80, Killingworth, CT 06419; 860-663-2030; http://www.ct.gov/dep.

—R. L.

TRIP 46
HAMMONASSET BEACH STATE PARK

Location: Madison
Rating: Easy
Distance: 3.0 miles
Elevation Gain: 20 feet
Estimated Time: 2.0 hours
Maps: USGS Clinton, Hammonasset Beach State Park map available online

Although not your classic woodland hike, three short trails—one loop, two out and back—traverse the extensive salt marsh, picturesque rocky shore, sandy beach, and isolated sandy uplands of this state park. Two trails with viewing platforms are fully accessible, also making it perfect for young children. Best avoided in summer, unless you enjoy the large crowds that patronize one of the state's most popular swimming beaches, this 919-acre park, replete with a diverse fauna and flora, is a great place from which to observe the fall bird migration spectacle.

DIRECTIONS
From I-95 in Madison, take Exit 62 and turn south at the end of the ramp (right if you're coming from the west, left from the east) onto Hammonasset Beach State Park connector. Travel south and cross Route 1 at 1.3 miles. The park entrance is located 0.3 mile farther. From the entrance station, follow the signs to Meigs Point for 1.7 miles, past a rotary, to a large paved lot on the left adjacent to the nature center.

TRAIL DESCRIPTION
After parking at Meigs Point Nature Center—located on a knoll overlooking a salt marsh—walk past the nature center and down the one-lane paved road. The roadway is lined with tall common reed (Phragmites), bayberry, poison ivy (its white berries are a favorite of many birds), and goldenrod. Soon reach the picnic area at the pavement's end. The 0.9-mile-long Willard's Island Nature Trail begins on the left. Interpretive leaflets may be available from a box at the trailhead as well as at the nature center when it is open. Both sides of the wide, level macadam path are vegetated with a thick growth of red cedar (juniper),

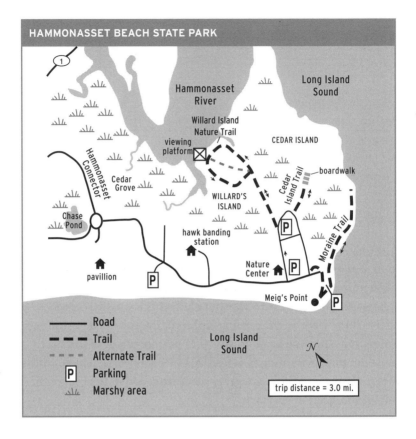

HAMMONASSET BEACH STATE PARK

Long Island Sound

Hammonasset River

Willard Island Nature Trail

CEDAR ISLAND

viewing platform

boardwalk

Hammonasset Connector

Cedar Grove

Cedar Island Trail

WILLARD'S ISLAND

Chase Pond

hawk banding station

Moraine Trail

pavillion

P

Nature Center

P

Meig's Point

P

——— Road
■ ■ ■ Trail
- - - Alternate Trail
P   Parking
⏦   Marshy area

Long Island Sound

N

trip distance = 3.0 mi.

wild rose, shining sumac, bayberry, poison ivy, aromatic sweet fern—not a fern at all—*Phragmites*, and goldenrod. The first five produce nutritious fruits consumed eagerly by many species of birds and mammals.

This relatively narrow strip of higher ground is surrounded by salt marsh (not accessible without a permit). Spartina grasses grow along the water channels in the rich mud, as do the odd segmented spikes of glasswort, which in late summer take on a translucent reddish hue. The high salt content of this plant has engendered a fitting nickname: pickleweed. You'll find blackgrass on slightly higher ground near the marsh edge. Not a grass at all, it is actually a rush whose dark brown fruiting capsules inspired its common name. Reach a three-way split in the asphalt path; follow the right branch. Virginia creeper, or woodbine, twines up the pyramidal forms of red cedar, its crimson fall foliage contrasting with the supporting evergreens. Small flocks of perky crested cedar waxwings utter high-pitched calls as they move about in search of fruit. The bluish berries, which also give gin its distinctive taste, are among their favorites. A stately multi-branched pear tree (certified to be the state's largest) left of the path is a reminder that Willard's Island was once an orchard. In early autumn, the remaining, fermenting fruit give off a noticeable but not unpleasant fragrance.

A trio of woody plants with Asian origins—autumn olive, Japanese honeysuckle, and Oriental bittersweet—thrives in the sandy soils. Autumn olive shrubs, planted years ago for erosion control and as wildlife food, are numerous. These are among the few nonleguminous (pea family) plants that fix nitrogen in the soil by means of bacteria ensconced in root nodules. All three Oriental species are now more or less invasive, to the detriment of native shrubs. To the right stands a big red maple, a species with wide moisture tolerances; the trail then curves left. Several apple trees with fruit in season appear surrounded by a dense thicket of rose, honeysuckle, sumac, dogwood, and young peach trees. Grapevines and Virginia creeper vines use the shrubs for support and to clamber up to sunlight. Bumblebees crawl back and forth over the goldenrod flower masses, gathering pollen. A grove of spindly sassafras trees grows on the right. A screech owl nest box, the entrance hole enlarged by a gray squirrel, is mounted on one of the trees.

Come to a split in the trail; stay straight rather than going left. Almost immediately reach a four-way intersection. Take the right branch, which forks again in 30 feet. Follow the right branch—a loop of fine gray gravel—to a salt marsh viewing platform. In addition to the tree, shrub, and vine species already mentioned, crab apple, white oak, and shad (Juneberry) now join the mix. The wooden viewing platform is located alongside Dudley Creek at the far end of the loop. Interpretive panels inform visitors about Willard's Island, salt marsh fish, ospreys, the heron family, and ducks. From here, enjoy expansive views of the Hammonasset River's biologically rich salt marsh and tidal-flat system. If the tide is low or falling, you can spot ribbed mussels protruding from the dark, peaty banks of the stream. The mussels, inundated twice daily by a salty broth, siphon microscopic creatures from it.

Gaze farther out and notice masses of sun-bleached sticks on channel buoys and on top of specially erected tall tripods. These are the nests of ospreys—large brown-and-white birds of prey that plunge feet-first into salt or fresh water to gaff live fish. In summer, osprey pairs raise two to three chicks to fledging on the structures. Once endangered by persistent pesticides, habitat loss, and even shooting, these noble birds have made a heartening comeback. The ramped platform and a bench along the trail are wonderful places to relax and have a snack while enjoying the scenery and wildlife passing by. When ready to carry on, follow the path past tall grasses and sunflowers back to the paved main trail. Gray catbirds give catlike meows from the thickets, which in fall include bright-red-fruit-laden winterberry.

The blue waters of Long Island Sound lie beyond the granite boulders and glacially deposited promontory of Meig's Point.

Turn right at the paved main trail and follow it through a dense growth of shrubs, sassafras, autumn olive, red cedar, grape, bittersweet, and Virginia creeper vines. Virginia creeper's stems and clusters of five leaflets add a bold dash of red color to the scene. Grapes fermenting in the warm sunlight of late summer waft their aromatic vapors over the footpath. Welcome shade on hot days is provided by a large red maple on the right. A migrant Swainson's thrush, a denizen of dark, cool northern forests, plucked ripe black cherries in rapid succession as I watched one late September day. The nature center comes into view as you continue along. Turn right at the intersection to retrace your steps to the trailhead. You can then turn right to return to your vehicle or head left for a one-way distance of 0.3 mile through the picnic area to the terminus of the Cedar Island Trail at an accessible viewing platform.

The Cedar Island trailhead is not obvious. Cross the mowed picnic area to its far corner and look for a graveled path that enters a strip of trees. Sassafras, pignut hickory, oak, black cherry, and basswood form a canopy over your head, with granite boulders beneath. Notice the cork-studded bark of a hackberry tree immediately left of the path. After proceeding through the woodland, the view opens up, affording fine vistas of the surrounding salt marsh. Cross a wooden bridge; a vigorous stand of poison ivy, its foliage already rusty in late summer, grows tall on the right, while patches of seaside goldenrod, a favorite nectar plant of migrating monarch butterflies, show off their flower clusters at both ends of the bridge. The path then gains ground gradually, and as a result the soil becomes drier. Shad, white oak, hickory, black cherry, huckleberry, lowbush blueberry, and azalea predominate. The shad trees—so named because they bloom in April, when the annual migration of shad fish up coastal rivers to spawn is underway—have multiple smooth, lithe gray trunks. Bracken fern, wild sarsaparilla, and striped wintergreen grow beneath the woody vegetation. The trail ends at a large, new platform with benches surrounded by salt marsh.

Clinton Harbor is visible to the right from this unobstructed vantage point. Two large, pinkish granite boulders, dropped by the receding glacier of the last ice age, stand as mute testimony to its power. A clump of seaside goldenrod has colonized the top of one. High above it I watched an aerial ballet in the form of thirteen snowy egrets spiraling up into the cobalt-blue sky, perhaps to begin their autumnal migration. When ready, retrace your steps to the picnic area and your vehicle beyond, or continue on to the Moraine Trail.

To reach the 0.8-mile out-and-back Moraine Trail and Meigs Point, cross the two-lane, paved park road, traverse a wide boardwalk to the bathhouse (watch for salt marsh sharp-tailed sparrows in late spring and summer here), turn left, and walk over the sand along the beach to a boardwalk. Interpretive brochures are available here. Climb steps to a viewing platform atop the point for an excellent view over granite boulders of Long Island Sound. This knoll is a glacial moraine created when the ice sheet dropped a load of debris during its slow and halting retreat. Seaside goldenrod, poison ivy, bayberry, shining sumac—whose leaf surfaces are highly reflective—and wild rose blanket the knoll. Signs identify many of the plants lining the path. Descend the gravel path on the opposite side, and continue straight after the dip past a number of side paths that intersect the main trail from the parking area on the left. Thickets of beach plum help stabilize the glacial soil. A picturesque view of the rocky point and beach lie ahead.

Descend to the rock-and-sand beach and walk along the boulder-strewn shore, making your way between large chunks of 600- to 800-million-year-old granite and dark green clumps of bayberry, or wax myrtle. The wax-covered fruits of this aromatic shrub constitute important fuel for migrant tree swallows and wintering yellow-rumped (myrtle) warblers, among others. Just offshore big, black double-crested cormorants fly low over the water. These common fish-eating relatives of pelicans also possess a pouched throat, albeit a much smaller one. A granite rock 80 feet out serves as a convenient loafing site for the birds. Salt marsh vegetation advances right to the shoreline at one point. The Cedar

AERIAL HIGHWAYS

Each autumn nature presents one of her most incredible and captivating spectacles—the long southward migration of birds and a few insects to areas where more clement weather and abundant food supplies enable these creatures to overwinter with relative ease prior to returning to breeding areas in the north.

As the multitudes move southward by day, hawks and monarch butterflies tend to follow time-honored corridors created by rivers and other landforms. Along submerging coastlines, such as along Connecticut's shore, where points of land jut out into the sea, the migrants tend to be funneled by such narrow appendages. Hammonasset is such a place. And when the winds are auspicious—that is, out of the northwest—thousands of hawks and even a few eagles may pass down to Meig's Point and then along the shore of the Long Island Sound in a single day. These are the days birders wait for eagerly.

For each bird it is a significant expenditure and a great risk, but one that must be taken. Their form and behavior allows them to take advantage of certain atmospheric conditions. They float upward on the elevators of rising air currents created when the sun warms the earth, and ride the updrafts born of wind-powered air masses striking ridges. Incredibly keen vision enables these raptors to spot prey from high above the ground and (especially in the case of the pointy-winged falcons) to drop or stoop upon it with dizzying speed. The master of this art is the peregrine falcon. Peregrine means "traveler," and indeed each year of their lives these striking birds must make a round-trip journey of up to 18,000 miles!

Be sure to glance up occasionally, especially if you visit from late August to early November. In late September for instance, if the weather cooperates, you are sure to see long-tailed sharp-shinned and Cooper's hawks; dainty American kestrels, small relatives of the peregrine; ospreys; bulky red-tailed hawks; and perhaps even a bald eagle on flat, 7-foot wings. Sometimes the hawks pass by high overhead, and at other times they streak low over the grassy fields into the teeth of a brisk wind. It's definitely a spectacle worth seeing.

Nor are hawks or, for that matter, shorebirds and songbirds the only winged sojourners passing through the area each fall. Big orange monarch butterflies make an even more monumental journey (for an insect weighing less than a fraction of an ounce) of 2,000 or more miles to the transvolcanic mountain range of central Mexico. Although some of the birds have followed their migration routes before, none of the butterflies ever has—or ever will again. Covering 40 miles per day on the average, the monarchs take 2 months or more to complete the trip. The fat-rich nectar of goldenrods and asters provides the fuel for their wing muscles at stopover points such as this.

After spending the winter months in the cool, high-elevation evergreen forests of the Mexican mountains, the butterflies mate. The females fly back only a relatively short distance before laying their eggs on milkweed plants and then die. The hatching caterpillars feast, grow rapidly, pupate, and then as adults continue the northward odyssey. It is the third generation of butterflies you first see in New England fields in early summer. A later migrant generation, removed from the previous year's travelers by five generations, begins the long southward journey by the end of August.

Island Trail boardwalk is visible out in the marsh. Climb to another point of land thick with bayberry, sumac, greenbrier, wild rose, vines, grasses, and goldenrod. In September, monarch butterflies wing by and alight on the goldenrods to take on fat-rich fuel for their perilous journey to central Mexico. The trail ends at the water's edge. Retrace your steps to the bathhouse and your vehicle.

MORE INFORMATION

Open 8 A.M. to sunset Memorial Day to Labor Day, and weekends from late April to Memorial Day and from Labor Day to the end of September. Weekends $9 per resident vehicle, $14 nonresident vehicle; weekdays $7 per resident vehicle, $10 nonresident vehicle (subject to change). There is a camping fee. Restrooms and boardwalk are accessible.

Also available are a nature center, picnic shelters and tables, and a cartop boat launch. A campground, showers, and concessions are available seasonally. Leashed pets are allowed in the picnic area, but not on the beach or in the campground. Meigs Point Nature Center's summer hours are Tuesday–Sunday 10:00 A.M.–5:00 P.M.; Tuesday–Saturday 10 A.M.–5 P.M. in spring and fall; and Tuesday–Friday 10 A.M.–4 P.M. during winter. Hammonasset Beach State Park, 1288 Boston Post Road, P.O. Box 271, Madison, CT 06443; 203-245-2785; 203-245-8743; http://www.ct.gov/dep.

—R. L.

TRIP 47
MCKINNEY NATIONAL WILDLIFE REFUGE
(SALTMEADOW UNIT)

Location: Westbrook
Rating: Easy
Distance: 1.1 miles
Elevation Gain: 100 feet
Estimated Time: 1.0 hour
Maps: USGS Essex

One of the more than 545 national wildlife refuges, a federal system comprising more than 96 million acres, the McKinney refuge is made up of 8 units along 60 miles of Connecticut coast. This pleasant stroll on the Saltmeadow Unit winds through shrubby fields, under massive woodland giants, and offers views of tidal salt marsh, a diminishing natural community. This is a great hike with young children.

DIRECTIONS
From I-95, take exit 64 in Clinton to Route 145 (Horsehill Road). Turn south and drive less than 0.1 mile to a flashing four-way red light at Old Clinton Road. Turn left (east) onto Old Clinton Road and follow it for 1.0 mile to the refuge entrance on the right, marked by a sign.

TRAIL DESCRIPTION
From the gravel parking area turn left and follow the accessible treadway past bird feeders and two handsome stone structures, once the hope of Esther Lape—the donor of the property—and now refuge headquarters, to a covered kiosk where a trail map is posted. No restroom is available on weekends. To begin the hike, backtrack 20 feet to a grassy path. Turn right and continue straight toward the brushy field ahead, rather than turning at the bench. The refuge staff is allowing this field to revert to shrubland, a scarce habitat type on the refuge. In spring and summer listen and watch for lovely eastern bluebirds that nest in the provided boxes. Other shrubland denizens include eastern towhee and gray catbird. Cherry, winged sumac, honeysuckle, and bayberry produce abundant fruit and in fall fruit-gobbling robins and cedar waxwings fatten up on the bounty. Little bluestem grass, goldenrod, and butterfly

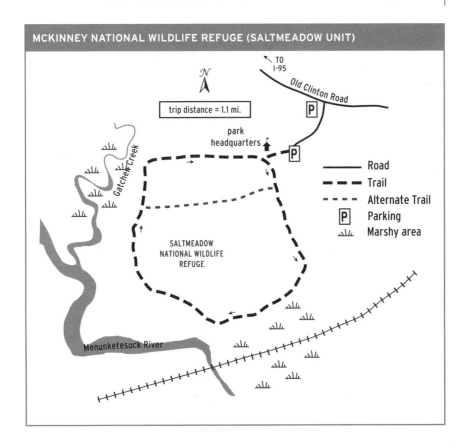

milkweed are slowly being crowded out. This clearing marks the "summit" of modest Murdock Hill.

As you pass through a stone wall gap, note the rough-barked tupelo (black gum) trees growing along the wall. Invasive exotic oriental bittersweet vines create quite a tangle. Enter an oak woodland where arm-thick grape vines are suspended from tree limbs and reach another stone wall (fence actually) where the trail bears right. Morrow's Honeysuckle, another invasive exotic Asian shrub, is abundant. The path parallels a wall that once bordered a sheep-filled meadow. After leaf fall a few homes and the salt marsh beyond are visible. After descending a few steps, note a gneiss (pronounced *nice*) boulder on the right that contains some very hard quartz crystals. The shiny, veined basal leaves of round-leaved pyrola brighten the forest floor here in fall. And note the thicket forming common greenbrier that warns off intruders with its stout thorns.

Two sets of railroad tracks form an unnatural corridor between the woodland and the salt marsh. Amtrak commuter trains often speed past. In addition

Butterflyweed, an orange milkweed that nourishes Monarch caterpillars and provides nectar for countless other insects when succulent, dries and offers up its seed for wind dispersal in autumn.

to oaks and hickories, sassafras trees with rugose trunks are common. Tall, planted spruces rise up on your left. Most of the native hardwoods have trunk diameters less than 1 foot, and they are very straight, indicating that they matured in a dense forest rather than in the open. At a bench, the trail turns right. You find many black or sweet birches in this forest disfigured by large fungus-caused cankers, which eventually kill the trees. A few short side paths lead down to the salt marsh. Ditches dug in the marsh decades ago to combat mosquito breeding actually exacerbated the situation by negatively impacting the small fish that dine on the insect's larvae. The tallest and most massive of eastern forest trees is the tulip tree. A truly impressive specimen with a 3-foot diameter stands 20 feet left of the path, before you pass through a stone wall gap and reach a trail split.

Turn left to parallel the marsh edge where stands of invasive common reed grow tall. A few azaleas, which produce exquisite blossoms in spring, grow

Once the stately home of Esther Lape, who donated her property, the stone house now serves as refuge headquarters.

along the trail. Farther on, you'll come upon formal gardens complete with stone fountain that hint at an earlier time. Horticultural remnants include arborvitae, pachysandra, yew, and coastal sweetbells, the latter shrub forming a thicket that threatens to engulf all in its path. An inscribed rock near the fountain commemorates the friendship between the former owner and Eleanor Roosevelt. An observation tower is under construction on the left where the trail turns right and passes under tall rhododendrons. You pass more trails under construction before reaching a row of European larches bordering the old roadway on the right, and another path not yet open.

After passing a bench, a log cabin under rehabilitation is just ahead. Close the loop at the map kiosk. The stone table and bench shaded by a flowering dogwood in front of the headquarters building is a fine place for lunch or a snack.

MORE INFORMATION

Open year-round, ½ hour before sunrise to ½ hour after sunset. No fees charged. Restrooms may not be available on weekends. Stewart B. McKinney NWR, 733 Old Clinton Road, Westbrook, CT 06498-1760; 860-399-2513; http://www.fws.gov/refuges/profiles/index.cfm?id=53546.

—R. L.

TRIP 48
BLUFF POINT COASTAL RESERVE

Location: Groton
Rating: Easy
Distance: 3.75 miles
Elevation Gain: 100 feet
Estimated Time: 2.0 hours
Maps: USGS New London; Bluff Point State Park & Coastal Reserve map available online

Enjoy excellent beachcombing, wildlife viewing, and woodland strolling along the rock-strewn coastline, barrier beach, and salt marsh system of this 806-acre property. You are also treated to fine views of Fishers Island Sound and Long Island Sound along this loop hike.

DIRECTIONS

From Interstate 95 in Groton, take Exit 88 and follow Route 117 south for 1.0 mile. Turn right onto Route 1 and drive 0.3 mile to the traffic light. Turn left onto Depot Road and follow it for 0.3 mile under the railroad overpass. Just beyond the overpass, the road becomes dirt; continue for 0.3 mile to the large gravel parking area.

TRAIL DESCRIPTION

From the parking lot, pass the picnic area and a sign on the left that enumerates park regulations. This old gravel cart road is lined with mixed oaks, black cherry, greenbrier, shining sumac, and multiflora rose. Many trees are draped with Oriental bittersweet vines. In late summer, goldenrod plants bloom profusely with pollen-filled, yellow-orange blossoms. Soon reach a short side path that leads to the water's edge. Windrows of dry, brown eelgrass, looking like masses of tangled recording tape, pile up along the Poquonnock River shore. The living green plant is an irreplaceable component of the estuary ecosystem. On the opposite shore is the Groton–New London Airport, often busy with aircraft landings and takeoffs. This is a pleasing vista nonetheless because the back side of the barrier beach and the green mounds of Bushy Point Island are also visible.

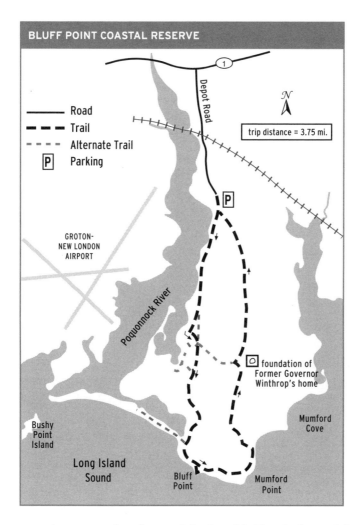

BLUFF POINT COASTAL RESERVE

——— Road
– – – Trail
– – – – Alternate Trail
P Parking

trip distance = 3.75 mi.

GROTON-
NEW LONDON
AIRPORT

Poquonnock River

foundation of
Former Governor
Winthrop's home

Bushy
Point
Island

Mumford
Cove

Long Island
Sound

Bluff
Point

Mumford
Point

Return to the cart road and turn right (south). Shortly, keep right at the trail junction. A grove of big-tooth aspen stands near the riverside. The aspen leaves shine golden in autumn. Sassafras trees and huckleberry and arrowwood shrubs line the cartway. On warm late-summer days, male cicadas fill the air with mechanical buzzing. Mockernut hickories join the oak trees, while 6-inch-high spotted (striped) wintergreen grows along the brushy edge. Note also poison ivy and bracken fern—one of the few ferns that tolerates dry, sterile soils. A slope rises up to the left covered primarily with immature trees.

Arrive at an open river view. Bayberry shrubs, some with multiple clusters of wax-coated berries where the branches meet the shrub's main stem, do well in the sandy soils. The only large trees are oak. Reach a clearing on the left where raspberry and sumac shrubs are overhung with masses of exotic, invasive Oriental bittersweet vines. Looking right reveals a pebbly beach and, beyond it, a wooden osprey nesting platform with a mass of sticks on top. Pass a gravel clearing on the left where little bluestem grass flourishes and then walk by concrete slabs that indicate former settlement. An open beach view may reveal people clamming in the rich mud when the tide is out. Hard- and soft-shell clams (actually the same animal during different parts of its shedding cycle) and oysters are still sought recreationally. Receding tides strand schools of small fish—mummichogs and Atlantic silversides—in tiny tide pools surrounded by salt marsh cordgrasses. Here they are easy prey for herons, egrets, greater yellowlegs in migration, and other long-legged waders. A bit farther along is a small enclave of salt marsh ditched years ago in an effort to control mosquito reproduction. Ditching disrupts the salt marsh ecosystem and is detrimental to the small fish that eat mosquito larvae.

Pass bayberry bushes heavy with fruit in late summer and enter shaded forest. The trail now forks, with the cart road being the left tine and a less traveled footpath constituting the right. Smooth-barked hickory, shad trees, and black birch stand between the parallel paths. To avoid bicyclists and joggers and even a few horseback riders who share the reserve with walkers, take the right path. Here I witnessed a male downy woodpecker gulping down blue-black arrowwood berries. Gain an open area dotted with red cedar, or juniper, trees. A plant with beautifully pink-purple, bell-shaped flowers and very slender leaves—gerardia—shows off its blossoms here in late summer. In this damp place, you stand at the farthest reaches of the highest tides, which occur but twice each month. The glasswort and blackgrass in this salty earth likewise indicate the extent of ground inundated by salt water. Just beyond the clearing, the path becomes quite overgrown, so backtrack a short distance and cross over to the higher and drier cart road. Continue south on the cart road, which is bordered on the right by an old stone wall, now in disrepair. Pass a big granite boulder on the left. Some of the sassafras trees, with their deeply furrowed brown bark, are quite large. Their spicy leaves come in three shapes—single, mitten, and three-lobed. Come to a slight rise where bittersweet weighs down the trees and shrubs; it spreads both by runners and seed. The yellow fruit husks split open in fall to reveal showy orange-red berries consumed and dispersed by birds.

Reach a fork in the trail; the left branch leads uphill over a rougher woods road to join the high cart road you walk later back to the start, but stay straight. At a grassy track on the right that leads to the river, stay straight as well. Shiny-

Enjoy a fine view out over the Poquonnock River soon after leaving the parking area.

leafed common greenbrier with clawing green stems fills the sunlit clearing. Invasive, exotic Japanese barberry, a low, prickly shrub with coral-red fruits, joins bittersweet in these disturbed soils. Reach a ditched salt marsh and past it a finger of water, then one of sand, with Long Island Sound beyond. The horizon may be studded with white triangles when wind conditions are favorable for sailing. The roadway now winds beneath oak and hickory. In addition to the drone of cicadas, you may hear the measured explosive pops of a propane cannon emanating from the airport runways—an effort to disperse bird flocks. The cart road curves sharply right, while a rockier track leads straight and slightly uphill into the woods. Follow the cart path; a view of the water is just beyond. A few holdover apple trees now provide food for wildlife. A tidal pond bordered by salt marsh vegetation is on the right.

At 1.6 miles reach Bluff Point, from which there is access on the right to Bluff Point Beach and Bushy Point Beach beyond. This pebble-and-sand, mile-long barrier beach shields the salt marsh behind it from the full storm surge and saltier waters of Long Island Sound. Great masses of empty slipper (lamp or boat) shells—more than we have seen anywhere else in New England—distinguished the wrack line on a day in early September. A small jellyfish lay among them. To the left, the beach below Bluff Point is composed of small, smooth granite pebbles with big angular granite boulders beyond. The plump

SEA OF GRASS

Below the usually placid waters of coastal estuaries, where fresh water from the uplands mingles with the salt water of the sea to produce a growth medium rich in nutrients, flowing green grasslands of a different sort give rise to a highly diverse natural community. The major food-producing plant of these undersea pastures is eelgrass, which is really not a grass at all. It is a marine flowering plant that produces its flowers and seeds totally underwater. It spreads mostly by means of runners, however.

Fertile pastures of eelgrass, stimulated both by abundant sediments brought from far inland by rivers such as the Poquonnock and by mineral-rich sea water, constitute the essential base of the life pyramid of estuaries. And when they decay, the organic material released provides nutrients for many other organisms. Even when lifeless and washed up on the beach, eelgrass continues to harbor small crustaceans and insects that shorebirds rely on for food. Eelgrass plays another important role in that its root systems anchor the sandy or muddy bottom soils of estuaries and coastal shallows and reduce wave erosion.

Eelgrass grows in vast dense beds that also harbor among their multitudinous blades a myriad of tiny creatures. The leaf surfaces themselves support a living film of algae and other microscopic life forms that nourish and sustain the higher animals that in turn become food for small fish and crustaceans—hermit crabs and pipefish, for example. These in their turn become food for still larger creatures, which then become food for you and me.

Thus estuaries are true nurseries for many of the shellfish and finfish that humans harvest commercially, and eelgrass is the mother's milk of that nursery. During the early 1930s a mysterious and fatal illness struck the eelgrass colonies of America's East Coast as well as those of Europe. Once vast beds of eelgrass were decimated. This, of course, had a domino effect upon the entire estuarine community dependent upon it. Wintering brant geese—smaller, darker relatives of the familiar Canada geese that graze almost exclusively upon the ribbonlike leaves of the plant when they winter in our estuaries—and bay scallops in particular were hard hit.

The cause of the plant's decline never has been fully explained, although a fungus and a slime mold were implicated. Changes in the temperature of sea water may have been a contributing factor. However, recent decades have seen a marked increase in eelgrass production in marine ecosystems in most areas, and brant geese and the multitude of other creatures that depend upon it directly or indirectly for sustenance and protection are the better off for it.

red hips and dark green foliage of exotic salt-spray rose shrubs shone in the sunlight behind the rocks that provided seating for our lunch that day. The big blossoms bloom pink or white.

The rocks at the low end of the tidal zone exhibit a blackish patina of life that the high-and-dry boulders do not possess. Across the water to the west lies the verdant, tree-covered mound of Bushy Point Island. You may want to explore the tidal pond behind the barrier beach by following an optional short trail on the back side of the sandy beach. Bush-like sea lavender adds its bouquet of tiny flowers to the scene along the edges of the salt marsh, while hermit crabs, safely ensconced in their borrowed mollusk shells, crawl about in search of edible bits. Superbly camouflaged, their small dark shells resemble beach pebbles. Until they move, they remain virtually invisible! Some of their shells support a living fuzz known as snail fur, which is actually made up of tiny microorganisms called hydroids. There are also small fish in the shallows and masses of snail-like periwinkles grazing algae off the mud in the brackish (mixed salt/fresh) water like a herd of tiny buffalo. A 4-inch-diameter moon jellyfish lay stranded in the pond.

The dunes separating the pond from the ocean are vegetated with beach grass, beach pea, and salt-spray, or rugosa, rose. A wooden boardwalk connects both sides of the barrier beach; do not cross the thin strip except via the boardwalk, as that can lead to erosion. When the path narrows, return to the main trail, which then curves left. A rocky track goes right and up to the top of Bluff Point, affording you a pleasant view of both the Fishers Island and Long Island Sounds. Goldenrod, huckleberry, sumac, greenbrier, and arrowwood crown this headland. The bluff is composed of easily eroded glacial till dropped by a receding glacier 20,000 years ago. Pinkish granite boulders litter the shore. A bench, installed in 1988 to commemorate the 50th anniversary of the great hurricane, is a convenient place to relax and enjoy the view.

Walk down the back side of the bluff to continue on the main trail. A fine view of Split Rock, a glacial erratic cracked by ice and storm waves, is visible a short distance off Mumford Point. Anglers find the rock a convenient perch from which to cast. Northern porgy, or scup, was the catch of the day during an early-September visit. Follow the trail gradually uphill now through shrubbery, briers, and red cedar. Reach a point where a trail enters from the left; stay straight on the main dirt cartway. Small black cherry trees are full of ripe fruit in late summer—at least until birds and chipmunks strip the bounty. At this time of year, the fragrance of ripening wild grapes is in the air. Brown thrashers and gray catbirds relish the fruit.

Arrive at a trail junction. A lesser path leads to the right, but stay on the main trail and curve sharply to the left. The diets of many insectivorous birds change in late summer to include fruit, as demonstrated by the black-capped chickadee I spied feeding on the dark fruits of arrowwood. Another path goes right, toward the shore, and you may want to follow it for a different scenic vista. Back on the main trail, you soon pass a fenced exclosure where the effects of deer browsing are being studied, and then curve left, walk down a gentle slope, and bear right. A stone wall that once bordered Governor John Winthrop's (served 1698–1707) pastureland now provides support for clinging vines and briers. Hay-scented, or boulder, fern softens the rock fence, which you soon pass through. This land was farmed until the 1950s. The old cart road winds among more red cedar and black cherry, two trees whose seeds require full sunlight for germination. Black knot fungus disfigures the branches of the cherries. Numerous informal side paths lead off in both directions, but stay on the main trail and arrive at a large shrubby clearing. A smaller trail turns left at 2.7 miles as the main trail bears right. Eastern towhees and gray catbirds— thicket specialists—skulk in the thick cover.

Another path heads off to the right as stone walls border both sides of the old roadway, which curves left. New York fern, Virginia creeper, and greenbrier all grow thickly along it. Some rather sizable black birches appear as you enter woodland that also includes oak, hickory, and black cherry. Gray squirrels busily harvest hickory nuts in late summer. The sound of nuts falling as they are cut down by the rodents is familiar at that time. Occasional granite boulders in the forest bespeak the ice sheet's legacy. The forest itself is rather open, with reduced underbrush. This may well be due to the once large population of hungry deer. Notice that you are walking downhill now. In the distance, water is visible through the trees. Black birch, characterized by smooth, dark bark, is the dominant tree, and unpresumptuous, white-blooming woodland aster is the ubiquitous flowering plant in the late-summer woods. The forest slopes downward to the left and up to the right. The roadway descends more noticeably now and curves left, passing between two concrete fence posts. Reach the junction with the low road and continue straight back to the parking area.

MORE INFORMATION

The park and reserve are open from 8:00 A.M. to sunset, year-round. No charge. There is a picnic area near the parking lot, and a public toilet located near the picnic area and at Bluff Point. Bicycles and leashed pets are permitted. Bluff Point State Park, c/o Fort Trumbull State Park, 90 Walbach Street, New London, CT 06320; 860-444-7591; http://www.ct.gov/dep.

—R. L.

TRIP 49
DENISON PEQUOTSEPOS NATURE CENTER

Location: Mystic
Rating: Easy
Distance: 2.3 miles
Elevation Gain: 70 feet
Estimated Time: 1.5 hours
Maps: USGS Mystic, Denison Pequotsepos Nature Center and Trail Complex map available online

This is a loop hike on a privately owned 300-acre sanctuary with surprisingly varied natural communities that offer great birding, ledge outcrops, and a natural history museum—a wonderful destination with young children.

DIRECTIONS

From I-95 in Mystic, take Exit 90 (note signs for Marinelife Aquarium/Mystic Seaport). Follow Route 27 south for 0.1 mile. Turn left onto Coogan Boulevard and drive 0.7 mile to its terminus at Jerry Browne Road. Turn right onto Jerry Browne Road and drive 0.3 mile to Pequotsepos Road on the right at the top of the hill (just before the large water tower). The nature center entrance and parking are 0.5 mile ahead on the left.

TRAIL DESCRIPTION

From the map kiosk immediately southwest of the nature center, turn left on the red-blazed Forest Loop Trail and pass Quarry Pond to the right. Submerged logs are often crowded with painted turtles basking in the sun shell to shell. In late fall, these reptiles retreat to the muddy pond bottom, surviving there in an amazing state of suspended animation. Continue past the pond and an unmarked trail that circles it and past a red-blazed junction, also on the right. Walk straight ahead and pass another junction on the same side. Climb gradually for a bit to the first intersection with the white-blazed Ledge Trail on the left; continue on the Forest Loop Trail for now. Pass the first ledge outcrops in this forest of oak, birch, and hickory.

Soon reach the other end of the Ledge Trail and turn left onto it. Dense thickets of greenbrier dominate this rather open oak woodland's shrub layer. Sassafras, huckleberries, lowbush blueberries, and a few azaleas also flourish

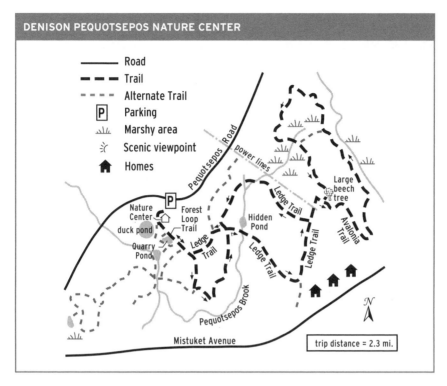

DENISON PEQUOTSEPOS NATURE CENTER

——— Road
▬ ▬ ▬ Trail
▬ ▬ ▬ ▬ Alternate Trail
P Parking
⸜⸝ Marshy area
☼ Scenic viewpoint
🏠 Homes

Pequotsepos Road
Power lines
Nature Center
duck pond
Forest Loop Trail
Quarry Pond
Ledge Trail
Hidden Pond
Ledge Trail
Ledge Trail
Large beech tree
Avalonia Trail
Pequotsepos Brook
Mistuket Avenue

N

trip distance = 2.3 mi.

in the sour granite soils, made even more acidic by tannins from decaying oak leaves. A rounded granite outcrop, its former angularity softened by an over-riding ice sheet more than 10,000 years ago, rises on the left. American chest-nut roots continue to sprout here, although most die before they can produce the characteristic prickly fruits. Follow the trail as it bends left and climbs to the top of the rocky spine. Indian pipes and striped wintergreen poke through last year's leaves, and beaked hazel bushes produce tasty nuts akin to filberts.

Caution! The earth drops off to the right; watch your footing, as these rocks can be slippery when wet. That same moisture brings life to dormant lichens clinging to the rocks. Maple-leaf viburnum and huckleberry shrubs cap the tough granite outcrop.

Descend and continue straight on the white-blazed trail through open woodland of black birch, red maple, oak, and hickory. As the trail climbs again gently, pass a granite boulder on the left. Reach a short side path, marked Over-look, which leads 35 feet to the cliff edge. No panorama here, but rather a nice bird's-eye view of the wet woodland below. The Ledge Trail continues through dry oak woods and over the top of another ledge. In fall, the crimson and or-ange leaves of Virginia creeper, or woodbine, stand out against the somber-hued trunks up which they twine. White oak trees sprout profusely along their trunks,

Eastern painted turtles line up on a Quarry Pond log to bask in the sun.

producing 1- to 2-foot-long limbs with leaves. I hadn't seen this degree of trunk sprouting anywhere else; perhaps it is in response to periodic defoliation by gypsy moths or drought. Walk easily downhill and bear right. More thick greenbrier and huckleberry are in evidence as you pass another low rock ledge on the right. White-breasted nuthatches hitch down the trunks of white oak looking for secure bark crevices to store tidbits for later retrieval.

Come to the edge of an outcrop bordered by beech. The trail swings left, where you gain a view of the damp woodland below, traversed by an intermittent brook. Fragments of green hickory nut husks left by industrious gray squirrels litter many of the rocks in fall. In addition to the ubiquitous greenbrier thickets, Solomon's seal, a member of the huge lily family, produces pairs of pendant, greenish-yellow flowers along its stalk in spring and blue-black berries in late summer. Descend gradually from the ledges and bear right through oak, red maple, and greenbrier to a T intersection at 0.4 mile. Take a right to continue on the Ledge Trail. Cross a small wooden bridge where Hidden Pond on the left may be without water during dry seasons. As a vernal pool, it provides essential breeding habitat for spotted salamanders and wood frogs in early spring. A postmounted wood duck box provides shelter for other creatures. Tickseed sunflowers bloom profusely in the black muck of autumn; arrowwood, winterberry, and abundant sweet pepperbush thrive in the damp soil.

Leaving the low spot, the path climbs gradually through rock-strewn woods of black birch and oak. Some of the densest greenbrier thickets yet flourish on either side of this old woods road. Pass through an old stone wall and come to a T intersection; turn left to continue on the white-blazed Ledge Trail. After leaf-fall, houses along Mistuxet Avenue are visible on the right. Red cedar growing here indicates former grazing. Cross a fallen stone wall; the trail parallels a wall on the left. Greenbrier has colonized these former pastures with a vengeance. Eastern towhees scratch for morsels within the relative safety of the thorny greenbrier patch. Arrive at a Y intersection and bear right on the white-blazed trail. A white oak clutches a boulder in a fashion reminiscent of an octopus tentacle clutching a clam just before you come to a narrow power-line clearing. Across the cut, the white-blazed Ledge Trail meets the orange-blazed Avalonia Trail at 0.75 mile. Reenter woods of white and red oak, hickory, and black birch on the Avalonia Trail on property owned by the Avalonia Land Conservancy and managed by the nature center; turn right just before you reach a stone wall.

Turn left, pass through a stone wall, and curve right. Hay-scented and New York ferns and tiny dark green, treelike club mosses grace the forest floor shaded by red maple, as greenbrier is much reduced. Reach a split (both sides blazed orange) in the trail at a large American beech tree, its trunk blackened by graffiti scars. You will return to this tree later. Stay to the right and cross a boulder, with a rock wall at the right. Tall cinnamon ferns require permanently moist ground, as you find at the point where the trail turns left, then right. You walk through damp red maple woods (some trees quite large) with sweet pepperbush and azalea shrubs. On an early-October visit my wife, Chris, found a tiny, perhaps recently emerged, wood frog whose coloration blended in perfectly with its surroundings. Hatched in ephemeral vernal pools, these frogs, as their name implies, are often found far from water later in life. Bog bridges lead through the wettest sections, which may well be dry by late summer. Bear left and cross more such bridges through a swale, then climb gradually up the opposite slope. Curve right, toward a stone wall, and then left along it. Cross over the top of another outcropping. The cliff drops off steeply on the right to a small valley cut by a part-time stream. Two houses are visible beyond. The path swings left.

While inch-long spring peepers called like chicks from the trees, I found another black-masked wood frog exactly the color of the decaying leaves. No telling how many others I might have missed. Pass another low rock outcrop on the right that has white wood asters blooming on it in fall; a higher ledge is visible on the other side of the small ravine. The path swings right and leads down into the ravine, across which a small stone wall runs diagonally. The wall even crosses the brook that flows near the outcrop's base. On the far side of the ravine, I discovered an eastern phoebe's old moss-covered nest under a crevice

STRANGER THAN A FAIRY TALE

Wood frogs defy logic. They aren't the standard fairy-book characters that sit on lily pads. Instead, wood frogs roam the forest floor, snatching up insects and other tasty invertebrates. While most species of frogs are green like Kermit in order to blend in with their verdant aquatic surroundings, female wood frogs are usually a pinkish tan. In contrast, the skins of males are generally dark brown. In either case, a still wood frog is virtually invisible. Only sudden movement betrays it. Reaching 3 inches in length in the case of the larger female, wood frogs are also distinguished by their trademark dark-brown, raccoon-like masks.

In early spring, when the first "warm" rains and melting snows begin to penetrate the ground, the seemingly lifeless frogs emerge to create another generation. Instinctively they move to temporary pools of rain and meltwater that collect in woodland depressions. Wood frogs and several species of salamanders court and reproduce only in such vernal pools. Male wood frogs advertise for mates with uncanny, duck-like quacking calls. The larger females, heavy with unfertilized eggs, follow the sounds to the pools where the males are waiting. In a frenzy of mating activity, males tightly clutch the females' torsos with their forearms. As the female lays her mass of up to 1,000 jelly-covered eggs, usually at the site of a submerged twig, the male releases his sperm into the water. After she has deposited all her eggs, she leaves the pool.

The fertilized eggs, and the tadpoles into which they develop in about 3 weeks, must grow rapidly before the heat of summer dries the pond. The tiny larval frogs, sporting tails and breathing with gills, feed on the minute organisms of the pool for about 2 months. The basic energy source of vernal pools is created and fortified by the constant addition of organic matter—leaves, twigs and the like—that winds up in the depression. If they escape predators and the pool retains its water long enough, the tadpoles eventually absorb their tails, develop lungs, and crawl out of the primordial slime ready for a life on terra firma, a life which may last for at least 3 years after emergence.

When cold weather strikes, these frogs seek shelter under logs and leaf litter and within burrows. But they have an ace up their sleeves: an amazing ability to freeze solid and survive. Water is somehow shunted from within the animal's cells into its body cavity so that those same cells don't rupture because of the formation of ice crystals. The return of warmer temperatures in early spring provides the magic kiss that revives the torpid creature from its slumber. Indeed, this is how a "cold-blooded" animal that ranges north of the Arctic Circle—farther north than any other member of its kind—has mastered its frigid environment. Thus, the lowly wood frog, remarkable in so many ways, lives an existence far stranger than any that could have been imagined by the Brothers Grimm.

overhang. This bird is just one of at least 69 species that have nested in the sanctuary. The trail follows the brook and reaches the border of the Avalonia Land Conservancy Nature Preserve. Follow the orange blazes through a stone wall in the oak-maple woods and bear left. Princess pine and cinnamon fern are now familiar, and a few clumps of sphagnum moss appear.

Reach a Y intersection. The left fork is a shortcut across the end of the Avalonia Trail; continue straight ahead through abundant hay-scented fern and scattered highbush blueberry, spicebush, and huckleberry shrubs. Princess pines, looking like miniature versions of their namesakes, bear candle-shaped strobules that produce the highly flammable spores once used by pioneering flash photographers. Pass through a stone wall in the mixed deciduous woodland, where greenbrier once again flourishes. Follow the orange-blazed trail as it turns left. Pass through another stone wall and bear left at a low ledge. The path continues to curve left in a sort of hairpin turn and then compensates somewhat in the other direction. As I passed by in early October, an eastern chipmunk watched my every action from its leaf-lined burrow entrance, without moving so much as a muscle or uttering a sound—a charming encounter. More small granite outcrops rise as the trail turns right. Black birch has found footholds among the rocks. Striped wintergreen, with its thick, variegated green-and-white leaves and white flowers in spring, is common in these woods.

Now descend easily to the right, around the end of the outcrop. This side of the ledge is higher, steeper, and more imposing. Curve left and pass through another stone wall. Agricultural fields in colonial times were generally only a couple of acres each, making for a lot of wall building, something in great evidence here. The level landscape is clothed by black birch, oak, and a few small beech trees. Breach another stone wall and note a depression on the forest floor on the right—the site of another vernal pool. Continue on as huckleberry, greenbrier, and pepperbush form a shrubby layer. Cross a couple of bog bridges and reach a small trail junction on the right; stay left on the main trail.

Eventually come to the now familiar graffiti-marred beech tree at a T intersection at 1.75 miles. Go right and retrace your footsteps across the power-line cut. Continue to a junction on the right with the white-blazed Ledge Trail and turn onto it through a stone wall gap.

Tufted titmice—pert, crested relatives of the smaller black-capped chickadee—sing their loud whistled *peter-peter-peter* in spring and summer. The trail leads gradually downhill through greenbrier thickets Uncle Remus's Br'er Rabbit would have been tickled to hide in. Spring peeper tree frogs pipe single shrill high notes during mild days—even in fall. You are walking now amid oak and smooth-trunked black birch. The small seeds of black birch can germinate only on bare ground; hence, bare earth created by logging and wind throws is essential for its reproduction. But thin-skinned black birch is also susceptible to fire, and its abundance in these woods indicates an absence of fire for some years. Amble downhill through a thick growth of huckleberry whose sweet blue-black fruits are highly prized by mammals. As soil moisture increases, sweet pepperbush, bearing spikes of small white flowers in summer, cinnamon fern—named for the color of its fertile fronds—and highbush blueberry line the path.

Tread on wooden walkways strategically placed in a damp fern-filled spot and cross a modest wooden bridge (you are just north of Hidden Pond). Now walk up a short hill with ledges to the right and come to a small boulder at the junction of an unmarked crossover trail; bear right. A couple of red cedars that once invaded an abandoned pasture now seem out of place. Bear left at a T intersection to follow the white-blazed trail. A house is straight ahead along Pequotsepos Road, beyond the T. Walk gradually downslope with stone walls to the right and come to an unmarked intersection on the left. Continue straight through maple, birch, and oak woodland on the Ledge Trail. At 2.2 miles, reach the intersection with the red-blazed Forest Loop Trail. Turn right onto it, retracing your steps to the nature center.

MORE INFORMATION

The Denison Pequotsepos Nature Center features an all-new natural history museum with exhibits and outdoor flight enclosures with live owls. Picnic tables available. Leashed dogs permitted; dog owners must clean up after their pet. Bicycles not allowed. Trails open dawn to dusk; nature center's hours: Year-round, Monday–Saturday 9:00 A.M. to 5:00 P.M., Sunday 10:00 A.M. to 4:00 P.M. Admission $6 per adult, $4 per senior (65 and over), child (12 and under). Denison Pequotsepos Nature Center, 109 Pequotsepos Road, P.O. Box 122, Mystic, CT 06355; 860-536-1216; http://www.dpnc.org/.

—R. L.

TRIP 50
BARN ISLAND WILDLIFE MANAGEMENT AREA

Location: Stonington
Rating: Moderate due to length
Distance: 5.3 miles
Elevation Gain: 65 feet
Estimated Time: 3.5 hours
Maps: USGS Watch Hill, Mystic

This is an out-and-back hike in a very biologically rich and scenic 1,013-acre area of extensive tidal wetlands, deciduous woodland, and shrublands. Barn Island ranks as the state's single largest coastal property managed for wildlife conservation and a recognized globally significant Important Bird Area.

DIRECTIONS
From Exit 91 off I-95 in Stonington, take Route 234 (North Main Street) west for 0.4 mile and turn left (still North Main Street). After 1.5 miles, turn left onto Route 1 and follow it for 1.7 miles to Greenhaven Road. Turn right and then immediately right again onto Palmer Neck Road; continue for 1.5 miles to the trailhead off the pavement on the right.

TRAIL DESCRIPTION
Before beginning the main hike, take a side trail west (right) for a few hundred yards for a picturesque view of Wequetequock. Follow the grassy path from the pedestrian parking area through thickets of greenbrier, Oriental bittersweet, and arrowwood. As you proceed, honeysuckle, sassafras, black cherry, black oak, and shining sumac also become abundant. Gray catbirds are common summertime residents and feel at home in this dense growth. Listen also for the sharply accented *chick-a-per-weeoo-chick* of a skulking little white-eyed vireo. After initially walking in shade, emerge into sunlight where goldenrods bloom in late summer and wild grapes ripen on vines festooning the shrubs and small trees.

Soon emerge at the shore, where the smell of salt is in the air. At low tide, notice that the shoreline is composed of tiny sand beaches interspersed with miniature islands of marsh peat, a sign of a sinking coastline. Rocks draped with rockweed are also visible then. The wrack line (material left by the last high tide)

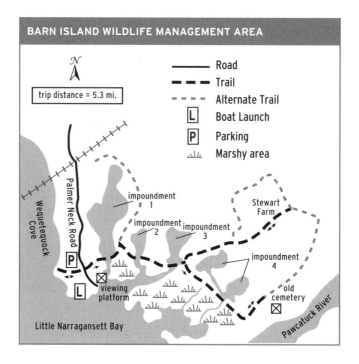

may contain slipper and shiny jingle shells, various crabs, horseshoe crab (not a true crab at all) carapaces, eelgrass, and the seaweeds codeum (green fleece) and Irish moss. Salt marsh cordgrass and the shrub marsh elder occupy the narrow tidal zone between dry land and bay, while seaside goldenrod, groundsel tree, wild rose, and poison ivy (away from the trail) thrive on terra firma. Large, black double-crested cormorants often stand on rocks just offshore with their wings extended for drying, and gray-and-white herring gulls are ubiquitous. To the left are the beach and dunes. In late summer and early fall, migrant monarch butterflies sip nectar from goldenrod's feathery spikes.

Backtrack to your vehicle. The main trailhead is on the opposite side of the asphalt roadway at an iron gate. A memorial stone here reads, "In Appreciation Of Louis Bayer For His Efforts In Preserving The Barn Island Marshes." Follow the graveled path as it curves left and gently down along a fringe of big bluestem grass (the indicator species of the Midwestern tallgrass prairie) and past a stand of skeletal red pines on the right. Sassafras trees become more numerous, and old man's beard lichen hangs from a few branches. Mockernut hickory trees and some large red oaks up to 2 feet in diameter appear. Curve right to walk down a dike bordered on both sides by salt marsh. Eye-catching snowy egrets use their sharp black bills to snatch fish stranded in small pools by a receding tide.

A few granite boulders dot the marsh, which 200 years ago was agricultural land. A steadily submerging coastline has inundated what was once dry land. The leafless stems of glasswort, or pickleweed, take on a reddish hue in late summer along the fringes of the marsh. At low tide the mud flats of the tidal creek on the left are exposed to migrant shorebirds and other creatures seeking a meal. A big culvert channels water under the dike. The natural tidal flow, once restricted, has been restored with the installation of this larger culvert. The nutrient-rich tidal salt marshes serve as veritable nurseries, spawning grounds, and feeding areas for myriad finfish, shellfish, and crustaceans. Cormorants and other fish-eating birds frequent the channel as their prey becomes easier to catch. Deciduous woodland rings the landward side of the salt marsh, while on the right the marsh opens to the salty waters of Little Narragansett Bay.

Reenter woods after a few hundred yards. Among the flora are pin oak; tupelo with shiny green leaves that change to red, yellow, and orange in autumn; and moisture-loving cinnamon fern. Climb a few feet among oak, hickory, and sassafras. Non-native autumn olive, once planted to provide wildlife food, and bracken fern also grow in the drier soil. Note the old apple trees, which hint at the land's former uses. Reach an intersection and stay straight. In late summer, arrowwood offers blue-black fruits to birds, and winterberry shrubs are heavy with bright red fruits; black cherry also provides a bounty for wildlife. Oriental bittersweet vines and honeysuckle shrubs are ubiquitous invasive exotics; birds disperse both. This woodland also contains a few overtopped red cedars that began life in what was then a pasture.

Emerge onto another dike that created a second impoundment on the left. Great egrets, impressive white waders nearly the size of great blue herons and sporting impressive yellow-orange bills stalk for frogs in the shallows. The sour odor of fermenting goldenrod nectar and the slightly sulfurous aroma of salt marsh decay mingle here in late summer. Cross drainage channels, and during low tides note the exposed clumps of ribbed mussels holding fast to the peaty banks. Well adapted for daily exposure to the drying effects of air, these animals retain some water within their shells after the tide recedes. By slightly opening their shells, they are able to effect gas exchange (breathe) even when "high and dry."

After about 100 yards, enter black cherry, tupelo, red maple, and black oak woodland and curve right. Huckleberry and prickly greenbrier flourish beneath the trees. Come to a stone wall on the left at the edge of the next impoundment. The twisted and gnarled trunks of the tupelos are aesthetically appealing. Tall, plumed common reed (*Phragmites*) lines this short dike. Cross

Two-hundred-year-old gravestones repose in a small cemetery slowly being reclaimed by sassafras, oak, cherry, and buckthorn.

the very modest drainageway and reenter woods. Here tiny spring peeper tree frogs emit high-pitched peeps until cold weather silences them. Emerge at another impoundment. An osprey nesting platform is mounted on a pole out on the bay side, while northern harriers (marsh hawks) course low over the marshlands listening for rodents. Cross another flowage where spindly-legged greater yellowlegs catch fish in the shallows during migration. I glimpsed a lovely buckeye butterfly here during a mid-September visit. Buckeyes display a series of eyespots on their upper wing surfaces that may fool predators. The dike curves left near a copse of white oak. The marsh is especially extensive on that side. Salt-spray rose and bayberry line the path.

Enter woodland once again as the land rises slightly. Reach a Y fork at 1.3 miles; remember it because you will be returning here later to strike off in another direction. Follow the right fork for now and reemerge into the open bordered by salt marsh. Visibility is limited and common reeds line the roadway. Big green darner dragonflies patrol the marsh, snatching numerous salt marsh mosquitoes. Reach a large culvert and a view of the waterway on the left. A few barnacles encrust the rocks at the culvert's mouth. In late summer, numerous white-blooming groundsel trees along the dikes attract butterflies, while goldenrods also entice bees and wasps. Notice that the salt marsh on the bayside has been ditched. Once done in an effort to eliminate the breeding grounds of pesky salt marsh mosquitoes, this alteration also reduced the population of mummi-chogs and other mosquito-larvae-eating fish that act as natural controls. In the long run, ditching has proven to be detrimental to salt marshes. Measures are now being taken to return the natural tidal flow. The dike curves left. Even when the path has not been mowed recently, it is easily passable on tracks.

A stone wall out in the marsh on the right frames what were cornfields two centuries ago; these former fields, now inundated by tides, are graphic evidence of the relatively recent rise in sea level. If you hear a crow giving a nasal *caa*, you are hearing a fish crow (a smaller relative of the very familiar American crow) which is generally found only near tidal rivers. Reenter woods of black locust, red maple, oak, flowering dogwood, and sassafras where red-orange wood lilies bloom in summer. Non-native thicket-forming multiflora rose is abundant. Eastern towhees scratch the ground in forest openings. Curve left past scattered red cedars and between rock walls. Arrive at a cellar hole on the right, just below the wall, constructed of mortared granite blocks, now overgrown. Head gently downward from the cellar hole under white pine, red maple, and oak that are once again of taller stature.

At 2.1 miles, reach a 0.5-acre clearing on the right occupied by a small cemetery. Some two dozen headstones, the oldest apparently dating from 1795, are still standing. The old burying ground, bounded by stone walls, is being reclaimed by sassafras, oak, cherry, and alder buckthorn. In sharp contrast to the tranquility of this spot, posted signs warn that Barn Island was once a bombing target range and may still contain old buried ordnance. While I was contemplating this, a gray tree frog uttered a trill from nearby. At the far end of the cemetery are imposing masonry gateposts. Beyond here, the old roadway eventually becomes paved Stewart Road and leads to a residential area.

When ready to move on, turn around and retrace your steps to the Y intersection located between the third and fourth impoundments (2.9 miles). Here you can continue back to your vehicle (0.9 mile) or turn right and walk through oak woodland as the road curves left. If you turn right, soon reach a trail junction on the left but continue straight on the old roadway under oak, tupelo, and red maple. Cinnamon fern, sweet pepperbush, azalea shrubs, and alder fill the low-lying areas. Cross a drainageway where Joe-Pye weed and sedges thrive, and then curve and "climb" to slightly higher ground occupied by white and black oaks, red maple, and black birch. Reach a trail intersection on the left, but curve right to enter a former pasture regenerating to white pine and red cedar where pretty American copper butterflies fly.

Arrive at picturesque hayfields with blooming red clover that attracts hordes of cabbage white and sulfur butterflies in late summer. Continue your

THE JAWS OF DEATH

As my wife and I made our way back to an incoming tide, we were treated to quite a spectacle in the salt marsh—one we had never seen before. Dozens of small silvery fish were jumping en masse a few inches out of the water repeatedly as if fleeing the jaws of some formidable predator. The energy contained in that scene was remarkable and caused us to stare almost transfixed at the spectacle. Like a handful of skipping pebbles hurled across the water's surface, each jump took the school approximately one linear foot across the water before they fell once again into the watery realm they were attempting to escape. Sometimes we witnessed two quick jumps in immediate succession. A bit farther along in the tidal creek we saw smaller groups of the same species making three jumps in very rapid succession. It was really quite captivating.

Only later did we learn that our hunch had been correct: what was making these schools of Atlantic silversides fish act like jumping beans was that they were being hotly pursued by the highly predatory bluefish. Although hatched far offshore, by late summer young bluefish, known as "snappers," enter tidal marshes and feed voraciously upon the abundant small fish. It was this life-and-death struggle we were witnessing. No wonder, then, that small, vulnerable species like silversides travel in schools that reduce any one individual's chances of being slashed by a predator.

By the end of their first summer, snappers may reach 12 inches in length on a diet of Atlantic silversides and other bait fish. Eventually these large-mouthed tigers of the sea return to open water, where they may attain a length of 3.5 feet. Here they are among the species most sought by anglers.

gradual climb through the Stewart Farm hayfields that afford nice, open vistas. Reach an iron gate as the track curves right and joins a gravel road going right. At this point turn around and retrace your steps to the Y intersection where you began this part of the excursion. At the Y, stay right to return eventually to the parking area.

MORE INFORMATION

Barn Island Wildlife Management Area is open sunrise to sunset. No charge. Exercise caution during the hunting season—September 1 to the end of February (the major hunting season is October 15 to December 1). No hunting on

Sundays. A new marsh viewing area and native plants demonstration garden is located about 100 yards before the entrance to boat launch parking area. Another salt marsh observation platform as well as portable toilets are located at the boat-launch parking lot a short distance down the road from the trailhead. Only vehicles with boat trailers may park there. Connecticut Department of Environmental Protection, Wildlife Division, Eastern District Area, 209 Hebron Road, Marlborough, CT 06447; 860-295-9523; http://www.ct.gov/dep, http://www.lisrc.uconn.edu/coastalaccess/site.asp.

—R. L.

INDEX